American Genealogical Research at the DAR
Washington, D.C.

Second Edition

by Eric G. Grundset and Steven B. Rhoc

DAR Library Studies in Genealogy and History, Number 1

National Society
Daughters of the American Revolution
1776 D Street, N.W.
Washington, D.C. 20006–5303

Published June 2004

★★★★★★★★★★★ ACKNOWLEDGMENTS FOR THE FIRST EDITION (1997)

The President General, Mrs. Charles Keil Kemper, the Librarian General, Mrs. David W. Ulrich, and the entire Executive Committee, have been most supportive of the concept of this book from the beginning. The DAR Library Centennial Committee, Mrs. Richard Powell Taylor, National Chairman, has funded the publication costs through various projects, and its support of the Library's publishing efforts is greatly appreciated. DAR National Parliamentarian, Mrs. Frank B. Surber, kindly proofread the copy and made many helpful comments.

Many DAR staff members have provided insight and information on the workings of DAR offices and records. In particular, the following deserve special thanks for their assistance: Glenna Acord, Rachel Ashby, James E. Barker III, LaKeitha Clarke, Elva Crawford, Diane Dunkley, Janice Fitzgerald, Belva G. Geist, Kathleen Hale, Rose Hall, Betty Humphrey, Darlene T. Hunter, Hazel F. Kreinheder, Elisabeth W. Schmidt, Margaret Turner, and Gerald S. Walker. Edith Rianzares has taken the rough copy of the book and transformed it into a polished product.

Without the support for DAR collections from Daughters around the country for over a century, the research center, which has evolved in Washington, D.C., would not be the storehouse of information it is today and this book would be unnecessary. Their dues and contributions have funded all the work to arrange this material since 1890, and their dedication to the purposes of the National Society have resulted in a long influx of materials to the Nation's Capital. With their books, periodicals, manuscripts, research notes, indices and files, DAR members have built a great repository of American history.

The public, which has had access to DAR collections since shortly after 1900, has also contributed greatly to the growth of DAR collections with donations of books and other materials. Many researchers have placed copies of their completed family histories and other works in the DAR Library to give these publications national exposure.

★★★★★★★★★★★ ACKNOWLEDGMENTS FOR THE SECOND EDITION (2004)

Over eight years have passed between the first and second editions of this guide. Researchers made the first edition a popular publication, and we are grateful for this reception. The President General, Linda Tinker Watkins, the Librarian General, Charlotte Bayliss Edson, and the entire Executive Committee of the Millennium Administration, have been very supportive of the DAR Library and the preservation of the DAR's historic research materials. The President General's Project has funded the digitization of the membership application papers and supplemental applications, indexing of membership records and the Genealogical Records Committee Reports, and the creation of several important internal databases to manage these sources. Through their support of this project, many DAR members have enabled this vital work to progress.

Special thanks are due various people, who have contributed their thoughts, editing, and a little writing to the text. In particular, Glenna Acord, Diane Dunkley, Elva Crawford, and Terry Ward deserve thanks in helping update the information in the second edition. Christopher Castleberry and Edith Rianzares have overseen the final production of the volume.

PHOTO CREDITS

Pages 6, 8, 12, 27, 36: Eric G. Grundset
Pages 17, 29: Robert W. Fones, Jr.
Page 79: Helga Photo Studio; Mark Gulezian

Artwork on pages 123, 124, 126, 127, 133, 138 and 145 is from Elroy McKendree Avery. *A History of the United States and Its People from Their Earliest Records to the Present Time.* Cleveland: The Burrows Brothers, 1908.

★★★★★★★★★★★★★★★★★★★★★★★ CONTENTS

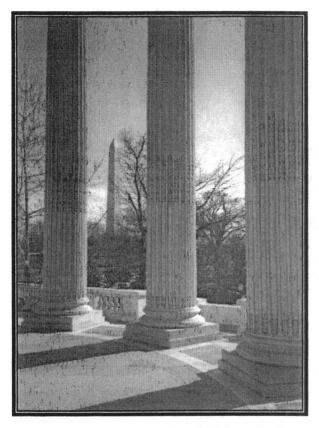

**The Washington Monument from the C Street Portico,
Memorial Continental Hall**

This book had its beginnings in the late 1980s with proposals to write a guide to research in DAR collections. Unfortunately many other projects had priority. With the celebration of the Centennial of the founding of the DAR Library in 1996, the composition of a guide to genealogical research at the DAR was a timely commemorative project. It was also long overdue. DAR had "hidden its light under a bushel" for far too long. American genealogists needed a clear understanding of the many family history treasures DAR owns and makes available for research. The first edition was published in April 1997. There have been many changes and additions to the collections at DAR in the subsequent eight years. The need for a revision became apparent in the past few years. This second edition updates arrangements, procedures, and other important information relating to DAR collections and offices.

Portions of the information contained herein have appeared in print in various DAR publications over the years. Finding it in all of these scattered places is not easy. Condensing over a century of collecting into a guidebook has been a fascinating challenge. With no precedent, we gathered everything from scratch over many years in preparation. Writing and research continued right up to the final minute.

Others have written guides to genealogical research in the major repositories in the Nation's Capital, including DAR of course. Such accounts of DAR's collections have been particularly lacking. These authors have generally not consulted the proper staff in each research center for the proper information. Consequently, emphasis has been uneven, accuracy has suffered, and omissions are glaring. This leads to misinformation for genealogists and difficulties for staff assisting them. To insure accuracy and to present the full picture of DAR's role in genealogical research, this guide is essential.

American Genealogical Research at the DAR is not a general guide to genealogical research in the United States. There are ample introductory and advanced guides on the market and in libraries nationwide. Instead, this DAR publication serves as a manual discussing the collections at DAR Headquarters in Washington, D.C. within the broader scope of American genealogical sources and subjects. Explaining what is available at DAR and how a researcher will be able to use it in his or her search for their family's place in American history is the book's purpose.

Chapters on the major departments at DAR Headquarters that maintain genealogical collections, including the DAR Library, begin the guide and provide detailed information on holdings, procedures, and finding aids. Chapter 13 presents portions of these DAR collections arranged in subject categories to highlight the interconnections between the departments and to inform researchers of the many unique and less well-known sources.

Many people assume that because of the appearance of the word "Revolution" in the society's name that only material on the American Revolution will be found here. While the War of Independence is, naturally, a major focus, DAR collections are much broader in their coverage and include materials from the past four centuries of American history. Even as recently as few years before this book first appeared, a colleague at another Washington research center was surprised to learn that the DAR Library owned a very large collection of American county histories. He had been telling researchers that these were only available in Washington, D.C. at the Library of Congress. Unfortunately, this was not atypical at the time. DAR collections are not as well known as they should be — yet another reason for this publication. People simply do not know what is behind the marble walls and columns.

Similarly, many researchers are surprised to learn that DAR collections are not limited to famous individuals, supposedly "blue–blood" families, and those with colonial English ancestry. American history and records are the result of a great mixture of peoples and traditions, and the same applies to DAR collections. Interspersed throughout are major holdings relating to many European immigrant groups, to African Americans and to Native Americans.

The staff at DAR is always surprised that even today many people are unaware of the fact that the DAR is open to researchers and has been since shortly after 1900. It is a common misconception, even among long–time Washington area residents, that only DAR members may use DAR collections. One does not need special permission to visit. The door is open to all.

Generally, DAR collections compliment and partially duplicate those of the Library of Congress and the National Archives. Although much smaller than these massive institutions DAR is no less important to the average American genealogist. So much unique material resides at DAR that researchers frequently comment that they have found genealogical gold they could not find anywhere else.

The holdings themselves, which do not circulate, coupled with open book stacks in the Library, quick processing of new materials for use, and major in–house finding aids, draw researchers from across the nation every day. *American Genealogical Research at the DAR* presents the DAR's research materials, gathered for over a century, to American genealogists with the hope that more will visit and find what *they* could not find elsewhere. After all, the point of building a historical collection is preservation for future generations. We are at once the future generation the DAR's founders had in mind when they began these collections and the preservers for still other future generations of Americans who will likely be interested in their family history.

Eric G. Grundset
Library Director
May 2004

THE NATIONAL SOCIETY
DAUGHTERS OF THE AMERICAN REVOLUTION

The National Society Daughters of the American Revolution (NSDAR, and hereafter simply DAR) was established on October 11, 1890 by four women interested in preserving the memory of the men and women involved in the birth of the United States. It was incorporated under the laws of the District of Columbia on June 4, 1891 and incorporated by an Act of the United States Congress in 1896. Since 1890, over 826,000 women have been members. The DAR is a nonaffiliated service organization dedicated to the support of historic preservation, the promotion of education, and the encouragement of patriotic endeavor.

Membership is by invitation to

> any woman ... who is not less than eighteen years of age, and who is lineally descended from a man or woman who, with unfailing loyalty to the cause of American Independence, served as a sailor, or a soldier or civil officer in one of the several Colonies or States, or in the United Colonies or States or as a recognized patriot, or rendered material aid thereto; provided an applicant is personally acceptable to the chapter. [Bylaws of the National Society of the Daughters of the American Revolution, Article III, Section 1]

Memorial Continental Hall from the Ellipse.

The DAR is headquartered in a block–sized group of connected buildings in downtown Washington, D.C. a few blocks from the White House. Memorial Continental Hall (1905-1910), Constitution Hall (1929), and the Administration Building (1921-1923; 1947-1950) are the components of this complex.

The National Society is comprised of nearly 170,000 members grouped into state organizations and nearly 3,000 local chapters; Units Overseas in the United Kingdom, France, Germany, Spain, Canada, Italy, Japan, Australia, Mexico, Bermuda, and the Bahamas; and members at large. Many of the state organizations and some chapters maintain their own buildings and offices, but the National Society is the primary repository for the DAR collections examined in this guide.

The history of the DAR has been told several times. The most recent account, by Ann Arnold Hunter, *A Century of Service: The Story of the DAR*, was published for the National Society's Centennial and chronicles the development of the organization and its programs. *American Spirit Magazine* is the official serial publication for the Society. This bimonthly publication features articles on history, historic preservation, genealogy and education. It is available in libraries nationwide and by subscription. A separate newsletter, *Daughters*, provides current information to the membership on the business of the National Society.

During the past century the DAR has worked to collect, to preserve, to transcribe, to index, and to arrange much material documenting the historical development of the country and the genealogical history of its families during the past four centuries with a natural, but not limited, concentration on the Revolutionary era. Researchers have known the value of DAR materials for the better part of the twentieth century, but the size and scope of the collections was never presented in a collected fashion until the first edition of this book in 1997.

1.1
CONTACTING THE DAR

The DAR's address is 1776 D St., N.W., Washington, D.C. 20006–5303. The main telephone switchboard number is 202–628–1776. DAR's homepage on the Internet may be reached at **www.dar.org**. The DAR Library's email address is **library@dar.org**.

1.2
GENERAL INFORMATION ON THE DAR

Readers interested in more information on the DAR should visit the DAR's website or contact the DAR Store, Office of the Corresponding Secretary General and request some of the available literature and publications. See Chapter 11 for more information on the DAR Store.

1.3
BECOMING A DAR MEMBER

Those interested in membership should visit the DAR's website and fill out the *Prospective Member Information Request Form* under "Membership" on the splash page. A paper version of this form is also available from the DAR at the following address. Completed forms should also be sent to the same address.

Prospective Member Services
NSDAR
1776 D St., NW
Washington, DC 20006-5303

1.4
A DAR GENEALOGICAL TIMELINE

1890   The National Society Daughters of the American Revolution was founded in October.

1892   *The DAR Magazine* begins publication.

1895   DAR publishes volume one of its *Lineage Books*.

1896   The DAR Library was established in February.

1900   First appearance of the "Genealogical Column" of *The DAR Magazine*.

1902   The public is permitted to use the DAR Library in its first home on F Street.

1905   DAR purchases the Chalkley Manuscripts of early records from Augusta County, Virginia.

1910   DAR moved into the Memorial Continental Hall in February. The Library was then located in the office now occupied by the Genealogy Department.

1911   After much debate, DAR publishes the Chalkley Manuscripts as *Chronicles of the Scotch–Irish Settlement*.

1912   DAR begins effort to urge the U.S. Congress to establish a national archives.

1913   Genealogical Research Committee established; name changed in 1932 to Genealogical Records Committee.

1919   The Bureau of the Census makes its first transfer to the DAR of original volumes of various special schedules from United States censuses.

1920   First book catalog of the DAR Library published.

1929   DAR Library moves into new quarters on the second floor of Constitution Hall.

1930 DAR transfers the special census schedules to the manuscript collection at Duke University's Perkins Library.

1933 Daughters nationwide urged the United States Congress to preserve, restore, and microfilm aging federal census records, especially those for 1800, 1810, and 1820.

1934 Congress appropriates money for census microfilming and preservation.

1936 The Works Progress Administration begins donations of its valuable records guides to the DAR Library.

1937 DAR receives another shipment of mortality schedules from the Bureau of the Census.

1939 The DAR Library's "wear and tear" fee begins for non–member researchers.

1939 DAR publishes the final volume, number 166, of the *Lineage Books,* which contains members' lineages up to 1920.

1940 Second book catalog of the DAR Library published.

1946 The DAR Library celebrates its fiftieth anniversary.

1947 The Library completed acquisitions of microfilm of the 1850–1880 federal censuses, a process that was stalled by World War II microfilm shortages.

1949 The DAR Library moves into its present location in the converted auditorium of Memorial Continental Hall.

1950 The first genealogical index to *The DAR Magazine* appears: *Genealogical Guide*.

1956 The National Archives transfers original 1880 population census schedules for twelve states to DAR.

1956 Dr. Jean Stephenson begins writing articles of genealogical methodology in *The DAR Magazine*.

1958 First publication of *Is That Lineage Right?*

1962 DAR begins microfilming membership application papers.

1966 The first *DAR Patriot Index* is published.

1970 DAR's Seimes Microfilm Center is established.

1972 A two–year project by the Genealogical Society of Utah to microfilm many unique materials in the DAR Library comes to an end after producing nearly 2,800 rolls.

1977 Requirement begins for documentation for membership applications for the first three - generations, including the applicant herself.

1980   DAR transfers its holdings of census mortality schedules to the National Archives and the 1880 population schedules to state archives or historical societies.

1982   The first volume of the third book catalog of the DAR Library is published: *DAR Library Catalog: Volume One: Family Histories and Genealogies.*

1986   The second volume of the third book catalog of the DAR Library is published: *DAR Library Catalog: Volume Two: State and Local Histories and Records.*

1986   The American Indian Committee

1987   and the Librarian General developed a new section for the Library, The American Indian Collection.

1989   The DAR Museum presents an exhibit, "Family Record: Genealogical Watercolors and Needlework."

1992   The third volume of the third book catalog of the DAR Library is published: *DAR Library Catalog: Volume Three: Centennial Supplement, 1986–1992.*

1994   The Centennial Edition of The DAR Patriot Index is published.

1996   The DAR Library celebrates its Centennial with publishing projects and development of a computerized catalog.

1997   *American Genealogical Research at the DAR* is published, the first detailed guide to the National Society's extensive resources.

1998   Indexing begins on the GRC reports.

2001   The DAR publishes *African American and American Indian Patriots of the American Revolution*, a collected edition of several smaller studies begun in the 1980s.

2001   The President General's project to digitize many of DAR's historic research sources begins.

2003   The DAR hosts "Forgotten Patriots: African American and American Indian Patriots in the Revolutionary War," a historical seminar accompanying a 2002-2003 exhibition by the same name in the DAR Museum.

2003   The National GRC index makes its debut in a searchable online version.

2003   The DAR Library receives the donation of the library of the National Huguenot Society.

2004   The second edition of *American Genealogical Research* at the DAR is published.

2004   The National Genealogical Society donated its manuscript collection to the DAR.

2004   The first digital images of DAR application papers become available to researchers.

VISITING DAR HEADQUARTERS

Limited public transportation and minimal parking complicate a visit to the DAR Headquarters, but the trip is worth the effort!

DAR Headquarters is located at 1776 D Street on the block bounded by 17th, 18th, C and D Streets, N.W. in downtown Washington. Use the D Street entrance to the building. The historic main entrance, now used only for special events, faces 17th Street and the Ellipse south of the White House. Besides the President's home, DAR's neighbors include the Red Cross, the Organization of American States, and the U.S. Department of the Interior.

The 1776 D Street Entrance to DAR Headquarters.

Access to the building for the disabled is at 1776 C Street. This entrance into the lower level of the administration building is in the center of the block behind the DAR Founders' Memorial. Presently, those with disabled license plates or stickers must park at meters and pay meter fees unless they possess a District of Columbia permit.

1. DAUGHTERS OF THE AMERICAN REVOLUTION
2. AMERICAN RED CROSS
3. CORCORAN GALLERY OF ART
4. ORGANIZATION OF AMERICAN STATES
5. DEPARTMENT OF INTERIOR

DAR's location is highlighted on this map of downtown Washington, D.C. and immediate neighborhood near the White House.

2.1
DRIVING AND PARKING

Street parking in this part of Washington is very limited and fills up very early in the morning on weekdays. Metered parking is available on C, D, 17th, and 18th Streets, but is valid for only two hours. Be sure to bring plenty of change, because the DAR is not able to provide change for meters. There are no meter fees on weekends, but events in Washington frequently result in full streets by the time the DAR opens at 9:00 a.m. or shortly thereafter on Saturdays. Parking restrictions may apply on some nearby streets. READ POSTED SIGNS to avoid tickets or towing. Meter readers monitor the streets carefully and frequently. Parking around the Ellipse is by government permit only. There are parking garages located in the area on 18th Street above F Street. Please be aware of safety and security restrictions in the area of the White House and throughout downtown Washington. Events can change quickly and new restrictions can affect traffic and parking without warning.

The Metropolitan Police Department frequently restricts parking on streets for specific hours or days. Watch for their "Emergency No Parking" signs attached to meters and carefully read the restrictions noted on them. Little, if any, advance notice is given for these closings. In addition, when major events such as marathons, parades, demonstrations, or rallies occur on the Mall or the Ellipse, parking can be restricted, banned or available only at a premium. The police may also close streets to through traffic without notice or for reasons of national security. Maintain an awareness of events planned for downtown Washington before driving into the city.

If you are planning to drive to DAR Headquarters from points North, take I-95 South or I-295 (Baltimore-Washington Parkway) to the Capitol Beltway, I-495. Take I-495 West towards Northern Virginia. (From the B/W Parkway, the Beltway will be called I-95 North/495 West). Take exit 30, Georgia Avenue/29 South, the 3rd exit after the intersection with 95. Go approximately 2 miles to 16th Street South. This is a large intersection with 16th Street veering off to the right. Go approximately 10 miles to "I" Street and turn right. At the 2nd light, turn left onto 17th Street. Turn right on D Street. The main entrance is in the middle of the block. Go up the stairs to enter the museum.

If you are traveling from Western Maryland, take I-270 South to I-495 West towards Northern Virginia. Cross the American Legion Bridge, then take the immediate next right exit to the George Washington Parkway. The Parkway will take you across the Theodore Roosevelt Bridge and put you on Constitution Avenue. Turn left on 18th Street, go three very short blocks. Turn right on D Street. The main entrance is in the middle of the block.

Visitors coming from the West should take I-66 East towards Washington. This will take you across the Roosevelt Bridge. Follow the directions in the preceding paragraph for Constitution Avenue. During the week between 6:30 and 9:00 a.m. I-66 east-bound is HOV-2 (High Occupancy Vehicles with 2 riders). Between 4:00 and 6:30 p.m., I-66 west-bound is HOV-2. Cars *must* have at least two passengers to use these routes during these hours. This freeway experiences frequent back-ups in the opposite direction from the HOV restrictions and just before and after those restrictions end because it is only two lanes in each direction.

If coming from the South, visitors should take I-395 North from Springfield, Virginia into Arlington County. After passing the Glebe Road exit, get in the second lane from the right to the Washington Boulevard/Memorial Bridge exit and go past the Pentagon and Arlington National Cemetery. Get in far left lane as you pass the Pentagon. This will take you across Memorial Bridge. Cross the bridge in the center lane. At the Lincoln Memorial bear left and follow the road to the left on Henry Bacon Drive (past the Vietnam Veteran's Memorial) until it ends at Constitution Avenue; make a right onto Constitution. Turn left onto 18th Street, go three very short blocks. Turn right on D Street.

2.2
PUBLIC TRANSPORTATION

Metrorail
The DAR was not consulted when the Metro subway system was constructed or when bus routes were laid out! The park-like area that has been DAR's home since 1910 is, therefore, unfortunately several blocks from the closest Metro stations. These are:

Farragut West (Orange and Blue Lines) – 6 blocks due north of the DAR at 17th and 18th Streets and I ("Eye") Street, N.W. Get off at the Farragut West Metro stop. Exit the station on 17th Street, and walk south on 17th Street towards Constitution Avenue and the Washington Monument. Turn right on D Street. On Saturdays and Sundays, you must use the 18th Street exit from this station; walk south on 18th Street and turn left on D Street.

Farragut North (Red Line) – 7 blocks due north of the DAR at 17th and K Streets and Connecticut Avenue, N.W. Get off at the Farragut North Metro stop. Exit the station from the K Street/17th Street end, cross K Street, and walk south on 17th Street next to Farragut Square park. Continue on 17th Street towards Constitution. Turn right on D Street.

Metrobus
Metrobuses run during the morning and evening rush hours *only* on the following routes. There is little Saturday service on these routes. For exact schedules, routes, and fares call Metro at 202-637-7000 or visit Metro online at **www.metroopensdoors.com.**

Mornings
From the Pentagon Metro Station in Virginia (connections from many Northern Virginia Metrobuses, Alexandria DASH buses, Fairfax Connector buses, Prince William Transit and other commuter buses, and the Blue and Yellow Metro lines) the 13A bus crosses Memorial Bridge and goes east on Constitution Avenue. Stops at 19th and 17th Streets (eastbound) are two blocks south of DAR. The 13B bus begins at the Pentagon, crosses the 14th Street Bridge, connects with other District Metrobus routes at 7th and 10th Streets and runs westbound from points east of DAR on Constitution Avenue eventually returning to the Pentagon. It is not the quickest route from the Pentagon in the morning, but in the afternoon riders may pick this bus up at 19th Street and Constitution Avenue's northeast corner to return to the Pentagon. These buses run about every 15-20 minutes during rush hours.

The 80 line runs from the Kennedy Center to Virginia Avenue southeast to 18th Street and then north on 18th past DAR. The S1 line begins at Virginia Avenue and 22nd Street, NW and follows Virginia Avenue and then goes north on 18th Street past DAR. The 80 bus runs on Saturday at a reduced schedule. These routes connect DAR with the Metro stations at Farragut West and Farragut North, and the 80 route even goes all the way to Union Station for Amtrak and MARC Rail connections.

Afternoons
After 3:00 p.m. catch the westbound 13B bus at the northeast corner of 19th Street and Constitution Avenue (no afternoon stop at 17th Street) and return to the Pentagon Metro Station.

Catch the eastbound 13A bus at the southeast corner of 17th Street and Constitution (the corner closest to the Washington Monument).

To points in Northwest Washington, catch the L1 bus on C Street immediately behind DAR Headquarters. It is marked "Chevy Chase Circle," and stops at points enroute.

The 80 bus, which is marked "Fort Totten" and runs throughout the day, stops at 18th and C Streets and continues north up 18th Street to L Street, turns right and continues its route to Union Station and Fort Totten in Northeast Washington. This bus may be used to reach the Metro stations on the Blue, Orange and Red lines mentioned previously.

2.3
HOURS AND HOLIDAYS

DAR's regular hours are:

Monday-Friday	8:30 a.m. to 4:00 p.m.
Saturday	9:00 a.m. to 5:00 p.m. (The Library, Seimes Microfilm Center and the Museum are open; all other offices are closed).
Sunday	Closed (since June 1, 2002)
Closings	DAR is closed for all Federal holidays. Occasionally, there are other special closings as well. Call to verify hours.

DAR is open only to its members during several days in late June or early July each year prior to and during its annual convention, Continental Congress. DAR is closed to the public from the weekend immediately preceding the first day of Congress on Wednesday and through the weekend and succeeding Monday. Check our website for specific dates each year as they will vary.

Inclement Weather: Generally, DAR closes for bad weather when the Federal Government does. Call 202-879-1776 for a recorded message before attempting a visit. Always call to be certain DAR is open before making a visit near a holiday, special event, or in early July.

2.4
LUNCH FACILITIES

DAR has a lunchroom on the lower level with coffee, soft drinks, snack and hot food machines, and microwave ovens. Restaurants are in several nearby buildings or up 17th Street near Pennsylvania Avenue. The Department of the Interior Cafeteria, across 18th Street from DAR, is open to the public, but one must present a photo ID to gain entrance. During periods of heightened security levels, permission to enter the Interior Department may be denied by their security staff. Visitors in groups may have to register individually with DOI security to enter their building. All visitors to the Department of the Interior must pass through a metal detector at the security checkpoint when you enter the building, and the less you take in with you the easier your admission will be. During Continental Congress week, temporary catered lunch facilities are available in DAR's lunchroom.

2.5
GROUP VISITS

Group visits to DAR are welcomed and encouraged. Individuals planning a research trip to the Library may wish to check with local, state or national genealogical societies about participation in possible group visits to Washington, D.C. that these groups might sponsor.

When planning your group's visit please follow these guidelines for the DAR Library. Other research centers in the city will have similar requirements, but it is best to check with each for details, especially any relating to security considerations.

- All calls regarding visits by groups of over 5 people should be made to the DAR Library at (202) 879-3229. Please provide your name and telephone number or that of the group's leader as a contact in the event we need to call someone. Remember that weather conditions and holidays in your area may not be the same as in Washington, D.C. On occasion major events or security concerns in the Nation's Capital can lead to street closings, worse-than-normal traffic congestion, and general inconvenience for visitors. Groups need to be aware of the general situation in the city when planning a visit.

- Schedule your group's visit as far in advance as possible. This allows us to reserve the day you choose or to notify you of conflicts. The Library Office maintains a calendar just for group visits. Groups may not visit during the week before or the week of the DAR's annual Continental Congress. For 2004 through 2010, Continental Congress will be in late June/early July, *not* April. The DAR observes most federal government holidays. Give yourself plenty of time to adjust schedules.

- Please let the Library know what time you expect to arrive. The staff will give an orientation to the Library, *if* the group requests one in advance and once all group members are present.

- The best days for group visits are Tuesdays through Thursdays, but Mondays and Fridays can certainly be scheduled. We prefer not to have large group visits on Saturdays. The Library can be extremely crowded on Saturdays, and space is very limited. Orientations cannot be given on Saturdays. DAR is closed on Sundays.

- There is an entrance fee for non-members per day. There are no group fees or reductions for more than one day. If you have a large group, it is helpful for the person leading the group to collect the entrance fees from non-DAR members prior to arrival. Present the collected fees to the Library staff member at the reference desk. This prevents long lines when entering the Library. A check for the total is also acceptable and should be made payable to "Treasurer General, NSDAR."

- Visitors to the DAR must pass through a metal detector when entering the building. Bags, packages and briefcases are subject to inspection on entering *and* leaving the building. Please advise your group to leave their pocket knives, nail files, and similar items at home. Such items will be confiscated in any building they attempt to enter.

- All members of the group must wear some type of name badge when visiting any Washington research facility. Group members do not sign-in individually at the D Street entrance guard's desk, but everyone in the group must wear either a group name badge or a DAR Visitor's badge while visiting the building. We do ask that everyone sign in at the Library's register for statistical reasons. Please be sure that all of your members bring a photo ID with them to Washington. This is required for admission to many buildings, including the Department of the Interior, where the closest cafeteria is located.

- Should your plans change and you need either to shift your visit or cancel it please let us know by calling 202-879-3229.

- The Library can provide your group with pamphlets and other information sheets in advance to help prepare for your visit. Please state the number of copies you will need, and we will gladly send the appropriate material in advance for distribution to your group.

2.6
SECURITY AND SAFETY

Visitors to Washington, D.C. should exercise the same caution and awareness they would in any large city. DAR is located in an area with much street and pedestrian traffic. Security personnel in the area surrounding the White House add further vigilance. Basically, be aware of your surroundings. DAR members are urged not to wear their ribbons and pins walking down the street. This is simply a general precaution. The walk to and from the Metro stations is basically a comfortable and safe one.

At DAR, visitors must sign in at the guard desk at the D Street entrance. Each visitor must pass through a metal detector. Pocket knives and other sharp or potentially threatening objects will be confiscated at the time of entry. Each individual receives a visitor's badge, which they should wear in a prominent place at all times and should return at the end of the day. All DAR staff members wear an employee's badge displaying their name and picture. Bags, purses and briefcases are subject to search both upon entry and exit from the building. Photography is generally not allowed in the building. Additional new security measures have been implemented to protect the collections.

Like the neighboring federal agencies, DAR had emergency response procedures in place in the event of a disaster either natural or otherwise. These procedures are designed to safely protect all occupants of the DAR buildings. In order to be ready for an emergency, the DAR will on occasion conduct drills to test the emergency response of employees and visitors. *The DAR asks that all visitors to the buildings at the time of these drills to cooperate by participating in emergency response drills*. DAR staff will assist visitors in responding to these drills.

Please watch your step when walking in the Library; step stools are frequently in the aisles. Be careful when standing on step stools. Should you need assistance in reaching an item, please ask the staff to help you.

2.7
DAR HEADQUARTERS FLOORPLAN

FIRST FLOOR

SECOND FLOOR

★ ★

Chapter 3

THE DAR LIBRARY

**A view of the setting for the DAR Library in the former
Auditorium of Memorial Continental Hall.**

*Memorial Continental Hall, First Floor
Library Office telephone number: (202) 879-3229
(a recording only when the Library is closed)
Fax number: (202) 879-3227
Email address: library@dar.org
Reference desk **direct** telephone number: (202) <u>777</u>-2366
Acquisitions telephone number: (202) 879-3250
Serials telephone number: (202) 879-3228*

In early 1896, DAR established a library in its cramped offices in downtown Washington's commercial district. The primary purposes at the inception were to provide reference material to assist with the verification of membership applications and preservation of historic documents. Not long afterwards, the general public was granted access, thereby expanding the library's purpose to include providing genealogical services to non-members as well as to DAR members. Early in 1910 the offices and the Library moved to Memorial Continental Hall, the National Society's new building. The Library moved again to space in Constitution Hall in 1929 but returned to the converted auditorium of Memorial Continental Hall in 1949 where it remains today.

The DAR Library is a highly specialized collection focusing primarily, but not exclusively, on American genealogy and history. When the Library was established in 1896, the basic collection policy, which remains in place today, emerged:

> ... the field covered by the collection is that part of America represented by local history (state, county, town, and church), genealogies, biographies and vital records. Histories of all kinds relating to the American Revolution, including military and civil records are desired, everything in fact that will assist in throwing light upon the men of the Revolutionary period, including their family lines as well as their service, and connect them with their descendants of the present day.

During the past century, the Library, along with other DAR departments, has grown into one of the major genealogical research centers in the United States. Donations of books, research materials, periodicals, and other sources by Daughters and non–members alike have been the basis for this growth. The result is one of the "must visit" places for genealogists coming to the Nation's Capital.

3.1
USER FEES AND GENERAL GUIDELINES

The Library has been open to the public since the early years of the twentieth century. In 1939 DAR initiated a fee for non-members to support the Library's basic operations, including book purchasing and binding. This remains the case today. The Library charges a daily user fee to non-members of the DAR, SAR, SR, and CAR. Members of the latter three groups must present a *current* membership card to receive the fee waver; there are no exceptions to this policy. Members of the National Huguenot Society, which donated its library to the DAR in 2003, are also exempt from the entrance fee with a current membership card until 2013. Fees at lunchtime on weekdays are reduced. Cash, personal checks, and traveler's checks are accepted for the entry fee, but not credit cards. Fees are posted at the Library's entrance, and *the staff cannot negotiate their reduction or elimination.*

Researchers are welcome to bring their laptop computers. Surge protectors are mounted on the underside of the tables in the Library as a power source for laptops, but on crowded days, there may be a limited number of outlets available.

Photography within DAR Headquarters is generally not permitted. Personal hand-held photocopiers, scanners and digital cameras may not be used in any DAR department for the reproduction of materials.

The use of cell phones is not permitted in the Library.

3.2
CATALOGS AND SPECIAL FINDING AIDS

3.2.1
The Catalogs: Online, Card, and Published

The Library's catalog has had several different forms over the past century. These all warrant some discussion because most retain their value even today.

3.2.1.1
Online Catalog

The online catalog is accessible at the Library's portion of the DAR's website at **www.dar.org**. In Spring 2004 the latest version of this catalog was unveiled and provided researchers with expanded search capabilities.

Beginning in March 1996 the card catalogs in the Library and Seimes Technology Center were merged into an online catalog. Since then, all new materials acquired by the Library were entered electronically, and the card catalog was closed to new entries.

In the Library's reading room, the online catalog is available to the public at computers located next to the reference desk in the Library. The basic search functions are by author, title, or subject. The computerization of the catalog has allowed the Library staff to offer greater access to the collection than ever before.

A project initiated by the Library staff and utilizing the online catalog is proving helpful. The Library has a largely complete run of many of the standard *historical* journals (not the genealogical journals) for the United States and the individual states. Many of these journals contain articles relating to the American Revolution, family histories, local and church histories, etc. Starting in 2001, the staff began to catalog *some* of the articles in these journals that related to topics of importance to DAR members, staff and researchers. An entry in the catalog with quotation marks around the title is a reference to an article. This was seen as a way to unlock some information in underutilized publications.

In another ongoing project, the staff adds the contents of individual *Genealogical Records Committee Reports* to the online records as a means of improving access to these important sources. The contents are fully searchable in the online catalog by keyword. This is an excellent complement to the effort to index all the G.R.C. volumes, and in 2004 the separate, online GRC National Index was linked to the cataloging record for each volume to provide context for the index entries. This index may be found adjacent to the link for the online catalog in the Library's portion of the DAR website.

3.2.1.2
Old Card Catalogs to 1996

Prior to the late 1970's the Library had a very basic dictionary catalog with few subject tracings. There were not any call numbers or spine labels on the books to help locate items. The catalog was interfiled with the Analytical Index. In 1970-1971 the Genealogical Society of Utah microfilmed the entire finding aid. This microfilm has limited usefulness today because of the many subsequent changes and additions. In the mid-1980s the staff carefully and methodically removed the old cataloging records from the catalog leaving the Analytical Index alone in its place. The old catalog is still maintained in storage for occasional use in reference and cataloging work.

A "reclassification project" in the late 1970s and early 1980s and subsequent cataloging to 1996 produced the next card catalog. The time and expense of producing a card catalog became excessive in a period when computers could help perform this work. Consequently, the card catalog was "frozen" in March 1996. In 2004, this catalog was removed from the reading room and placed in storage. It has been superseded by the online catalog.

3.2.1.3
Published Catalogs of Library Holdings in the Twentieth Century

The DAR has produced published catalogs of its book holdings three times in this century.

1920: *Historical and Genealogical Works, National Society Daughters of the American Revolution Library, Memorial Continental Hall.*

1940: *Catalogue of Genealogical and Historical Works, Library of the National Society Daughters of the American Revolution.*

1982-1992: *DAR Library Catalog Volume One: Family Histories and Genealogies* (1982)
Supplement to Volume One: Family Histories and Genealogies (1984)
Volume Two: State and Local Histories and Records (1986)
Volume Three: Centennial Supplement: Acquisitions 1985-1991 (1992)

The three-volume set, *The DAR Library Catalog*, listed available titles through 1991 and superseded all previous catalogs. These books, which are owned by libraries nationwide, are now out of print and will not be reprinted. The online catalog has also superseded these publications.

3.2.2
ANALYTICAL INDEX

Beginning in the 1910s, Library staff and volunteers produced an Analytical Index amounting to over 300 card drawers. This index, typical of similar finding aids in libraries large and small, provides access points to many older county histories and to special book and file collections within the Library. *Genealogical Records Committee Reports* created prior to 1970 are also partially indexed here. As part of the continuing President General's Project to digitize DAR records and indexes, the Analytical Index will be digitized, indexed, and made available online to researchers.

The variety of indexing techniques used to create cards makes for some interesting entries. A title noted in 1930 may not really be the complete title of the book. Creative abbreviations abound. There are many cryptic references to information in this index, but, of course, the staff will help interpret these. Despite these drawbacks, this index is an invaluable finding aid. To locate information cited in the index, one must consult the online catalog under either the author or title for the book containing the desired reference. Then one must determine the proper call words for the volume, because very few cards in the Analytical Index contain call words for books.

3.2.3
SPECIAL INDICES

Various smaller and separate card indices lead researchers to information on such subjects as all names mentioned in selected Revolutionary War pension applications, the names of some Virginia women during the Revolution, and the library's manuscript collection of genealogical research materials. Other smaller card indices are also available. The staff suspects that several of these have been superseded by newer printed finding aids, but the indices remain available on the slight chance that a morsel of information may have been missed in the newer compilations.

Index to Names Appearing in Revolutionary War Pensions

This twenty-three drawer index contains references to the names of individuals which appear in abstracts of some Revolutionary War pensions. These abstracts were prepared by DAR staff and volunteers to help prove pending application papers prior to the early 1960s. It is not a complete index of all Revolutionary War pensions. Besides giving an abstract of a pensioner's papers, this index also provides the names of other pensions mentioned in the pension that can be valuable when searching for information on individuals living during the late eighteenth and early nineteenth centuries. The 340 volumes of pension abstracts indexed by this finding aid include 233 covering pensions of veterans from around the country; 101 for pensions of New Hampshire veterans; and 6 for pensions of Rhode Island veterans. Additional information on Revolutionary War pensions is in section 13.20.4.15. As part of the ongoing President General's Project, this index will be digitized and made available online.

Virginia Women in the American Revolution

Anne Waller Reddy, a genealogical researcher in Virginia during the mid-twentieth century willed her papers and files to the DAR Library upon her death in 1971. The material included this card index containing references to women living during the Revolution who Miss Reddy found in Virginia records and sources. Most of the actual records are not available in the DAR Library. See the next entry for further sources.

Index to the Ann Waller Reddy Collection

Miss Reddy's research papers during her residence in Richmond, Virginia from the 1930s to 1970 comprise this collection. Her lengthy files focus strictly on Virginia families, especially those in eastern and central parts of the state. The index provides access to the major names in each group of files.

Index to Jefferson County, Kentucky Marriages, 1784-1826

Maryland Marriages (miscellaneous): Baltimore City, Caroline County, Charles County, Frederick County, Harford County, Montgomery County, Prince George's County, Worcester County.

Contains miscellaneous records from the specified jurisdictions, mostly from the 1790s, early 1800s, and later in the nineteenth century.

Index to Miscellaneous Marriage References

This index was compiled many years ago, and the staff does not add to it. It contains marriage references arranged first by state and then by surname. We speculate that it was created as part of a defunct project and have no additional information on its sources.

Index to *Michigan Pioneer and Historical Collections*

This index provides access to this important set of forty books on early settlers in Michigan. It is also useful for research in New York, New England, and the Midwest.

3.2.4
INDICES TO LIBRARY MATERIALS ON MICROFILM

In the early 1970s, the Genealogical Society of Utah produced nearly 2,800 microfilm rolls of thousands of one–of–a–kind volumes in the DAR Library. **Printed indices** for much of this material exist, and although these are located in libraries throughout the country, many researchers are unaware of their value and purpose. See the Genealogical Records Committee discussion in Chapter 4 for further details. These four books are *The Vital Record Compendium, The Cemetery Record Compendium, An Index to Some of the Family Records of the Southern States,* and *An Index to Some of the Bibles and Family Records of the United States (excluding the Southern States).* The microfilms are available at DAR, the Family History Library in Salt Lake City, and the Allen County Public Library in Fort Wayne, Indiana.

3.3
THE ARRANGEMENT OF THE DAR LIBRARY

The DAR Library has a unique arrangement, which does not use the Dewey Decimal or Library of Congress classification systems to organize books on the shelf. Instead, a "term classification" system is in place, which utilizes "call words" instead of "call numbers." It is based on the existing arrangement of the books when the entire collection was reclassified in the early 1980s. This layout has an overall geographical focus and subject categories within it. The system is very conducive to browsing and easily adaptable to changing needs and new materials. Most researchers will find the arrangement very different at first, but many have also commented that they wish other libraries had such a "genealogy–friendly" system that does not rely on numbers.

There are four major subdivisions of the Library's book collection: General, Families, States & Regions, and Special Collections.

3.3.1
GENERAL SECTION

The General Section contains many subject breakdowns that contain books on general aspects of history and genealogy in the United States. The individual subjects are shelved within the General Section in alphabetical order. Within each subject there are further subdivisions as needed. The following list gives most of the subject subdivisions within the General Section and some representative examples of further breakdowns. Space limitations on the spine labels necessitate the use of some abbreviations or truncations in the "call words." A diagonal indicates the beginning of a new line, and therefore a new subdivision of a subject. Within each subject and subsection the final line of the "call word" will be the first three letters of the author's last name or of the first word in the title if there is no author.

- **Research**
  Research/Directories
  Research/Historiography
- **Adoption**
- **African American** (Studies of the African American experience with subdivisions)
- **Arch** (Architecture)
- **Arch-Lib** (Archives and Libraries)
  Arch-Lib/LC (Library of Congress)
  Arch-Lib/LDS (LDS Family History Library and System)
  Arch-Lib/NARA (National Archives and Records Administration)
- **Bibliogra** (Bibliography)
- **Biography** (Collected biographies, not the same as the "Biography" section.)
- **Cemeteries** (Cemetery locators and literature on cemeteries.)
- **Census** (Arranged by state, then by census year. Census indices in the collection are located in the Seimes Microfilm Center or on CD Rom behind the Reference desk).
- **Computers** (Computer applications for genealogy)
- **Dictionaries** (English and many foreign language dictionaries)
- **Emig** (Emigration and Immigration; arranged in a general section followed by national/ethnic groups in alphabetical order with a section of published passenger lists.)
- **Families** (Contains collected works on families and general studies on the history of the American family. It is not the same as the "Families" section below.)
- **Genetics**
- **Geography** (Contains atlases, gazetteers, and postal directories)
- **History** (United States history arranged chronologically)
  History/1607-1775 (The Colonial Period)
  History/1775-1783 (The American Revolution)
    History/1775-1783/African American
    History/1775-1783/Bibliogra
    History/1775-1783/Biography
    History/1775-1783/Claims
    History/1775-1783/Congress
    History/1775-1783/F: + a country's name (Foreign involvement in the Revolution by country in alphabetical order, i.e. History/1775-1783/F:France.)
    History/1775-1783/Folklore
    History/1775-1783/Geography
    History/1775-1783/Jews
    History/1775-1783/Loyalists
    History/1775-1783/Military
    History/1775-1783/Music
    History/1775-1783/Naval
    History/1775-1783/Newspapers
    History/1775-1783/Pensions
    History/1775-1783/Periodica
    History/1775-1783/Prisoners
    History/1775-1783/Records
    History/1775-1783/Religion

History/1775-1783/Spies
History/1775-1783/Vital
History/1783-1812
History/1783/1812-1815 (The War of 1812)
History/1815-1861
History/1815-1861/Mexican War
History/1861-1865 (The American Civil War with subdivisions)
History/1865-1917
History/1917-1918 (World War I)
History/1918-1941
History/1941-1945 (World War II)
History/1945- (The Library generally does not collect much post-World War II history material unless it is specifically genealogical.)

- **Index** (Major historical and genealogical indices)
- **Land** (Basic studies and sources on United States land records)
- **Military** (General studies and histories of the United States military)
- **Names** (Books on name studies)
- **Newspapers** (Information on United States newspapers)
- **Pensions** (Published compilations of pensions for various wars)
- **Periodica** (Major nationally-focused genealogical and historical periodicals filed in alphabetical order by title.)
- **Records** (General sources of United States historical records, mostly government publications.)
- **Reference** (Miscellaneous reference sources)
- **Religion** (General books on the history of religion in the United States followed by subdivisions for specific Christian denominations and Judaism)
- **Vital** (A miscellany of vital records covering the entire United States or major portions.)
- **Wills** (Some collections of wills from around the United States)

Typical "call words" in the General Section look like this in sequence on book spine labels:

GEN	GEN	GEN	GEN	GEN
ADOPTION	CEMETERY	EMIG	HISTORY	PERIODICA
SMI	AGS	POLISH	1607-1775	TAG
		KAM	JON	

3.3.2
FAMILIES SECTION

The family histories and genealogies are arranged on the shelf in alphabetical order by the main (or sometimes, first) surname in the title or contents. Cross-references in the catalog provide access points for other major surnames covered by each book. A "call word" for a Morrison family history by an author named Smith would look like this in the online catalog: FAMILIES/MORRISON/SMITH, and like this on the spine label of the book:

FAMILIES
MORRISON
SMITH

Interpreted, this means the book is in the Families Section in the "M's," in alphabetical order under "Morrison." The third line is the author's last name, and if there are multiple books on a surname, they are in alphabetical order by each author within the surname's section.

3.3.3
STATES AND REGIONS SECTION

Within the Library's collection, the states, regions and District of Columbia are arranged in alphabetical order within several larger sections of the country. East Coast states and a few others, such as Kentucky, Tennessee, and Ohio, occupy the majority of the Library's first floor. All others are on the Library's balconies. The "northeastern" regions of New England and New Netherland are on the first floor interfiled in alphabetical order with the states. "The South" and the "Midwest" regions are on the balconies.

Each state and region has subsections, which in most cases are the same as the subsections of the General Section listed above. Books on specific cities and towns are located in the county in which they are located. Independent cities, such as Baltimore, Maryland and those in Virginia, are located in the counties that surround them. New York City has its own section with subdivisions and precedes the New York state section. The towns of the New England states are arranged in alphabetical order within the county in which they are located. There is some variation, however, in the subsections based on specific unique situations in certain states. The major subdivisions within the states and regions are:

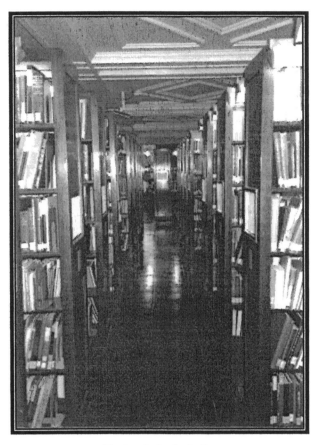

The bookstacks in the
State section of the Library.

- **African American**
- **Architecture**
- **Archives and Libraries**
- **Bibliography**
- **Biography**
- **Counties** (By far this is the largest portion of each state section. Regions do not have a "county" subdivision. The counties are in alphabetical order, and within each county's section the books are arranged in alphabetical order by the first three letters of the author's last name or of the title if there is no author. "Parishes" is the term used in Louisiana, of course, instead of counties.)
- **Education**
- **Emigration and Immigration**
- **Families**

- **G.R.C.** (the state DAR's Genealogical Records Committee set)
- **Geography**
- **History**
- **Land**
- **Law**
- **Military**
- **Newspapers**
- **Periodicals**
- **Records**
- **Reference**
- **Regions** (publications concerning recognized historic regions of a state)
- **Religion**
- **Vital**
- **Wills**
- **Women**

Representative call numbers in the Alabama section would look like this in sequence on book spines:

ALA	ALA	ALA	ALA	ALA	ALA
ARCH	COUNTIES	HISTORY	LAND	MILITARY	VITAL
BLA	JEFFERSON	GAN	GOL	HAM	GRE
	GAN	JON			

3.3.4
SPECIAL COLLECTIONS

The Library maintains several special collections that are housed in various locations. Each has its own separate subject subdivisions, but these are essentially the same as those in the General Section and the State and Regions Section. These Special Collections are:

A view from the Library's South Balcony.

- **American Indian Collection** is a significant collection of materials on the first peoples of North America focusing on genealogy, history, and culture. The books are arranged by general subject groups, but materials specific to a nation/tribe are organized first by broad Native American cultural areas and then by the nation/tribe name. See section 13.22.

- **Biography** contains studies of prominent historical Americans and collected biography. See section 13.3 for more information.

- **City Directories** number 1,100 volumes from around the United States, mostly from the early twentieth century. See section 13.6.

- **DAR Publications** include DAR State organization rosters and histories and *The DAR Lineage Books*. See Chapter 12.

- **Foreign Research** is a basic gathering of books to assist researchers with investigations beyond the United States. Refer to section 13.11.

- **National Huguenot Society Collection** focuses on the history and genealogy of French Huguenot immigrants to the American colonies and the story of Protestants in France. This collection was donated to the DAR Library in 2003.

- **Women's History** is a small collection on the history of women in the United States. This collection is located in the Library's office. See sections 13.20.4.6 and 13.29.

In addition to these Special Collections housed on the balconies, the Library has other Special Collections and special condition books stored in areas mostly accessible to the staff only. Please ask for assistance in locating materials in the following collections:

- **American Flag Collection** consists of a small set on the history of the American flag.

- **Lineage Society Collection** includes many but not all publications of other lineage societies similar to the DAR, such as the Sons of the American Revolution, the Sons of the Revolution, the Colonial Dames of the XVII Century, and others. See section 13.18 for more information.

- **"Locked Case" Books** are cataloged books that are locked in cases because of their age, rarity or value. Researchers must present one form of identification to use these volumes, leave the ID at the reference desk, and return the book to regain their ID. Watch for the initials "L.C." at the beginning of the call words in the catalog.

- **Oversize Section** houses books that will not fit easily on the regular shelves. Their cataloging records note "OV" before the call words. Oversized books for the eastern states are located mainly along the back wall of the Library. Oversized family books and books for the remaining states are found on the balcony areas.

- **"Poor Condition" Books** are cataloged books that are brittle or fragile and must be handled with care. Catalog records for poor condition books have the initials P.C. before the call words. Please request such books at the reference desk only. In most cases, photocopies cannot be made from these books.

- **W.P.A. Collection** contains a large percentage of the publications of the Historical Records Survey of the Works Progress Administration. Patrons who wish to use this collection must make a request at the Library Reference Desk. See section 13.10 for further information.

3.4
FILE COLLECTION

The Library's file collection is a mixture of materials that have come with DAR membership applications (see Chapter 6.7), subsequent donations by DAR members, and items given by the public. Innumerable Bible records, family studies, pamphlets, and research notes are included. Numbering an estimated 300,000 folders, the richness and variety of the collection covers the entire United States and concentrates on the eighteenth, nineteenth, and early twentieth centuries, with significant colonial records as well.

There are no published or in-house guides to the files, which grow by several boxes each month. The simple arrangement in one alphabet within each division of the files by the names of Revolutionary War ancestors or family surnames makes for relatively easy retrieval.

A miscellany of brief sources for each state including pamphlets, short typescripts, handwritten notes, published booklets, extracted journal and newspaper articles and clippings, and copies of original documents comprises the Library's "State File Collection." Cemetery records, military lists, church materials, local histories, and other historically useful materials are represented. Researchers must request staff assistance to browse through a state section for items of interest.

The library staff assists researchers in locating and copying material in the file collection. All files must be ordered and used in the Library at the tables adjacent to the reference desk. Most items in the files may be photocopied, but birth certificates, death certificates, and other vital records from state health agencies *cannot* be copied regardless of age.

Beginning in 2003, the DAR's digitizing project turned to the contents of the file collection. The results of this effort will be the entire retrospective conversion of the files into digital format, with the original papers being placed in off-site storage. The accessibility of these materials online at DAR headquarters will represent an enormous enhancement of research capabilities for American genealogists and the opening of much hidden information.

3.5
MANUSCRIPT COLLECTION

A growing manuscript library of genealogical research materials is one of the lesser-known components of the DAR Library. Each month sees the arrival of boxes and folders of documents, unpublished genealogies, research notes, and indexes. Examples include the Anne Waller Reddy Collection of Virginia family research performed by a Richmond genealogist in the mid–twentieth century; the Eunice B. Haden collection of genealogical research; the Frederick A. Virkus collection; and Lyman Chalkley's original annotated typescript for his three–volume publication *Chronicles of the Scotch–Irish Settlement in Virginia*, first published by the DAR in 1912.

Currently, the manuscript holdings of the Library amount to about 300 individual collections of varying size, some of which have been cataloged to the folder level. The Library's online catalog provides access to the manuscript collection.

The Library often receives requests from individuals for information on a relative's research materials that "were given to the DAR." Very rarely does the staff locate such a collection, but sometimes the search is successful. A possible solution may be that the relative gave it to the local DAR chapter or state organization. They in turn may have donated it to a local genealogical or historical society or kept the material for their own files. Such materials are unlikely to appear in indices

Genealogists of families that live in or passed through Virginia's Shenandoah Valley will all know the name of Lyman Chalkley and his three-volume work *Chronicles of the Scotch-Irish Settlement in Virginia Extracted from the Original Court Records of Augusta County 1745-1800*. Few will realize, however, that this set was originally published by the DAR in 1912, seven years after the National Society purchased the manuscript from Judge Chalkley.

Publication of the *Chronicles* was not without controversy, owing in large part to the fact that the abstracts comprising the book were by no means complete and were very selective. The *Proceedings* for both the 1911 and 1912 DAR Continental Congress contain lengthy discussions on the merits and drawbacks to publishing Chalkley's manuscripts. DAR even commissioned an independent review of the materials. This was performed by Thomas Forsythe Nelson, was entitled *Report on the Chalkley Manuscripts*, and concluded that while the work was useful, the pervasive gaps therein diminished its publication value.

After much discussion, the DAR decided to publish the material despite its limitations to make some information available from the extensive historical records of Virginia's Augusta County. Chalkley's set has assumed a major place in the historical and genealogical literature of the Shenandoah Valley. It has been reprinted several times. Researchers should be aware that there are many omissions from the original records and should not consider these books the final word from Augusta County's early records. Chalkley's original handwritten volumes and notes are part of the DAR Library's Manuscript Collection.

to manuscript collections such as online or print versions of *The National Union Catalog of Manuscript Collections (NUCMC)*. Researchers should exhaust all possible leads regarding such donations.

Some research notes and materials from individuals do exist on the shelves of the Library. In decades past, the staff took such loose papers, bound them together, and added them to the collection as a volume. These materials appear in the collection now as books.

With a functioning manuscript collection and proper donation procedures in place, the Library welcomes donations of research material. When such collections arrive, they are given a collection name (usually the name of the donor or compiler), accessioned, cataloged with subject tracings, and added to the Manuscript Collection for use.

3.6
SEARCH SERVICE

The DAR Library offers a research service to members and non-members. The "DAR Library Search Service" information sheet may be printed from the DAR web site at **http://www.dar.org/library** under "Search Services." Please consult the sheet for fees and procedures. These may change if necessary and without prior notice.

3.7
PHOTOCOPIES

The DAR Library has photocopiers available for patron use in the reading room. Library patrons may make photocopies from books and periodicals, but not from the files, manuscripts or maps. The Library staff will make photocopies from these materials at the request of the patron. To obtain a photocopy from files, manuscripts or maps, the researcher should fill out a "photocopy order slip" for each file. The request slips are available at the reference desk and at the tables adjacent to the reference desk.

Copyright is a major consideration in the duplication of materials. The DAR Library will not copy entire books or major portions of books for researchers, especially if a book is still under copyright. The staff will assist researchers in an attempt to locate current order information for a book. Researchers may request photocopies by mail from the Library's Search Service. See section 3.6.

On occasion, the staff will not make copies if the copying process will damage the item, or if there is some type of legal restriction on the item such as vital records from a state health agency. Researchers should expect this possibility, and their understanding is appreciated.

Personal hand-held copiers, scanners or digital cameras are not permitted to be used in any DAR department.

MEMORIAL CONTINENTAL HALL
LIBRARY

3.8
BOOK AND SERIALS DONATIONS

The Library welcomes donations of genealogical books and other materials by DAR members and the public. Please contact the Acquisitions Librarian to offer items to the Library (202-879-3250). Gifts to the DAR Library can be made using the "Gift Approval and Donation Form." Donors may obtain a copy of this form in the Library, by contacting the Library's acquisitions staff, or by printing the form from the DAR web site at **http://www.dar.org/library** under "Ways to Give." Books and periodicals need not be bound or indexed to be acceptable, but binding and indexing are always desirable. The general types of material acceptable to the Library fall into these categories:

- Genealogy and family history
- State history, record abstracts, etc.
- Records and histories of religious groups and denominations; church histories
- Historical and genealogical periodicals, newsletters, journals, yearbooks, etc.
- Ethnic-American history and genealogy
- Local history, record abstracts, etc.
- U.S. history, records abstracts, etc.
- Histories of the Revolutionary War era
- Biographies of major figures in U.S. history
- U.S. women's history
- Native American history and genealogy

One of the unanticipated but none-the-less desirable results of what I might call the ancestral-patriotic movement is the publication of a variety of fresh, delightful books relating to American history. Personally, I delight in these accessions to our Daughters of the American Revolution Library to such an extent that I have to add many of them to my private library, even though my shelves are filled to overflowing.

Anita Newcomb McGee,
First DAR Librarian General,
In her column "Our Library"
American Monthly Magazine, 1897, p.188-189.

Please **do not** send items in the following subject areas:

- Poetry
- Literature
- Cookbooks
- Illustrated historical calendars
- Chapter yearbooks/directories
- Historical fiction
- Foreign history, except Canadian, which is acceptable.

3.9
FINDING RECENT AND OUT–OF–PRINT BOOKS

Recent books often have order information printed on the back of the title page. The Library staff will help locate publisher information from this source and our acquisition records. Such standard sources as *Books in Print*, publisher catalogs, and the book review sections of major genealogical and historical journals assist with this type of search. There are also a number of sources online for new books. Most publishers now have their own web site for ordering. In addition, there are specialty bookstores and well-known clearinghouses on the Internet that deal in a variety of books and other materials.

Many, many books in the Library, however, are no longer available for purchase from the author or publisher, especially the family histories and genealogies. For copyright and staffing reasons the Library cannot copy entire books. Incredibly, some ask us to sell the books to them, which is, of course, impossible. Several genealogical publishers do republish older and out of print books, including family histories and at least one publisher will reprint family histories on demand.

The Library maintains many catalogs of recent publications and receives a number of catalogs from out of print/rare book dealers. Directories of these are also available such as the Burns' *A Guide to Used Book Dealers of the Mid-Atlantic*. Here again the Internet is a possible source as a number of used and rare book dealer consortiums maintain web sites, such as **www.abebooks.com** (Advanced Book Exchange). The DAR does not, however, endorse any of these sites.

Researchers should also check local yellow page listings under "Books-Used and Rare" for their home city or city in the locality of research interest. These dealers will check their own stock, and many will do searches.

GENEALOGICAL RECORDS COMMITTEE

The New York DAR's Genealogical Records Committee set contains nearly 1,000 volumes.

In 1913 DAR established the "Genealogical Research Committee" as an internal network to collect genealogical information for the DAR Library. The name changed to "Genealogical Records Committee" (G.R.C.) in 1932. The main function of this committee and its state and chapter chairmen is to copy, prepare in proper form, bind, and place in the Library information of genealogical value from unpublished sources such as family Bibles, gravestones, court records, etc. A small manual, *Instructions for Copying Source Records and Their Preparation for Library Use*, is available explaining how this work should be performed. Since its inception, the G.R.C. has worked to gather this information with great success.

4.1
G.R.C. REPORTS

Numbering over 18,000 typescript volumes, the *Genealogical Records Committee Reports*, as they are collectively called, comprise one of the most important and unique parts of the DAR Library's holdings. DAR members have gathered and submitted these unpublished compilations of Bible, cemetery, family, vital, county, town, church, and military records since the late 1910s. The pre–1972 books were microfilmed by the Genealogical Society of Utah, but an greater number have arrived since this filming. Because the work of the G.R.C. is on–going, users of the Library should expect to find new material throughout the year. State DAR organizations may also place copies of their reports in a library or libraries in that state. Frequently, these will be the state library, historical society, or a major public library. Sometimes there is a small State DAR library. The DAR Library in Washington is the only research center owning nearly all of the *G.R.C. Reports* comprising the national set. Approximately 300-400 new reports arrive each year. The Library has not been able to determine the locations of all of the state sets unfortunately. See Chapter 12 for a listing of known state DAR libraries and repositories.

The submission of information is simple. Members of the DAR provide previously unpublished genealogical information to their chapter G.R.C. chairman, who passes the properly typed version on to the state chairman. The material submitted may be for any state in the country, not just the state of membership or residence. The state chairman then submits the material collected from her state as one or more volumes to the national office at DAR Headquarters. Most states contribute at least one book of records each year, and several donate many annually. The size of each state's set of reports varies greatly from the nearly 1,000 volumes for both Texas and New York to a few for Alaska and Hawaii.

The importance of the *G.R.C. Reports* for genealogists cannot be overstated. Many privately owned, inaccessible records for families all over the United States have been transcribed. Bible records and cemetery inscriptions are the mainstay of the reports, but just about any kind of record might be found in them. Many cemeteries surveyed in the early twentieth century by the DAR no longer exist or the stones are now illegible. Numerous reports contain abstracts of complete county court books such as marriage registers, deed books, and probate records. Church records have been popular sources for abstracts and transcriptions. Every part of the county is not covered in depth, however, but researchers should investigate the possibility that the DAR may have collected exactly what they need. A chapter in one county may have been very active, while one in an adjoining county may not have produced any abstracts.

> The work of our Genealogical Records Committee is like the brook, it "goes on forever," and also like the brook it flows through interesting phases of the work and tedious shoals, but finally, gleefully and serenely, flows into the river as the finished volume gets to our National Library of the Daughters of the American Revolution.
>
> Nell Downing Norton, National Vice Chairman,
> Genealogical Records Committee,
> Central Division,
> In her article "Genealogical Records" in the
> *Daughters of the American Revolution Magazine*,
> December 1946, p. 641.

The varied nature of the contents of *G.R.C. Reports* makes indexing essential. A report from Oregon could conceivably contain records from any other state as well as items from Oregon. Consequently, much material is "buried" in volumes from states where records did not originate. Such is the nature of the genealogical material that any group of genealogists might have in their collection with fewer and fewer people living in the same locality where their ancestors did. Generally speaking, *G.R.C. Reports* from each eastern state tend to contain sources from that state, while the further west one goes the reports contain a greater variety of record origins.

Yet for many years access to the information contained in the *G.R.C. Reports* was difficult. The DAR Library's Analytical Index provides basic subject entries to many of the reports although indexing of many states' sets stopped in the late 1960s. Many individual *G.R.C. Reports* contain an index located somewhere within the book. In some books one finds the index at the front, in others at the back of the book, and sometimes only sections within the book are indexed. Until recently indices for all the reports from a particular state were few and far between. Several years ago a few DAR member volunteers started a project to create statewide indices for each state G.R.C. set. The volunteers began by indexing the Virginia records and then continued with Maryland and West Virginia. Other states have followed including Oregon and Kentucky.

In 2001, Linda Tinker Watkins, the President General of the DAR, incorporated G.R.C. indexing into her large "President General's Project" to create databases, indexes and finding aids for many DAR materials. By the summer of 2002, hundreds of members across the country were indexing the reports for their states under the direction of the National Chairman, Genealogical Records Committee, and in cooperation with the Library staff and the Information Systems Department of the DAR. All of the indexers are volunteers who use the same specific guidelines and the same indexing software. The individual indexes for each report are merged into an online master index.

This G.R.C. National Index has been available for searching on the web since mid-2003. Users can access this database through the DAR website at **www.dar.org** by following the Library link to "GRC National Index." The database already contains over nine million names with more being added with each new completed index. The index is searchable by surname, first name, state, series and volume number. Search results can be sorted by "Last name," "First Name," "State," "Series," "Volume," or "Page." Detailed instructions for searching and sorting are on the website. The "Page" sort enables the viewer to see all of the names that appear on the same page with the result of their search of the index. This provides a context for the name of interest. In 2004, a link was added to the index that takes the researcher to the cataloging record for the book in which the entry appears. In the future, plans call for digitizing of the actual text of each report and for linking these images to the index as well.

Please see Chapter 14 for information on the proper bibliographic citation of *Genealogical Records Committee Reports.*

4.2
LDS MICROFILMS OF *G.R.C. REPORTS*

In the early 1970s the LDS's Genealogical Society of Utah sent a microfilming team to the DAR Library and filmed most of the *G.R.C. Reports* then in the collection. Copies of these films are available at the DAR Library's Seimes Technology Center, the Family History Library in Salt Lake City and its Family History Centers, and at the Allen County Public Library in Fort Wayne, Indiana. There are nearly 2,800 rolls of microfilm. Each roll contains the pages of several volumes of *G.R.C. Reports*. Since completion of the filming in 1972, thousands more volumes have arrived in the DAR Library. These have not been microfilmed.

Researchers may be familiar with several printed indices to the microfilm of the G.R.C. Reports, but many may not realize that these books actually index a major portion of the DAR Library's collection. Use of these can still provide a genealogist with an early start on their visit to the Library, however, advances in cataloging and indexing at the DAR Library are rapidly making these volumes obsolete. These finding aids are:

- John D. and E. Diane Stemmons. *The Cemetery Record Compendium: Comprising a Directory of Cemetery Records and Where They May Be Found*. Logan, Utah: Everton, 1979. Not all cemetery records in this index are for the G.R.C. Reports on microfilm, only those followed by the film numbers to which is appended the note "DAR" [Example: G907987, DAR].

- John D. and E. Diane Stemmons. *The Vital Record Compendium: Comprising a Directory of Vital Records and Where They May Be Located.* Logan, Utah: Everton, 1979. Again, not every listing is for the G.R.C. Reports on microfilm, but many are.

- E. Kay Kirkham. *An Index to Some of the Family Records of the Southern States: 35,000 Microfilm References from the NSDAR Files and Elsewhere.* [Vol. 1]. Logan, Utah: Everton, 1979. The entries are for the G.R.C. microfilms.

- E. Kay Kirkham. *An Index to Some of the Bibles and Family Records of the United States (excluding the Southern States): 45,500 References as Taken from the Microfilm at the Genealogical Society of Utah (NSDAR).* [vol. 2] Logan, Utah: Everton, 1984. The entries are for the G.R.C. microfilms.

The four books listed above are not for sale by the DAR. Inquiries on availability should be sent to Everton Publishers, Inc., P.O. Box 368, Logan, UT 84323–0368.

Genealogists should check these guides to determine if records they need are in DAR collections, and they should also check the DAR Library's online catalog. Read the introductions to each volume carefully. The only exception in these introductions is the statement that the six–digit film numbers do not apply to the record's location at the DAR. This is incorrect, because a set of the microfilms is in the Seimes Technology Center, and the films are arranged by the LDS numbers. Copies from the microfilms may be ordered from the Center.

Reproduction of entire rolls from the DAR's G.R.C. microfilms is restricted by agreement between the Genealogical Society of Utah and the DAR. Requests for such copies must be approved by the DAR Library Director and will be considered on a case–by–case basis. Generally, approval for reproduction of DAR microfilms by GSU will be given only to another library and not to individuals. Concerns related to the protection of the DAR's intellectual property rights, unauthorized reproduction and publication of some *GRC Reports* by some individuals, and other issues surrounding the location of the reports in public institutions make approval for reproduction of these microfilms less likely in recent years. The DAR itself does not reproduce or loan these microfilms or the original books.

The contents of the G.R.C. microfilms are included in the "Family History Library Catalog," part of the *FamilySearch*™ database, by subjects or by roll numbers. Another older listing of the contents of the G.R.C. microfilms may be available to researchers in libraries around the country:

Ruby Lacy. *DAR Records on Microfilm Available in Salt Lake City Genealogical Society Library*, 4 volumes. Ashland, Oregon: R. Lacy, 1978, 1979.

Vol. 1: Alabama, Arkansas, Illinois, Indiana, Iowa, North Dakota, North Carolina
Vol. 2: Arizona, Connecticut, Delaware, Kentucky, Ohio, Oregon, Pennsylvania, Tennessee
Vol. 3: Colorado, Florida, Louisiana, Maine, Minnesota, Montana, Nebraska, New Hampshire, New Jersey, Rhode Island, Texas, Virginia
Vol. 4: California, District of Columbia & Miscellaneous, Georgia, Idaho, Kansas, Maryland, Massachusetts, Michigan, New York, Oklahoma, South Carolina, Vermont, West Virginia

According to the introduction to these catalogs, they have "been gathered from the reports of the camera operators of the Genealogical Department of the Church of Jesus Christ of Latter Day Saints in Salt Lake City, Utah as they microfilmed the DAR Library collections in 1970–1971." Ten states are not listed in Mrs. Lacy's catalogs; perhaps these were the ones filmed in 1972. While these catalogs are helpful in that they group together by state all of the randomly assigned film numbers, they naturally repeat the vague and very incomplete title information the film operators noted in their reports. From the viewpoint of the DAR Library, the titles of the books noted in these filming reports usually do not reflect the actual titles of the books as they appear on the title page. Abbreviated titles from the spine of the book may have been used. It is often very difficult and sometimes impossible to match the actual book in the DAR Library with a copy on a reel of microfilm because of these discrepancies.

4.3
THE GRANDPARENT PROJECT (1959-1983)

The Grandparent Project began in the late 1950s as a research aid enabling prospective DAR members to link their lineage to those of existing members with shared grandparents. Members were to copy their application papers starting with their grandparents and working back to the Revolutionary ancestor. Because this was a voluntary project among DAR members and because the project started when DAR was nearly seventy years old, many members are not represented in this source. Consequently, there is not a form for every ancestor listed in the *DAR Patriot Index*. The Genealogical Records Committee administered the project.

There are a total of 875 volumes of "Grandparent Papers." Whole number volumes 1 (1960) through 670 (1972; Series 12, vol. 57), which comprise the first twelve series of this set, were microfilmed by the LDS Church during its filming project from 1970–1972. Volumes 671 (1973) through 875 (1983) are only in book form. All books must be requested and used in the Library. While the project itself ended in 1981, papers completed before the termination continued to arrive, so there are volumes dated 1982 and 1983.

The indices to the grandparent papers are located in the DAR Library. There are two indices to the papers, one for the name of Revolutionary War ancestors and one for the names of the grandparents of members who participated in the project. The index to ancestors is complete, but that for grandparents is not. The indices refer to the twelve series and the volume numbers within each series, **NOT** to the sequential whole volume numbers added as a shelving device by the staff.

Please note that changes to records of ancestors' service in the Revolutionary War may have resulted in some ancestors being removed from the *DAR Patriot Index*. To verify service for any Revolutionary War ancestors appearing in the Grandparent Project, please contact the Office of the Registrar General.

The names of the grandparents are only completely indexed for the entire set through part of the letter "H". The names of grandparents in other parts of the alphabet are *partially* indexed. If the line goes through a grandmother, her **maiden name** is used, *not* her married name. Within Series 1–12, the grandparent papers are arranged in alphabetical order by the names of the grandparents within each series. Within volumes 671–875 the papers are arranged in alphabetical order by grandparent's name *within each volume!*

Researchers at DAR may request copies directly through the Genealogical Records Committee Office during their visit to the building. Those seeking access from a distance may write to the Genealogical Records Committee giving the name, birth date, death date, and name of spouse of an individual grandparent or the Revolutionary War ancestor. One may order copies from the Genealogical Records Committee Office for $2.00 per set. All checks should be sent with the request to the appropriate office and be made payable to "Treasurer General NSDAR."

Advances in indexing underway at DAR at the time of publication for this book will result in an index to all names in all lineages represented in DAR membership applications and supplemental applications. This developing index will also provide indirect access to the material in the Grandparent Papers.

SEIMES TECHNOLOGY CENTER

Administration Building, Lower Level
Telephone: 202–879–3246

The DAR established the Betty Newkirk Seimes Microfilm Center in 1970 and named it for the then–President General. In April 1978, the 87th DAR Continental Congress made the Microfilm Center a National Committee. In 1997 Seimes was made a part of the Library, and in 2004 the Center's name was changed to the "Seimes Technology Center" to better reflect the changing formats of materials available.

The existence and continuing growth of the Center is in conformance with DAR's purpose to collect and preserve documents and records relevant to the individual services of Revolutionary War soldiers and patriots and the lineage of members of proven descent. Originally, the Center combined existing microfilm holdings of the Office of the Registrar General and the DAR Library. Since then, the collection has expanded considerably and embraces many valuable research materials.

Visitors to Seimes should first sign in at the Library. After signing in, those who are not members of the DAR, SAR, CAR, or SR must pay the daily user's fee. This allows patrons for access to both the Center and the Library. Patrons entering Seimes should check in with the staff, obtain a reader assignment, and explain to the staff what they are researching.

The Center is equipped with microfilm and microfiche readers and printers and a CD–ROM computer. Copies may be made from all sources **except** DAR membership applications and supplementals. To obtain copies of these materials, please ask the staff about current procedures. New computer stations will enable researchers to view the digital images of applications, supplementals, and supporting documentation as the President General's Project progresses.

The microform collection has been cataloged. The resulting records are in the Library's online catalog. A book of Seimes' holdings, *Catalog of the Seimes Microfilm Collection,* was published in 2001, but newer additions are rapidly making this publication obsolete.

As the DAR's microform library, the Center contains a wide variety of microfilm and microfiche publications and special collections. DAR membership applications, state and federal records pertaining to the American Revolution, federal census records 1800–1900, and many sources from state archives not available elsewhere in Washington form the core of the collection. The major types of sources in the Center are:

DAR Membership Applications and Supplemental Applications: For many years, these were on microfilm and microfiche, but in 2004 the digital images of these unique resources became available for viewing in the Center. The microforms have been relegated to back-up reference materials. To view or to obtain copies of these papers, please consult the staff of the Center.

Census records: While the center houses microfilm of the1800–1900 censuses, including the 1880 and 1900 Soundex, the availability of federal censuses through online subscription services, makes the microfilm useful mostly as a back-up research tool. See the "Census Research" section in Chapter 12 for more information. A collection of printed census indices is in the Center, for the years 1790 to 1870, and for scattered places in later years. Again, these traditional sources are now back-ups to electronic searches. Microfilms of several state census records are also available in the center and represent surveys of the population in years between the federal decennial censuses. Records for some of the state censuses for Illinois, Massachusetts, Michigan, Minnesota, New Jersey, New York, North Dakota, Rhode Island, and Wisconsin are present.

Genealogical Records Committee Reports on microfilm: Between 1970 and 1972 the Genealogical Society of Utah produced nearly 2,800 rolls of unique DAR records. These films are in the Center along with printed indices. See Chapter 4.2 for details.

Special Collections: Most of these sets of microfilm or microfiche contain state and local records. For additional listings see Chapter 13.27.

- Draper Manuscript Collection
- Index to pre–1870 Vermont vital records
- South Carolina Combined Alphabetical Index and other South Carolina probate and land records
- Spanish Land Grants in Florida
- Illinois Name Index to Early Records and Index to Illinois County Histories
- Kentucky county tax lists (pre–1850)
- Maryland Prerogative Court Wills 1639–1777 and other colony- and state-level records
- Massachusetts Vital and Town Records on microfiche
- Missouri county records (indices to deeds, wills, marriages for most counties; 400 reels)
- New Jersey county ratables, 1778–1832, land records, and military records
- New Jersey State Census, 1850-1895, 1905
- New York State Census: From 1825 to 1875, the state of New York conducted its own census. The state also took a census in 1892 and then every ten years from 1905 to 1925. Seimes owns a number of these censuses on microfilm, but it does not have a complete set owing to availability and the restrictions of county authorities.
- North Carolina records of Revolutionary War accounts and Warrants and Surveys, Western Territory (Tennessee) 1778–1791
- New Hampshire indices to vital records to 1900
- Ohio Civil War Regimental Histories and Reunions
- Ohio County History Surname Index
- Passenger Arrival Lists for U.S. Ports
- Tennessee Index to Land Grants, 1775–1905
- Virginia county and city tax records (mostly for jurisdictions with major losses of court records)

Federal Revolutionary War records: Major microfilm publications relating to the American Revolution from the National Archives are available in the Center. Many similar sources from state archives are also available or planned for purchase.

- *Compiled Service Records of American Naval Personnel ... Quartermaster General and the Commissary General ... During the Revolutionary War, NARA RG–93, M–880*
- *Compiled Service Records of soldiers who served in the American Army during the Revolutionary War, NARA RG–93, M–881*
- *General Index to Compiled Service Records of Revolutionary War Soldiers, NARA RG–93, M–860*
- *Miscellaneous Numbered Records ... 1775–1783, NARA RG–93, M–847 Special Index to Numbered Records...1775–1783, NARA RG–93, M–847*
- *Papers of the Continental Congress, NARA RG–360, M–247*
- *Records of the Continental Loan Office, 1777–1791, NARA RG 53, M–247*
- *Revolutionary War Pension and Bounty Land Warrant Application Files, NARA RG–15, M–804*
- *Ledgers of Payments to U.S. Pensioners Under Acts of 1818 through 1858, NARA RG–217, T–718*

These are just a few examples of valuable sources available in the Center. The holdings in general complement those in the DAR Library. A continuing effort to acquire further materials from state archives promises to enrich the collection with sources not available in any other research center in Washington, D.C.

As the number of staff members in the Center is small, they cannot perform genealogical research. Please contact the DAR Library's Search Service for this assistance.

A valuable addition to the library during the past three years have been the microfilming of the state census records from 1850 through 1880. Thirty-one states have completed this project. We had hoped to have the number finished during this regime. We have just received a letter from the Acting Chief, Information and Publications, Bureau of the U.S. Census, telling us that because of the requirements of the armed forces "In order to avoid the possibility of rationing films you are strongly urged to photograph nothing but your most important work. The photographing of old records and similar documents should be postponed for the duration." Therefore it is with regret we announce that we shall discontinue microfilming the census records until such time as we can obtain films.

From the Report of the Librarian General, April 1945, *National Historical Magazine*, June 1945, p. 407.

OFFICE OF THE REGISTRAR GENERAL

The Registrar General's office is composed of the following sections: Genealogy, Record Information, Record Copy and Lineage Research. Some of the activities of these sections are pertinent to general genealogical research, while others are specifically internal.

The Mission Statement of the Registrar General's Department is to enhance the goals of the National Society through the timely, efficient verification of member-related applications. Basically, the Registrar General oversees the processing and approval of membership applications and the attendant materials that process produces. These materials represent a significant portion of the DAR's unique research sources. Genealogists should understand the arrangement, benefits, and limitations of these sources to make the most of their content.

6.1
THE GENEALOGY DEPARTMENT

The staff genealogists work specifically on the verification of application papers for pending members of the DAR and supplemental applications for members. Prospective members make their contacts with this office through the chapter and state registrars. The work of the Genealogy Department is vital to the continued admission of new members to the National Society. The office itself does not provide genealogical research or reference assistance to individuals either by phone, by mail, by e-mail, or in person. General researchers should not contact the Genealogy Department with these objectives in mind.

From a general research standpoint, however, the importance of the Genealogy Department is its production of verified membership applications. These become available to researchers and potential DAR members shortly after the approval process. The application papers, along with the supporting documentation that accompanies them, are some of the DAR's most basic and important research sources.

In addition to their primary responsibility of verification of application papers, the section is also responsible for corrections to the published *Patriot Index* and the Ancestor Database, new ancestor lists for publication in the DAR's newsletter, verification of an ancestor's service for grave marking requests, and the training of Volunteer Genealogists.

The Genealogy Department holds four one-week, in-house training seminars for Volunteer Genealogists. These volunteers assist chapters with the preparation of papers to be submitted to the section. In addition, two field seminars are held in the states to train members and registrars.

For an organization as old as DAR and with well over one million applications and supplemental applications, there is always the potential for errors and for corrections. Many of the older papers do not have much in the way of supporting documentation. The Corrections Team is responsible for handling lineage and service that is in error or suspected to be in error. Corrections are entered daily into the *Patriot Index* and Ancestor Database, which contain the most up to date information on the society's patriot ancestors.

6.2
LINEAGE RESEARCH NATIONAL COMMITTEE

The Lineage Research Office, which was established in 1961, assists prospective members who have been referred by the Genealogy Department or a State Lineage Research Chairman. The staff does not provide assistance to the public or help with supplemental applications for members.

For those who are seeking membership in the DAR, the staff will assist in locating a line to a Revolutionary War Patriot or in locating a substitute ancestor when the original application cannot be verified because of problems with lineage or service.

The Committee also assembles a "Lineage Research Kit" of information brochures, research aids and forms relating to genealogical research. This may be purchased through The DAR Store, Office of the Corresponding Secretary General.

6.3
RECORD INFORMATION OFFICE

Administration Building, First Floor, Room 108
Telephone: 202–879–3251

Traditionally, the R.G. Record Information Office was often a researcher's first stop when visiting DAR Headquarters. The staff maintained the actual ancestor card file of "The DAR Patriot Index" (see section 6.4) and served as the public contact point for access to membership applications and supplementals through the index. With the creation of internal online indexes covering all of this information, researchers may now obtain information to access DAR applications and supplementals at the reference desks in the Library and Seimes Technology Center, as well as in this office.

The staff of this office will also respond to requests for information from the index in writing and by telephone. Information provided by telephone will be limited, however, to verification of the fact that an individual is an established ancestor. National numbers will not be given over the telephone. Please do not request information by fax. All inquiries are answered in order of receipt. Researchers may also take advantage of the DAR's free online "Patriot Index Lookup Service" to obtain verification of an ancestor's presence in the index. Information on this service is on our website at **www.dar.org**.

It is very important to provide as much information as possible to help the staff identify the correct ancestor. Copies of *The DAR Patriot Index Millennium Edition* (2003) are available on the research table in this office, in the DAR Library and Seimes Technology Center, or in libraries nationwide to help begin the search. Earlier editions of this publication are not valid. One important piece of information is the name of a specific child through which a researcher seeks a lineage. Researchers may request three national numbers at a time and may request more later. If one is only seeking information on a patriot's Revolutionary War service, please state that.

Prior to the late 1980s, when the practice was abolished, some members closed their applications to viewing for personal reasons. Consequently, some applications may not be examined. The staff will state if the only paper on a particular ancestor is closed, but they cannot provide additional information on that paper until the member dies, resigns or personally lifts the restriction.

After receiving a national number, researchers must go to the Seimes Technology Center to view the digital images of the papers. See Chapter 5 for more information on the Center.

Copies of applications (record copy) must be ordered, however, through the Record Copy Office using the proper form. As of this writing, the cost for a copy of one set of application papers (four pages) is $10.00. Checks should be made payable to "Treasurer General, NSDAR." Mail order should be sent to "Record Copy," Office of the Registrar General, 1776 D St., N.W., Washington, D.C. 20006–5303.

Orders placed in person prior to 12:30 p.m. each day may be ready by 2:00 p.m. Those placed later will be ready the following day or may be mailed on request. Only six record copy orders may be placed at a time in person. There is no limit on the number that may be ordered by mail. Pre-payment is required.

Some restrictions apply on obtaining copies of DAR membership applications. Please see the order forms on DAR website. Click on "Membership" on the splash page, and then on "Application Paper Copy Requests form."

6.4
THE DAR PATRIOT INDEX

"The DAR Patriot Index" is a resource well known to many genealogists in its published form, but it is actually more than just a set of books. Basically, it is a listing of the established Revolutionary War ancestors of DAR members but not a list of all participants in the American Revolution.

On the DAR's website, researchers will find a "Patriotic Index Lookup Service" by clicking on "Membership" on the splash page and then on that link on the next page. Volunteer DAR members, who want to help others with their research, provide this free service. The request form appears on the same page, and submission is electronic.

The actual "DAR Patriot Index" was for decades a large file of 4" x 6" ancestor cards, which the Registrar General's staff maintained. In the first years of the twenty-first century, all of this information was reentered electronically and formed the basis for internal online indexes, particularly the Ancestor Database. This database is kept very current by the addition of new information daily. The appearance of a patriot's name in the index indicates that there has been at least one application or supplemental application since 1890 establishing that ancestor's service.

Each ancestor record provides space (although every space is not always completed) for the following basic information on established Revolutionary soldiers or patriots:

- birth and death dates and places

- place(s) of residence

- name(s) of spouse(s)

- place(s) of residence

- children through which DAR lineages have been established and associated national numbers needed to consult application papers

- type of Revolutionary War service and place or state

- notations by the staff explaining details about the ancestor and related application papers, such as "data in," "corrected copy," "future applicants must complete," or "Tory."

The "Patriot Index" has been condensed several times into the published *DAR Patriot Index*. The first was in 1966. It was followed by three paperback supplements between 1969 and 1976. The three supplements, plus additions and corrections were incorporated into volume 2 in 1979. A 1982 supplement followed. Finally, volume three was published in 1986. The subtitle of volume 3 is *An Index to the Spouses of the DAR Patriots*. **Please note that all of these volumes are superseded and contain records that have since been corrected or deleted.** The 1986 volume may still have some usefulness because it indexes the spouses of many valid Patriots. Use it with caution, however.

The next edition of *The DAR Patriot Index* was published in April 1994. This blue, three–volume "Centennial Edition" had a spine date and a title page date of 1990, but it contained names of established ancestors of DAR members through December 1993.

The most recent edition of *The DAR Patriot Index* was published in May 2003 in three red volumes. It supersedes all previous editions, which should be discarded by anyone or any libraries owning the earlier publications.

Updates to listings in the published index show newly established ancestors and appear several times each year in the DAR's newsletter. The listing of Revolutionary ancestors by DAR members changes constantly, and researchers should maintain awareness of these updates to keep apace of new information.

6.5
THE LINEAGE BOOKS OF THE
DAUGHTERS OF THE AMERICAN REVOLUTION

From 1890 to 1939 the National Society Daughters of the American Revolution published 166 volumes containing the lineages of accepted members through national number 160,000 (admitted in April 1921). The set is available in many large libraries around the country having been used by the DAR to exchange with other libraries for their publications. It is often the genealogist's first contact with DAR records, which, unfortunately, can lead to problems in further research and documentation of genealogies.

DAR recommends that researchers **USE GREAT CAUTION** when studying the *Lineage Books*. The staff genealogists of DAR no longer accept lineages cited in the *Lineage Books* as suitable proof for applications by potential new members. The set is useful only for clues to a lineage. The lineages contained in these books are quite old and deserve careful scrutiny. Consequently, there have been at least eighty-three years during which many new sources have become available to researchers. Nearly 665,000 applications for membership in DAR have been approved since the last published lineage from 1921.

Thousands of corrections have been made to the records in this set during this period. These corrections *have not* been published in supplemental volumes to the *Lineage Books*, and are therefore available only at DAR headquarters. Additionally, some older lineages listed in the set, may never have had another applicant associated with them to help identify errors and make corrections. All lineages, whether they are those in the *Lineage Books* or those submitted subsequently to them, should be verified with the Registrar General's office. Documented corrections may be sent to the Corrections Genealogist Team.

Although there are major limitations to the validity of information in the *Lineage Books*, researchers may find valuable clues hidden in the pages of this set of 166 volumes. A four–volume set of indexes was published between 1916 and 1940. In 1980 and several times since then, the Genealogical Publishing Company of Baltimore, Maryland has reprinted this set as *Index to the Rolls of Honor in the Lineage Books of the National Society of the Daughters of the American Revolution*. This set of books covers volumes 1–160, but not the last six volumes. Copies must be ordered directly from the Genealogical Publishing Company. Volumes 161 to 166 have been indexed in a separate publication: Ethel McNabb. *Index of the Rolls of Honor (Ancestor's Index) in the Lineage Books of the National Society of the Daughters of the American Revolution, Volumes 161–166* [S.l.: s.n.], 1965. This volume is not presently available from a publisher to our knowledge.

All volumes of the *Lineage Book*s have been out–of–print for many years. They will not be reprinted in either book form or microform. No copies are available for purchase from any office at DAR.

In any event, researchers should use this entire set with the greatest of caution. Some information is correct. Other information is not. The DAR Library has shelved its set of *Lineage Books* away from the main collection, but library users can certainly use the books if they so desire. The staff warns anyone inquiring of their location of the limitations and suggests that the Ancestor Database be checked for newer information. Librarians and researchers elsewhere should be aware of the limitations of this set of books.

> The [DAR] ... deserves great credit for pioneering in developing an interest in family history. At that time [1890] we were comparatively close to the Revolutionary patriots we wished to honor, the last of whom had died in 1868 at the age of over 104 years-these men and women who, who in the period 1775-1783, contributed physically or materially to the success of the struggle for independence, or established themselves as loyal to the American cause.
>
> Daughters and granddaughters of these patriots were living in 1890, and it was easy for them to remember, or, with the aid of family Bibles and tradition, to say who these parents and grandparents were. Genealogy as a science or profession had not been extensively developed. At the very beginning we asked of an applicant for membership in the Society only the names of her line and some service attributed to the patriot ancestor. What a loss that we did not require the birth, death and marriage dates, with reference as to where these occurred! The members could at that time so easily have supplied much that it now requires a great deal of research to find. If these had been given, it would have brought out the fact that the memory and tradition were often mistaken, and that for a father and son, brothers were sometimes given on these undated papers and accepted in good faith without proof. Sometimes a collateral relation, such as an uncle or nephew, would be claimed.
>
> No attempt was made to check the line with new records coming in. Also no attempt was made to identify an ancestor with the service claimed. When the service was checked by a pension, it frequently happened that the pension record itself was not obtained, but reference was made to a list of pensioners in which the soldiers name appeared, with no data to identify him as the one having the service claimed in the pension.
>
> Comments by Eleanor B. Cooch,
> Registrar General, 1941-1944,
> in her article "Papers Without Proofs and Lineage Books"
> in *National Historical Magazine*, April 1944, p. 206.

6.6
DAR MEMBERSHIP APPLICATIONS AND RELATED SOURCES

Care of Records by Chapter Registrars

It is of the utmost importance that proper care be taken of the duplicate verified application and supplemental papers, which are from time to time sent to the chapter registrar by the office of the Registrar General as they are approved by that office and the National Board of Management. They are priceless records of your chapter's growth and the genealogical background of your members, and should be safeguarded against fire or other damage. *These papers constitute a trust and should be so considered.*

If some catastrophe should occur in the Administration Building in Washington, which would destroy part or all of our application or supplemental papers filed there, we would look to the duplicates in the chapters to rebuild our records. We pray this may never happen, but at the beginning of the war steps to safeguard treasures were taken all over the country, since such damage was considered a possibility.

This explanation is given at length, because a few registrars have lately asked this office, *"What is the use of keeping these old papers?"*

We trust that we have made clear to present and potential future registrars that the need to take proper care of the papers of present and former members is very real and very important.

Comments by Eleanor B. Cooch in her article "Requirements of the Office of the Registrar General" in *National Historical Magazine*, February 1944, p. 79.

6.6.1
APPLICATION PAPERS

The result of the work of the staff genealogists is the verified application papers. The originals are stored off-site in a secure facility for safekeeping, and research copies are available in digital form on-line in the Seimes Technology Center. Researchers may go directly to the Center to view applications. If one knows the name of a DAR member and would like to view her application paper but does not have the national number, the staff of the Center will also be able to check DAR databases to locate the needed material online. If one knows the name of a Revolutionary War ancestor and wishes to identify which applications are associated with the ancestor, the staff will be able to provide this information as well.

Since the beginning, DAR application papers have been four pages in length. There have been various revisions to the content and detail of the papers over the years, usually to request more information for accuracy and clarity in the lineage. Generally, the structure of the papers is:

Page 1: identifies the applicant, her ancestor, and clerical information regarding the stages of the application through the final approval date.

Page 2: outlines the lineage of the applicant to the Revolutionary War patriot. Since 1890 spaces for such information as birth, marriage, and death dates, locations, and similar details were added.

Page 3: lists the documentation or sources

proving the lineage. Staff genealogists make notations here that have varied over the years. Some state "data returned" or "data in file case," explaining the probable location of supporting documentation. Page 3 of the current application also has a section for listing the children of the patriot.

Page 4: lists the service that qualifies the ancestor as a Revolutionary War patriot.

A free and helpful booklet, *Application Papers:*
Instructions for Their Preparation, describes an application in explicit detail and offers guidelines for its completion. Details on acceptable proof and acceptable Revolutionary War service are included. It is a very helpful discussion of applications for anyone completing an application or for researchers who study accepted applications. Every chapter registrar should own a copy as well. Copies are available from The DAR Store, Office of the Corresponding Secretary General.

Two other booklets provide additional instruction on completing application papers and insight to the information they contain. *Is That Service Right?* and *Is That Lineage Right?* examine specific problems one may encounter and offer solutions. Both booklets are available for purchase from The DAR Store.

Please see Chapter 14 for information on the proper bibliographic citation of DAR Membership Applications.

6.6.2
"SHORT–FORM" APPLICATIONS

Beginning in 1964, the DAR used "short–form" applications to allow applicants to "piggy–back" onto applications of their close relatives within four generations. Because they build on earlier papers and because recent documentation relating to individuals alive after 1930 is not open to research, proof for short forms is very limited.

6.6.3
SUPPLEMENTAL APPLICATIONS

Many Daughters have proven and recorded their lineage to more than one Revolutionary War patriot by submitting "Supplemental Applications." In the very early days these may have accompanied the original application. Now they are submitted later. Many of these early "supplementals" were not microfilmed. This once caused research problems. Generally, a notation on the first application paper will state that there are additional papers on file. Digital images of all supplementals and internal online indexes to every paper have eliminated earlier difficulties with these materials.

To solve the early problem of arranging the supplementals, the Registrar General's Office created "*Add Volumes*" to contain them. The first *Add Volume* starts in 1897. Supplemental papers are assigned the member's national number plus an *Add Volume* number, and this information appears in the Ancestor Database. The papers are filed within the appropriate *Add Volume* by the national number. Presently, each *Add Volume* contains 200 supplemental applications beginning with the lowest national number in that batch. Not every member submits these additional papers. Those who submit them do so whenever they chose. Consequently the numbering within each *Add Volume* skips many national numbers.

Please see Chapter 14 for information on the proper bibliographic citation of DAR Supplemental Application Papers.

6.6.4
DIGITAL IMAGES AND MICROFORMS OF APPLICATION PAPERS

Reformatting to microfilm of applications and supplementals began in 1961. All microforms have now been replaced by digital images that may be viewed in the Seimes Technology Center. All applications and supplementals were also reformatted on new microfiche beginning in 2003, but this form is only used as security back-up. This material is only available at DAR and is not available on inter–library loan through any facility.

6.6.5
CLOSED AND QUESTIONED LINEAGES

The staff genealogists may close lines or require new documentation if an error in the lineage or Revolutionary War service is discovered. Contact the Corrections Team for information. Refer to section 6.5 on the *DAR Lineage Books*, which definitely fall into the category of questionable sources.

6.7
SUPPORTING DOCUMENTATION FOR APPLICATIONS

Along with the application papers and supplemental papers themselves, prospective members and members respectively submit supporting documentation to back up the lineage and service in the paper. All of this material becomes the property of the DAR on receipt.

The Genealogy Department evaluates the documentation accompanying the applications and supplementals. When the genealogists complete their work, the file is now digitized, vital information on recent generations, including the applicant's, is blocked from public view, and the historical material becomes available for internal use online. The types of materials that are usually retained are pages or sections from published family histories not in the Library, deeds, wills, Bible records, photographs or transcriptions of tombstones, research notes, and other pertinent sources. Current documentation files fall under the control of the DAR Library's Documents Management Office after this work is complete. This office prepares the files for off-site storage once they have been digitized. It also provides the paper files to researchers in the Library following submission of a request at the reference desk.

While membership applications are prepared on acid–free, rag–content forms, the documentation will likely not be archivally sound. Some may fade and become difficult to read. Digitizing of this material will solve many problems of this nature.

Where are the supporting documents that were submitted with membership applications to prove the lineage? The *surviving* files of material are available for research in the DAR Library, which houses it in two sections. The first covers documentation files that came with applications prior to and including the DAR's October Board of 1958 (National Numbers 1 to 462457); the second covers those subsequent to that date. The files in each section are arranged by the names of the Revolutionary ancestors, **NOT** by national number or members' names. As the digitizing work progresses, the pre-1958 files will be reformatted first because they are not presently available in anything but paper form. Incoming materials will also be digitized as they arrive. The intermediate material covering roughly 1959-2001 will be reformatted when the beginning of this project is complete. All of this work will take several years to accomplish, but the results will be an amazing digital collection of genealogical materials searchable in the Seimes Technology Center on the DAR's internal online system.

Several years ago the Registrar General's office had a project to remove the remaining pieces of documentation from the original applications, place them in files, and add them to the Library's file collection. During the Watkins Administration, the Documents Management Staff completed this extraction work, prepared files for all of this previously hidden documentation, and arranged it for use prior to digitizing.

There are many gaps in the supporting documentation. With over 826,000 members since 1890, in theory, there should be an corresponding amount of material to verify the application papers of all of these members. This is not, however, the case. At this writing, the Library has 1,500 linear feet of documentation files—nearly three times the height of the Washington Monument! The Library staff estimates this to translate into about 300,000 files. Documentation in any one file may relate to several application papers. Estimating what percentage of papers have supporting materials is impossible. Suffice it to say, many papers lack this documentation.

Why are there gaps? In the early years of the National Society, the amount of proof required to support an application was small in comparison to what is needed today. The availability of historical sources was also much less than now. In the days before photocopy machines, originals sent in with the application were often returned because there were no other copies and members wanted their original materials. Some carbon copies and handwritten transcriptions were retained. Once photocopying became widespread in the 1960s less material was returned. Not until the late 1970s was proof for the first three generations beginning with the applicant herself required with the application. Consequently, many early papers do not have any proof to support them beyond what is written in on the paper itself. Vague references to "bible records, cemetery records, and family papers" may be the only clues that will appear. This is not to say that there is no proof available for early applications, but there is not a great deal. The Library staff will check for any file and report whether or not one was found.

More documentation files exist for applications in the middle and late twentieth century, but again, there are gaps. During some periods, the proof papers were returned to the member after her application was approved. The material was returned because of storage limitations, lack of staff for processing, and the reasons mentioned previously. This practice has not been followed since 1984. There also may be no file because a member joined on a "short–form" application, "piggy–backing" onto an established application paper. The necessary documentation would not be available in the research files because it relates to recent generations. DAR staff has removed documents accompanying papers prior to 2001 that are directly associated with the member or her immediate family and that post–date 1910. This information is not available for research purposes for privacy reasons. For 2001 to the present, all material has been retained, will be digitized, and the private information blocked from public viewing electronically. As this sensitive material ages and passes the 75-year limit for viewing, it will become available for research use.

Researchers must consider the possibility that an older application has been updated or superseded by a newer one, so there is the chance that files could appear in both sections of the files. Often, there is no file under an ancestor's name in either section of the files.

The contents of a file may relate to any individual in any generation of a member's lineage. There may not be much material clarifying the Revolutionary service of an ancestor, but then, there may be considerable proof. Each file is different, but Bible records and other vital records do predominate.

One may request a search for a particular file if they are visiting the Library and may obtain copies of older material included in the files. Mail inquiries are accepted, but the volume of such requests results in long delays before the staff can process such orders. Please direct all inquiries regarding the files to the DAR Library's Search Service.

The supporting documentation for membership applications represents a large, unique research collection in the DAR Library. Its processing by staff and careful use by researchers will insure the preservation of valuable information for future genealogists.

Please see Chapter 14 for information on the proper bibliographic citation of documentation supporting DAR Membership Applications.

6.8
NEW PROJECTS

Several projects developing in the early years of the twenty-first century will lead to greater access to information in the applications and supplementals. In particular, a "Descendants Project" will index every name in every generation in every lineage, thereby creating a new master index that has never existed before. Volunteer DAR members will prepare this index using digital images of these sources. When this index is completed, the old lineage books and other indexes will become completely obsolete.

OFFICE OF THE HISTORIAN GENERAL

Location: Administration Building, Second Floor, Room 206
Telephone number: 202–879–3256

Besides having responsibility for the National Society's official archives, for the "Special Collection Relating to the History of the NSDAR" and for various historical activities, the Office of the Historian General maintains the Americana Collection of approximately 4,000 accessions and several other sources useful for genealogical research. In addition, a small collection of books established in 1967, the Historical Research Library, is available.

7.1
AMERICANA COLLECTION

The Americana Collection had its beginnings in 1940 at the time of the celebration of the DAR's fiftieth anniversary "as a repository of manuscripts and imprints pertaining primarily to Colonial America, the American Revolution, and the Early Republic." Its collections focus on the seventeenth to the nineteenth centuries with some exceptions. Manuscripts of many types are preserved here, including Bible records, letters, diaries, court papers, and land records. Printed sources include books, almanacs, pamphlets, school books, newspapers and photographs. The "genealogical card index" provides access to information about accessions received prior to circa 1970, and researchers will find references to church records, deeds (mostly from New England), ledgers and account books, vital records for entire families, and many personal names associated with documents. The staff in this department has compiled in–house inventories of accessions focusing on the American Revolution and the Civil War.

A brochure is available on the collection, which says the following regarding access to materials:

> The contents of this collection are available for public inspection and for research. Requests for photocopies of material in the collection are handled by the Office of the Historian General. That office reserves the right to evaluate each request and to deny permission, in certain instances, such as when original copies are too fragile, bound in volumes, or restricted material. Exhibits are mounted in special display cases in the Americana Room and are changed periodically. Individuals and groups are welcome. Tours can be arranged by prior consultation with the staff of the Historian General's Office.

7.2
LOCATED AND MARKED GRAVES
OF REVOLUTIONARY WAR SOLDIERS AND PATRIOTS

**Revolutionary marker placed on grave of Joseph Harrison
by the Edward Buncombe Chapter**
Photo from the DAR Magazine, August 1929

An activity which has been foremost in the historic preservation efforts of DAR members since the early years of the National Society is the locating and marking of the graves of Revolutionary soldiers and patriots, their spouses and their daughters. Surveys and transcriptions of cemetery records in general have occupied the time of many Daughters in the Library, and the Library contains many volumes of these records. The Office of the Historian General, however, maintains several card files, or indices, of reported "located" graves and graves "marked" by the DAR. Please be aware of the fact that not all of the located and reported graves have been documented; errors do exist in these listings. The inclusion of a name in one of these sources does not serve as proof of Revolutionary War service. Use these indices for clues.

Index of Reported Located Graves of Revolutionary War Soldiers and Patriots
This index is a finding aid to the located graves, which have been reported by DAR members and others since the late 1890s. It provides access to those listings published in the Reports to the Secretary of the Smithsonian from 1898 to 1974 (see below), as well as

to others that have been listed since then. A few cards include photographs of the tombstones. Listings of located graves which appeared in the *Smithsonian Reports* were also collected, indexed, and published in a four volume, privately printed, non–DAR sponsored work by Patricia Law Hatcher, *Abstract of Graves of Revolutionary Patriots*, Dallas, Texas: Pioneer Heritage Press, 1987–1988. The DAR published lists in pamphlet form in the mid to late 1970s noting additional reported located graves. This pamphlet is entitled *Located Graves of Soldiers and Patriots of the American Revolution, March 1, 1974—March 1, 1976*. Some further lists appeared in *The DAR Magazine* in the years immediately after 1978. There have been no subsequent publications other than those in the magazine.

Index of Reported Marked Graves of Revolutionary War Soldiers and Patriots
The DAR Magazine provides researchers with frequent references to grave marking ceremonies by DAR chapters. No comprehensive index to these activities exists; however, any information concerning the date of placement and dedication of a marker may provide clues about when an article may have appeared in *The DAR Magazine* describing the event. Some of these entries include photographs of the ceremony. Since the late 1980s the Office of the Historian General has maintained files containing proof of these locations and markings.

Index of Reported Marked Graves of Wives and Daughters of Revolutionary War Patriots and Soldiers

Index of Reported Marked Graves of Signers of the Declaration of Independence

Index of Reported Marked Graves of DAR Members
This multi–drawer card index gives useful information relating to marked graves of deceased DAR members prior to the 1990s. It is not comprehensive since not all markings have been reported. Currently, all reports received of the placement of DAR insignia markers are entered into IMIS, an internal database at DAR headquarters.

Index of Reported Marked Graves of Real Daughters
This index notes the graves of DAR members who were actually daughters of Revolutionary War participants. See section 7.4 for more information.

Index of Reported Historical Markers Placed by DAR Chapters (arranged by state)

7.3
DAR REPORTS TO THE SECRETARY OF THE SMITHSONIAN INSTITUTION

One requirement made of the DAR in its 1896 incorporation by the United States Congress was an annual report to the Secretary of the Smithsonian Institution. The first was a "catch–up" seven–year report covering the years 1890–1897 and was published in 1899. After their submission, the reports became government documents, were submitted to the United States Senate by the Smithsonian along with annual reports of many other organizations, and included in the U.S. Serial Set. Each DAR Report is therefore available in any library that owns the Serial

Set. A complete set is available in the Office of the Historian General and a partial set is in the Library.

Besides the lists of graves of Revolutionary soldiers and patriots just mentioned, the early reports contain many other sources of genealogical interest. A few have been published as separate volumes, but most are not well known. The following details the contents of these reports.

Report, v. 1, 1890–1897 (1899), 55th Congress, 3rd Session. Senate. Document no.164
    This report does not contain historical records.

Report, v. 2, 1897–1898 (1900), 56th Congress, 1st Session. Senate. Document no.425
Appendix B:	Graves Identified by Dorothy Quincy Hancock Chapter, Bernardstown, Massachusetts
Appendix D:	Roster of women nurses enlisted for Spanish–American War by DAR Hospital Corps

Report, v. 3, 1898–1900 (1901), 56th Congress, 2nd Session. Senate. Document no.219
Appendix C:	The Ancient Burying Ground of Hartford (Names on the gravestones standing in 1835)
Appendix D:	Unpublished list of Massachusetts citizens who loaned money to the government during the Revolution
Appendix E:	Georgia Soldiers of the Line–Revolutionary War (from papers in the Office of the Secretary of State of Georgia)
Appendix F:	Alphabetical list of Georgia Revolutionary Soldiers of all ranks and names including Continental, Militia, Provincials, Minute Men, Rangers, Partisans, Mariners, Sons of Liberty, Independents, etc.
Appendix G:	Soldiers of the American Revolution and Pioneers of Broome County, New York
Appendix H:	List of Historic Spots in Lower Merion (Montgomery County, Pennsylvania)

Report, v. 4, 1900–1901 (1902), 57th Congress, 1st Session. Senate. Document no.447
Appendix A:	Some Rolls of Connecticut Soldiers
Appendix B:	List of Revolutionary Soldiers Graves, Worcester, Massachusetts
Appendix C:	Historical Collections of General Frelinghuysen Chapter, Somerville, New Jersey
Appendix D:	Entry from the Account Book kept by Capt. David Tarbox, Hebron, Connecticut
Appendix E:	Partial List of Delaware's Revolutionary Soldiers
Appendix F:	List of Historic Spots in Blockley, Pennsylvania
Appendix G:	Roll of General Sumters Regiment of South Carolina
Appendix H:	Record of Revolutionary Ancestors of Members of Ascutney Chapter, Windsor, Vermont

Report, v. 5, 1901–1902 (1903), 57th Congress, 2nd Session. Senate. Document no.210
Appendix B:	List of Revolutionary Soldiers, compiled by Capt. B.F. Johnson, Additional to List Published Under Appendix E in our Third Report, with Corrections of that list.
Appendix C:	Revolutionary Soldiers Buried in the Vicinity of Attleboro, Massachusetts
Appendix D:	Revolutionary Soldiers Buried at Hookset, New York

Appendix E:	List of Recruits from the Cape May Battalion and Revolutionary Soldiers of Cape May County, New Jersey
Appendix F:	Revolutionary Ancestors of members of the Knickerbocker Chapter, New York
Appendix G:	Revolutionary Soldiers Buried in Jefferson County, New York
Appendix H:	Revolutionary Soldiers Buried in Lake and Geauga Counties, Ohio
Appendix I:	Revolutionary Soldiers Graves, Located by Ox–Bow Chapter, Vermont

Report, v. 6, 1902–1903 (1904)

Appendix A:	Revolutionary Soldiers Buried in Derby, Connecticut
Appendix B:	Revolutionary Soldiers Buried in Massachusetts
Appendix C:	Records of Revolutionary Soldiers Furnished by General William Floyd Chapter
Appendix D:	List of Revolutionary Soldiers from Seneca County, N.Y.

Report, v. 7, 1903–1904 (1905), 58th Congress, 3rd Session. Senate. Document no.193

Does not contain separate appendices, but includes with the chapter reports a list of Revolutionary War pensioners from Steuben County, New York and located graves of Revolutionary War soldiers in West Virginia.

Report, v. 8, 1904–1905 (1906), 59th Congress, 1st Session. Senate. Document no.532

Does not contain separate appendices, but includes with the chapter reports lists of located graves of Revolutionary War soldiers in Indiana; Brockton, Massachusetts; Tilton, New Hampshire and a list of soldiers who served from New Milford, Massachusetts.

Report, v. 9, 1905–1906 (1907). 59th Congress, 2nd Session. Senate. Document no.400

Does not contain separate appendices, but includes with the chapter reports a complete payroll of the 1st South Carolina State Troops from 1782.

Report, v. 10, 1906–1907 (1908)

Report, v.11, 1907–1908 (1909), 61st Congress, 1st Session. Senate. Document no.117

Contains grave listings in the chapter reports.

Report, v.12, 1908–1909 (1910),

Contains grave listings in the chapter reports.

Report, v.13, 1909–1910 (1911), 61nd Congress, 3rd Session. Senate. Document no.856

Contains grave listings in the chapter reports.

Report, v.14, 1910–1911 (1912), 62nd Congress, 2nd Session. Senate. Document no.371

Contains grave listings in the chapter reports.

Report, v.15, 1911–1912 (1913), 63rd Congress, 1st Session. Senate. Document no.9

Contains grave listings in the chapter reports. Also includes a list of Revolutionary War soldiers from Massachusetts with information on parents, birth, death, marriage and name of spouse as compiled by the Molly Varnum Chapter of Lowell, Massachusetts.

Report, v. 16, 1912–1913 (1914),
> *Appendix B:*   List of Real Daughters
> *Appendix C:*   Classified List of [Graves of] Revolutionary Soldiers

Report, v. 17, 1913-1914 (1915), 63rd Congress, 3rd Session, Senate. Document No. 988
> *Appendix:*   Pierce's Register [Subsequently reprinted as a separate volume by other publishers.]

Report, v. 18, 1914–1915 (1916) to Report, v. 20, 1916–1917 (1918). These reports contain grave listings.

Report, v. 21, 1917–1918 (1919),
> *Appendix:*   A Pension List of Revolutionary Soldiers from Connecticut

Most of the remaining reports contain grave listings that have all been published and indexed as noted above.

Please see Chapter 14 for information on the proper bibliographic citation of these DAR reports to the Smithsonian.

7.4
"REAL DAUGHTERS"

All DAR members are called "Daughters." Those early members who were the actual daughters of Revolutionary War soldiers and patriots were known as "Real Daughters." More than 700 women enjoyed this distinction. The Office of the Historian General has the finding aid listed above as "Index of Reported Marked Graves of Real Daughters" as well as a photograph collection of some of these interesting women and a few files of additional information. Issues of *The DAR Magazine*, especially those published prior to the 1940s, also contain useful vignettes of Real Daughters, generally complete with likenesses of the women under discussion. The Historian General's Office has a listing of those Real Daughters who were honored by an article in *The DAR Magazine*. See section 13.8 for additional information on this subject.

Georgia's Real Daughter Sisters
Left – Mrs. Mary Pool Newson
Right – Miss Sarah Pool
Photo from the DAR Magazine, August 1929

7.5
THE HISTORICAL RESEARCH LIBRARY

The Office of the Historian General has a very small Historical Research Library containing a variety of materials on American history and historical subjects and individuals. Biographies of famous figures in American history, especially George Washington, are housed here. There is some duplication with the DAR Library's biography collection. Studies in women's history and the presidency are other areas of concentration.

An excellent and almost complete collection of the state guides in the "American Guides Series" is part of this library. These guides are the work of the Federal Works Agency of the Work Projects Administration and date from the late 1930s and early 1940s.

Some useful bibliographic sources for American imprints are in this collection as well. Shaw and Shoemaker's *American Bibliography: A Preliminary Checklist 1801–1834* (with indices), Jones and Leypoldts' *The American Catalog: Author and Title Entries of Books in Print and for Sale 1876–1910*, and similar compilations provide good information on this subject.

OFFICE OF THE
ORGANIZING SECRETARY GENERAL

Location: Administration Building, First Floor, Rooms 101 and 103
Chapter Services, Room 101
Telephone (202) 879-3325
Membership Services, Room 103,
Telephone (202) 879-3324

The Office of the Organizing Secretary General maintains records relating to chapter organization, national and state chairmen, chapter officers, and historical and current membership materials.

8.1
MEMBERSHIP RECORDS

Each woman who has become a DAR member receives a national number. Since 1890 there have been over 826,000 members, and the Office of the Registrar General assigns the national numbers in sequence as the member is admitted. To gain access to open application papers of members, one must obtain the national number of the member either at the Library reference desk or in the Seimes Technology Center where the applications may be viewed.

The development of the DAR's internal, online "All Member Index" in 2002-2003 incorporated the contents of several card and microfiche indexes that the Office of the Organizing Secretary General had maintained for decades. Visitors to the DAR may request information on early members of the DAR at the Library reference desk. Inquiries of this nature by mail should be sent to the Organizing office.

This office also maintains a file on the former and current National, State and Chapter Officers of the DAR. If an ancestor or relative were an officer, information on her activities may be available.

8.2
ADDRESSES

In recent years, the DAR has limited the distribution of addresses of members. Generally, addresses of officers of the National Society and State Societies are available to researchers with legitimate reasons for contacting these members. Addresses of individual members may not be distributed. The DAR does not distribute any membership lists in any form to anyone.

8.3
WAS SHE A DAR MEMBER?

This question is a frequent one received by several offices at DAR. The Library staff has the ability to search the new Ancestor Database, an internal database of member names. While they cannot reveal member's addresses (either current or historical), they can attempt to verify whether or not a woman were a member. The results of such searches can be mixed.

Frequently, however, there is some family memory that a woman was a member of a lineage society, and researchers assume this to be the DAR because it is the largest and most well known of these groups. Actual membership in such groups as the Daughters of the Revolution, the United Daughters of the Confederacy, the Colonial Dames, and other groups is often the basis for these inquiries. Although it may not always be possible, researchers should try to verify which organization an individual joined before contacting any lineage society including the DAR.

Some applications for DAR membership are not approved. A woman may have gone through the application process and had her paper returned for additional proof or clarification. She may never have completed the work and resubmitted the paper. As a result, there may be a memory among family members that this happened. The DAR does not maintain records of individuals whose membership application was not successful.

Name changes and other variations on a person's name can prevent the staff from determining whether a woman were a DAR member or not. Please provide as complete information as possible in your inquiry to help overcome these stumbling blocks to research. State and city of residence at the time of membership, or more than one if relocations occurred, are additional important facts the staff needs to know.

Other sources for membership records include state and chapter historical rosters and histories produced by the state DAR societies/organizations and local chapters. The Office of the Organizing Secretary General does not maintain these publications. Most state histories and historical rosters are available through either the Library or the Office of the Historian General. Chapter publications are, however, usually only available from the chapter and are not considered public information. A collection of these is not maintained at DAR headquarters with the small exception of a few in the custody of the Historian General.

AMERICAN SPIRIT, THE DAR MAGAZINE

Since 1892 the DAR has published a periodical that contains many articles and notes of genealogical and historical interest. Large libraries nationwide own a full set of this magazine, which has had several titles in its history and one continual numbering system.

- *The American Monthly Magazine*, v. 1 (July 1892)-v. 42 (June 1913)
- *Daughters of the American Revolution Magazine*, v. 43 (July 1913)-v.72 (December 1938)
- *The National Historical Magazine*, v. 73 (1939)-v. 79 (1945)
- *The Daughters of the American Revolution Magazine*, v. 80 (1946)-v.135 (2001)
- *American Spirit*, v.135, no.6 (July/Aug. 2001) to the present
- [**Note:** Until v. 51 (July–December 1917) a volume comprised half a year or six issues.]

In 2001, the *DAR Magazine* changed in content and format to become *American Spirit* a bimonthly, full color magazine. *American Spirit* focuses on American history, historic preservation, patriotism, genealogy, and education. The magazine also features articles on antiques and collectibles, current events, influential public personas, women's issues, and book reviews. The business of the society is now covered in a separate newsletter, *Daughters*, which is distributed to the membership with each issue of *American Spirit*.

Several regular features of early volumes of *The DAR Magazine* are especially useful to genealogists. Although genealogical information has appeared in the publication since 1892, the "Genealogical Department" column began in 1900 and ran until June 1957 with that title and as "Genealogical Source Material" from July 1957 to July 1961. This column contained record abstracts and articles addressing particular research areas and methodology. Afterwards, the succeeding column has tended to be mostly genealogical queries. The columns' title was changed to "More Genealogy" beginning in April 1984. Researchers should be aware that there are no correspondence files relating to any queries published in *The DAR Magazine*.

In more recent years, the staff of the Genealogical Records Committee (G.R.C.) abstracted genealogical information from documentation files in the DAR Library on specific surnames. These abstracts were published in the "More Genealogy" column. They appeared as time permitted and abstracts were available. Any researcher could submit a query for publication. Guidelines for submission appeared at the beginning of each column in each issue of the magazine.

The *DAR Patriot Index* is discussed in detail in the section on the Office of the Registrar General, but additions and corrections to this publication appear regularly in the DAR's newsletter *Daughters*. Lists of "New Ancestors" registered by members through applications or supplement applications approved by the staff genealogists are printed in the newsletter three issues after the month in which the new applications are approved at the DAR's National Board of Management meetings (February, April, June, October, and December). Corrections to the *Patriot Index* are compiled semi–annually and published on a space–available basis. More detailed information on new ancestors and corrections is available from the Office of the Registrar General.

Please see Chapter 14 for information on the proper citation of articles in *The DAR Magazine/American Spirit*.

9.1
INDICES TO *THE DAR MAGAZINE*

In 1998, the DAR published a master index to *The DAR Magazine* in three volumes. The index covers volumes 1 through 132 (1892-1998). The three volumes have specific content:

> Volume 1: General Subject Index
> Volume 2: Genealogy and Necrology
> Volume 3: Advertisements, sites and names, and "interesting information."

This source should be the first place a researcher looks to find information in this long-published journal.

Until 1998, there was no single index to *The DAR Magazine*, and several publications provided varying levels of indexing for this journal. All of these older indices are out of print. The quality and depth of coverage in these finding aids vary considerably, but researchers should consult them for the details they may contain.

- Elizabeth Benton Chapter, NSDAR. *Genealogical Guide: Master Index of Genealogy in the Daughters of the American Revolution Magazine, v. 1–84 (1892–1950)*. Washington, D.C.: DAR, 1951.
- Elizabeth Benton Chapter, NSDAR. *Supplement to Genealogical Guide: Master Index of Genealogy in the Daughters of the American Revolution Magazine, v. 85–89 (1950–1955)*. Washington, D.C.: DAR, 1956.

These two publications were reprinted as one book as *Genealogical Guide: Master Index of Genealogy in the Daughters of the American Revolution Magazine, volumes 1–84 (1892–1950) with Supplement, volumes 85–89 (1950–1955). Combined Edition.* Baltimore: Genealogical Publishing Company, 1994. This edition also contains a introduction which explains the benefits and limitations of the indices.

- Mary Emery, Ervil Norton, and Ruth Gee. *Index to Genealogical Records in the 1956 DAR Magazines, v. 90.* [S.l.]: Seminole Chapter, NSDAR, 1957.
- Martha Porter Miller. *Index to the Genealogical Department of the Daughters of the American Revolution Magazine, v. 91 (1957).* Washington, D.C.: M. P. Miller, 1958.
- Martha Potter Miller. *Index to the Genealogical Department of the Daughters of the American Revolution Magazine, v. 92 (1958).* Washington, D.C.: M. P. Miller, 1961.
- John Frederick Dorman. *Index to the Genealogical Department of the Daughters of the American Revolution Magazine, v. 93 (1959)—v. 101 (1967).* 9 annual volumes. Washington, D.C.: J. F. Dorman, 1961–1968.

The preceding entries represent a consistent run of indices to *The DAR Magazine* through 1967. Subsequent volumes have not been indexed in these forms. Several other indices to parts of *The DAR Magazine* also are available:

- Mrs. Balfour N. Clark. *An Index to Genealogical Data in the Daughters of the American Revolution Magazine 1926–1946.* Corsicana, Texas: James Blair Chapter, DAR, 1947.
- Mary Knight Crane. *A Condensed Index to the Genealogical Material, Marriage and American Revolutionary War Records Contained in the Daughters of the American Revolution Magazine, v. 1 to 55 Inclusive* [1892–1921]. Erie, Pennsylvania: M. K. Crane, 1922.
- Louise H. Rainey. *Index: American Monthly Magazine, Daughters of the American Revolution Magazine.* New York: L. H. Rainey, 1938. This index appears to cite articles beginning with v. 17 (1900) and ending with v. 71 (1937).
- Katie–Prince W. Esker. *The Genealogical Department: Source Records from the DAR Magazine 1947–1950.* Baltimore: Genealogical Publishing Company, 1975.
- Lorena Wildman. *Genealogical Guide to the Daughters of the American Revolution Magazine volume[s] 95–99 (1961–1965).* Spokane, Washington: Eastern Washington Genealogical Society, 1981.
- Ellen Smith Long. *Partially Annotated Index of Articles of Bicentennial Interest Published in the Daughters of the American Revolution Magazine 1956–1975.* Waycross, Georgia: E.S. Long, 1976.
- Barbara Schull Wolfe. *Federal and State Records, DAR Magazine from Beginning to May 1976, with Supplement to 1982.* Indianapolis: Ye Olde Genealogie Shoppe, 1984.
- Mrs. Frank R. Mettlach. *Listing of Historical Articles in the Daughters of the American Revolution Magazine 1892–1970.* Washington, D.C.: DAR, 1970.

Other published indices to genealogical periodicals have included the DAR's publication.

- *Genealogical Periodical Annual Index, v. 1 (1962)* to the present. Bowie, Maryland: Heritage Books, 1962– .
- Michael B. Clegg and Curt B. Witcher, editors. *Periodical Source Index (PERSI).* Fort Wayne, Indiana: Allen County Public Library Foundation, 1987– ; in CD-ROM; and presently online through a subscription service.
- Kip Sperry. *Index to Genealogical Periodical Literature, 1960–1977.* Detroit: Gale, 1979. Gale Genealogy and Local History Series, v. 9.

OFFICE OF THE CURATOR GENERAL
DAR MUSEUM

Location: Administration Building, Third Floor, Room 303
Telephone: 202–879–3288

The DAR Museum is a collection of early American decorative and fine arts and crafts. While not a genealogical department like many others at DAR, it does have, nonetheless, a genealogical presence because of the composition of the collections, the general atmosphere in which they reside in the building, and the simple fact that it belongs to the DAR.

Among the Museum's treasures are a small number of family record needlework pieces, which are excellent examples of this highly personal art form. Additionally, some family histories have accompanied other donations to the Museum and are kept on file with the object records. These provide a family context in which to view the items. Questions regarding these sources should be directed to the Museum Registrars in the Office of the Curator General.

Over the years the DAR Museum has mounted many exhibits which have focused on women's history, the American Revolution, genealogy and related subjects. Descriptive checklists or catalogs were prepared for some of these and are available in the Museum Office and the DAR Library. Background information for these exhibits may also be available from the Office of the Curator General. Among these exhibits were:

- *Lafayette in America* (1979)

- *The Jewish Community in Early America: 1654–1830* (1980–1981)

- *When You See This, Remember Me: Early American Samplers* (1982)

- *Old Line Traditions: Maryland Women and Their Quilts* (1985)

- *Childhood Lessons: Educating Through Toys, Dolls and Books of the 19th Century* (1988–1987)

- *First Flowerings: Early Virginia Quilts* (1987)

- *For My Little Ones* (1988)

- *Family Record: Genealogical Watercolors and Needlework* (1989)

- *Magnificent Intentions: Decorative Arts of the District of Columbia, 1791-1861* (September 1991-March 1992)

- *Kinsmen, Clay and Commerce: The Exeter Pottery Works* (June-August 1992)

- *Souvenirs from the Voyage of Life* (October 1992–March 1993)

- *True Love and a Happy Home: Cultural Expectations and Feminine Experiences in Victorian America* (June-December 1993)

- *George Washington: The Man Behind the Image* (February–October 1994)

Sampler made by Emily Tarr, 1835, of Georgetown, Maine.
Photograph by Helga Photo Studio

- *Classical Quilts* (September-October 1995)

- *American Women, American Fashion: Costume from the DAR Museum Collection* (June-September 1996)

- *Bound for the West: Women and Their Families on the Western Trails, 1840-1880* (October 1996-April 1997)

- *American Case Furniture: 1680-1840* (June-October 1997)

- *Youth is the Time for Progress: The Importance of American Schoolgirl Art, 1780-1860* (December 1997-May 1998) (Copies of the catalog for this exhibition are available through the DAR Museum Shop)

- *Costume Myths and Mysteries* (May 1998-January 1999)

- *Pleasing Things Made in Her Honor: Martha Washington and the Colonial Revival* (February-September 1999)

- *The Historical Precedent for the Art Quilt* (October 1999-February 2000)

- *As Centuries End* (April 2000-October 2000)

- *The Art of Upholstery* (October 2000-Mary 2001)

- *Feminine Images: American Portraits 1750-1860* (June 2001-November 2001)

- *The Stuff of Childhood: Artifacts and Attitudes, 1700 to 1900* (2001-2002)

- *Forgotten Patriots: African American and American Indian Patriots in the Revolutionary War (2002-2003)*

- *Degrees of Latitude: Maps from the Colonial Williamsburg Collection* (2003-2004)

- *Something Old, Something New: Inventing the American Wedding* (April 2004-September 2004)

- *Of Thee I Sing: Needlework and Quilts from the DAR Museum Collection* (October 2004-Early 2005)

In 1989, the DAR Museum presented an exhibit "Family Record: Genealogical Watercolors and Needlework" and published a catalog with the same title written by Gloria Seaman Allen, then–Director and Chief Curator. The exhibit and the catalog, which is now out of print, offered excellent examples of this artwork gathered from many collections and annotated entries with descriptive commentary. A sample from the exhibit follows and is representative of the Museum's holdings and of some of the items in the Historian General's Americana Collection.

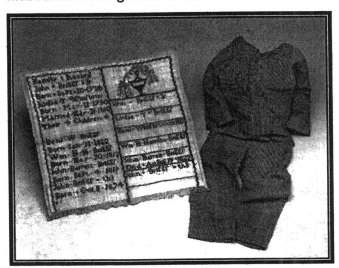

Child's suit made by Lydia Winslow Briggs, 1822, of Sumner, Maine, and needlework family record, attributed to Lydia Briggs
Photograph by Mark Gulezian

In 2003, the DAR Library and the Museum offered a symposium on minority participation in the Revolutionary War. This symposium coincided with the Museum's exhibit "Forgotten Patriots: African American and American Indian Service in the Revolutionary War" and the publication by the DAR in 2001 of a reference book by the same name.

The Museum Reference Library is a small collection of books on pertinent subjects. Among these are titles on American artisans, clockmakers, pewterers, gunsmiths, furniture makers, and painters. Books on ceramics, silver, brassware, glassware, textiles, quilts, folk art, needlework, costume and toys combine with others on U.S. history, Women's studies, architecture, interior decoration and antiques to provide general background for the Museum's areas of specialization. Genealogists researching individuals in such fields *may* gain insight from the materials in this library. Plans are underway for the holdings of the Museum Library to be accessible through the DAR Library's online catalog.

THE DAR STORE
OFFICE OF THE CORRESPONDING
SECRETARY GENERAL

Location: Administration Building, Lower Level, Room LL3
Telephone: 202–879–3218

This office functions as the DAR's "book shop" and sells all DAR publications including:

- *The DAR Patriot Index*

- *Is That Lineage Right?*

- *Is That Service Right?*

- *"A Century of Service:" The Story of the DAR*

- *African American and American Indian Patriots of the American Revolution*

- *Daughters Overseas: A History of Units Overseas*

Request a copy of "DAR Publications and Supplies" for a full and current listing of these materials. DAR publications are only available for purchase from the National Society's Corresponding Secretary General.

The Lineage Research Kit, prepared by that committee and available from the Corresponding Office, contains various collected guides for basic genealogical research. Basic genealogical charts and pedigree charts are also for sale here.

The DAR Store also distributes various free information sheets including the following on DAR or related to genealogical research:

- *Application Papers: Instructions for Their Preparation* (1995)

- *All About the DAR* (formerly *DAR in Action*)

- *DAR Policies*

- *DAR Fact Sheet*

PUBLICATIONS AND SOURCES
OF THE STATE DARS AND CHAPTERS

Most of the State DAR societies or organizations have produced various publications of research value. Historical rosters and organization histories predominate, although some states and chapters have published volumes of record abstracts and historical sources. Please note that lineages published in these state books are not necessarily acceptable to DAR staff genealogists in support of membership applications.

The most significant state–produced compilations are the *Genealogical Records Committee Reports* discussed in detail in Chapter 4. The DAR Library staff has attempted several times in recent years to determine the locations of the state copies of these reports. The results of these surveys have been mixed. The following libraries or research facilities have been identified by DAR state librarians as having holdings of DAR materials. These do not include membership applications, but rather, *G.R.C. Reports*, some state publications, and other historical and genealogical materials collected by Daughters in each state. Collections will vary in size and content, but only a few are considered large. Addresses for the public institutions mentioned in the following list are found in such publications as *The American Library Directory* or by searching for their website.

12.1
STATE DAR COLLECTIONS AND LIBRARIES

Alabama
> Most of Alabama's GRC books may be found in the Birmingham Public Library. The Mobile Public Library and the Huntsville Public Library also have DAR holdings.

Alaska
> No separate DAR state library

Arkansas
> DAR materials are housed in the Little Rock Public Library, and the Central Arkansas Public Library System and some are also in public libraries in Jonesboro, Fort Smith, Pine Bluff, Fayetteville, and Texarkana. A collection of chapter records and a scrapbook from the Marion Chapter, Arkansas DAR is on file at the University of Arkansas, Fayetteville.

Arizona
> No DAR state library. Some DAR materials are in the Tucson Genealogical Library, the Genealogical collection of the Arizona State Library in Phoenix, and the Sun City Genealogy Library.

California

The California DAR Library is located at 201 West Bennett Avenue, Glendora, CA 91740. This library was established in 1988. Other materials are in the California State Library in Sacramento, its branch in San Francisco, the Sutro Library, and the Genealogy Department of the Los Angeles Public Library.

Colorado

No separate DAR state library. Denver Public Library holds the DAR Collection.

Connecticut

The Connecticut DAR has a library in the Oliver Ellsworth Homestead, 778 Palisado Ave., Windsor, CT 06095. No separate DAR state library. The Connecticut State Library in Hartford has some DAR material, as does the Connecticut Historical Society Library also in Hartford.

Delaware

No separate DAR state library. Some materials are at the Delaware Historical Society in Wilmington and at the Delaware Archives in Dover.

District of Columbia

The D.C. DAR has a small library in its headquarters in Washington, but District Daughters have supported the DAR Library since its founding in 1896.

Florida

The Florida State DAR Collection is housed in the Orange County Library System, Genealogical Department, 10 North Rosalind, Orlando, FL 32801. There is also a DAR collection at the University of West Florida Library, Pensacola. Other libraries with some DAR materials are Polk County Historical and Genealogical Society Library in Bartow; Palm Beach County Genealogical Society Library in West Palm Beach; Miami–Dade Public Library, Genealogy Collection in Miami; Bay County Public Library, Genealogy Collection, Panama City; and Tampa Public Library.

Georgia

The Georgia Genealogical Records Committee Reports are available in their entirety at the Georgia Department of Archives and History, in Morrow, and partial sets of these compilations in the Georgia Historical Society in Savannah and the Washington Memorial Library in Macon.

Hawaii

Aloha Chapter House and Memorial Library, 1914 Makihi Heights Drive, Honolulu is the state's main genealogical facility.

Idaho

The Idaho State Genealogical Library, 325 State Street, Boise, holds some DAR volumes.

Illinois

The C.E. Brehm Memorial Library, 101 South Seventh St., Mt. Vernon, IL 62864 is home to the Illinois State DAR Library. A number of Illinois GRC books are available at the Newberry Library in Chicago.

Indiana

No separate state DAR library. Some materials are in the Allen County Public Library in Fort Wayne and the Indiana State Library, Genealogy Division, in Indianapolis.

Iowa

No separate state DAR library. Some materials are in the Iowa State Genealogical Library, Iowa City; the Iowa Historical Center, Des Moines; and the Iowa Genealogical Society Library, Des Moines.

Kansas

Kansas DAR Library, Village Square Mall, Lower Level, 2601 Central, Dodge City.

Kentucky

The John Fox Jr. Library, Duncan Tavern in Paris and the Kentucky Historical Society in Frankfort own some DAR materials.

Louisiana

The Annie Laurie Moody LSDAR Collection is held by the East Baton Rouge Public Library. Some material is also in the Louisiana State Library, Baton Rouge.

Maine

No separate DAR state library. The Maine State Library in Augusta and the Bangor Public Library own some DAR materials.

Maryland

The Maryland DAR State House in Baltimore holds some materials but is not open to the public, and some items are in the Maryland Historical Society, Baltimore.

Massachusetts

The bulk of the Massachusetts DAR's collection was removed from the New England Historic Genealogical Society several years ago and placed in the Haverhill Public Library, Haverhill. Some material, however, remains at NEHGS.

Michigan

The Michigan DAR has placed its compilations in the Burton Historical Collection of Detroit Public Library and in the Library of Michigan in Lansing.

Minnesota

DAR materials are in the Minnesota Historical Center in St. Paul, the Minneapolis Public Library, St. Paul Public Library, and Duluth Public Library.

Missouri

The Missouri State DAR Library Collection is housed at Missouri University Library in Columbia. Some materials are also in the Mid-Continent Public Library in Independence and the Springfield Public Library.

Mississippi

The Mississippi State DAR Library Collection is housed in the Eudora Welty Library in Jackson.

Montana

No separate DAR state library

Nebraska

Edith Abbot Memorial Library in Grand Island houses the Lue R. Spencer State DAR Collection.

Nevada

No separate DAR state library

New Hampshire

No separate DAR state library. DAR materials are held in the New Hampshire State Library, Concord.

New Jersey

The New Jersey DAR Collection is housed at the Special Collections Department of the Alexander Library at Rutgers University, New Brunswick. Some materials are also in the New Jersey State Library, Trenton.

New Mexico

Some materials are in the Special Collections of the Albuquerque Public Library.

New York

Collections are housed in the New York Public Library in New York City, and the New York State Library in Albany.

North Carolina

Some materials are in the North Carolina Department of Archives and History in Raleigh.

North Dakota

Collections are in the North Dakota State Archives in Bismarck.

Ohio

Collections are in the Ohio Historical Society in Columbus.

Oklahoma

The Oklahoma DAR Collection is in the Oklahoma Historical Society, Oklahoma City.

Oregon

The Caples House Museum in Columbia City is the Oregon DAR's state library. Other materials have been placed in the Genealogical Forum of Oregon Library in Portland, the Oregon Historical Society in Portland, and the Oregon State Library in Salem.

Pennsylvania

Some materials have been placed in the Genealogy/Local History Section of the Pennsylvania State Library in Harrisburg.

Rhode Island

Some materials are in the library of the Rhode Island Historical Society in Providence.

South Carolina

The South Carolina DAR Collection is housed at Camden Archives in Camden. Some materials are also in the South Carolina Department of Archives and History in Columbia and the South Carolina Historical Society in Charleston.

South Dakota

Some materials are in the South Dakota State Archives in Pierre.

Tennessee

Some materials are in the Tennessee State Library and Archives in Nashville.

Texas

Some materials are in the Clayton Library Center for Genealogical Research, Houston Public Library. Other local libraries receive materials from chapters.

Utah

No separate state DAR library, but the Family History Library in Salt Lake City holds microfilm of many DAR GRC Reports. See Chapter 4.

Vermont

Materials are placed in the Vermont Historical Society's Library in Montpelier.

Virginia

Some materials are in the Library of Virginia in Richmond.

Washington

The Washington State Society DAR's collection is housed in the Yakima Valley Genealogical Society Library in Yakima. Other materials are available in the Spokane Public Library, the Seattle Public Library, and the Washington State Library in Olympia.

West Virginia

Various materials have been placed in the West Virginia and Regional History Collection at West Virginia University in Morgantown, Marshall University Library in Huntington, the West Virginia Department of Archives and History in Charleston, and the West Virginia Room of the Waldmore Library in Clarksburg.

Wisconsin

The Wisconsin Historical Society in Madison holds many DAR materials. *GRC Reports* may be found at the main branch of the Milwaukee Public Library.

Wyoming

Materials are in the Wyoming State Library in Cheyenne.

12.2
SELECTED STATE DAR PUBLICATIONS

Many of the DAR State Organizations/Societies have published rosters and histories that may contain information useful to genealogists researching Daughters in their family histories. Please remember that the records in these volumes may not always coincide with the information that the National Society now considers to be accurate. Like the *DAR Lineage Books* and other similar publications, corrections and additions may have occurred since publication. Most states have also published annual reports of their activities, often called yearbooks, and many individual DAR chapters have also produced histories and rosters of their members. The National Society does not own complete sets of these state and chapter publications.

Alabama (Alabama Society of the National Society Daughters of the American Revolution)
- *Alabama DAR Chronological History 1894–1970* (1970)
- *Membership Roll and Register of Ancestors*, 6 volumes (1949-)
- *Roster of Revolutionary Soldiers and Patriots in Alabama* (1979)

Alaska (Alaska Daughters of the American Revolution)
- No rosters or histories are in the DAR Library or DAR Archives.

Arizona (Arizona Society Daughters of the American Revolution)
- *Arizona State History of the Daughters of the American Revolution* (1930)
- *Historical Markers Placed in Arizona by the Arizona Society and by Chapters of the Daughters of the American Revolution* (1965)
- *Arizona Daughters of the American Revolution, Territorial Days to 1990* (1990)
- *History of the Arizona State Society DAR 1930–1980* (1980)
- *1996 Arizona Daughters of the American Revolution with Arizona Lineage before Statehood* (1996)

Arkansas (Arkansas State Society National Society Daughters of the American Revolution)
- *Roster of the Arkansas Society and Register of Ancestors, 1893–1968* (1968) with 3 supplements (1978, 1988, 1998)
- *History of the Arkansas State Society DAR* (1931)
- *Arkansas Historical Markers Including Revolutionary War Soldiers Commemorated by the Arkansas State Society Daughters of the American Revolution* (2002)

California (California State Society of the National Society Daughters of the American Revolution)
- *California DAR Ancestry Guide* (1976)
- *Autobiographies of Members, California DAR*, 4 volumes (1928)
- *California History of the DAR, 1891–1938, Volume I* (1939)
- *California History of the DAR, 1938–1968, Volume II* (1969)
- *California History of the DAR, 1968–1980, Volume III* (1981)
- *California History of the DAR, 1981-1994, Volume IV* (1994)
- *Deeds Not Dreams: One Hundred Years of Service by California Daughters* (1991)
- *California's Seventy–five Historic Years, DAR 1891–1966* (1966)

Colorado (Colorado Daughters of the American Revolution)
- *Colorado DAR Member and Ancestor Index* (1981)
- *Colorado DAR Member and Ancestor Index and Supplement to October 10, 1984* (1987)
- *Supplement to the Colorado DAR Member and Ancestor Index, 1979–1984* (1987)
- *History of the DAR of Colorado, 1894–1941* (1941); *1953–1971* (1971); *1971–1987* (1987)

Connecticut (Connecticut Daughters of the American Revolution, Inc.)
- *Chapter Sketches, Connecticut DAR: Patriots' Daughters* (1904)
- *Connecticut State History of the DAR* (1929)
- *A Glance Back: Connecticut DAR Historical Directory, Vol. 1* (1969)
- *Honoring NSDAR: Connecticut Members and Their Revolutionary Patriot Ancestors* (1995)

Delaware (The Delaware State Society Daughters of the American Revolution)
- *Roster and Ancestral Roll Delaware DAR* (1940)

District of Columbia (District of Columbia Daughters of the American Revolution)
- *State History District of Columbia DAR, 3 volumes* (1934)
- *Diamond Jubilee Chapter Histories District of Columbia Society Daughters of the American Revolution, 1892–1966* (1966)

Florida (Florida State Society, National Society Daughters of the American Revolution)
- *Florida State Society NSDAR Historic Chapter Names 1895–1995* (1995)
- *History 1892–1933 Daughters of the American Revolution of Florida, Volume 1* (1933)
- *History 1933–1946 Daughters of the American Revolution of Florida, Volume 2* (1946)
- *History 1946–1958 Daughters of the American Revolution of Florida, Volume 3* (1958)
- *History and Roster Florida State Society of the DAR, Volume 4* (1968)
- *History and Roster Florida State Society of the DAR, Volume 5* (1978)
- *History and Roster Florida State Society of the DAR, Volume 6* (1988)
- *History and Roster Florida State Society of the DAR, Volume 7* (1998)
- *Florida State Society National Society Daughters of the American Revolution: Historic Chapter Names 1895–1995* (1995)

Georgia (Georgia State Society of the National Society Daughters of the American Revolution)
- *Membership Roll and Register of Ancestors of the Georgia State Society NSDAR* (1946, 1956, 1966, 1976, 1986)
- *Histories of Revolutionary Soldiers Contributed by Georgia Chapters, 26 volumes*
- *Revolutionary Soldiers Buried In Georgia*
- *Chapter Histories DAR of Georgia 1891–1931* (1931)
- *History of the Georgia State Society DAR 1899–1981* (1982)

Hawaii (Hawaii State Society, National Society Daughters of the American Revolution)
- *History of the DAR in the Hawaiian Islands* (1928)

Idaho (Idaho Daughters of the American Revolution)
- *History and Register 1904–1934 Idaho State Society DAR* (1934)
- *History 1963–1987 Idaho State Society DAR* (1987)
- *Idaho DAR State and Chapter History* (1931)
- Ancestor Index, Idaho State Daughters of the American Revolution (n.d.)

Illinois (Daughters of the American Revolution of Illinois)
- *Illinois State History of the Daughters of the American Revolution* (1929)
- *Illinois State History of the Daughters of the American Revolution* (1969)

- *Illinois State Directory of Members and Ancestors DAR* (1957)
- *Supplement to Illinois Ancestral Directory Members and Ancestors DAR* (1962)
- *Bicentennial Supplement to Illinois Ancestral Directory of Members and Ancestors DAR* (1976)

Indiana (Daughters of the American Revolution of Indiana)
- *Roster of Soldiers and Patriots of the American Revolution Buried in Indiana, Volume 1* (1938)
- *Roster of Soldiers and Patriots of the American Revolution Buried in Indiana, Volume 2* (1938)
- *Roster of Soldiers and Patriots of the American Revolution Buried in Indiana, Volume 3* (1981)
- *A Roster of Revolutionary Ancestors of the Indiana Daughters of the American Revolution, Volumes 1 & 2* (1976)
- *Members and Ancestors of Some Disbanded Daughters of the American Revolution Chapters in Indiana* (1987)
- *History of the Daughters of the American Revolution in Indiana* (1984; 4th edition)

Iowa (Iowa Society Daughters of the American Revolution)
- *Revolutionary War Soldiers and Patriots Buried in Iowa* (1978)
- *Biographies of State and Chapter Regents of the Iowa Society DAR* (1930)

Kansas (Kansas Society Daughters of the American Revolution)
- *Roster, Kansas Society Daughters of the American Revolution* (1970)
- *History of the Kansas Society Daughters of the American Revolution, 1894–1938* (1938)
- *Looking Back: Trails to the Second Century: The Centennial History, 1896-1996, Kansas Society Daughters of the American Revolution* (1996)
- *Kansas State Society of the NSDAR History 1944–1986* (1986)

Kentucky (The Kentucky Society, Daughters of the American Revolution)
- *Graves of Revolutionary Soldiers, Their Wives and Children, Buried in Kentucky* (1943)
- *Ancestor Roster of the Kentucky Society DAR* (1986)
- *History of the DAR in Kentucky 1890–1929* (1929)
- *History of the Kentucky Society DAR* (1969)
- *Beginning a Legacy: Chapter Histories of Kentucky Society Daughters of the American Revolution* (1983)
- *Revolutionary Ancestors of Kentucky Daughters of the American Revolution* (1958)

Louisiana (Louisiana Society of the National Society Daughters of the American Revolution)
- *Revolutionary Ancestors of the Louisiana Society of the NSDAR 1895–1989* (1991)
- *Roster Louisiana State Society DAR* (1954)
- *History of the Chapters of the Louisiana Society DAR* (1951)

Maine (Maine State Organization, National Society Daughters of the American Revolution)
- *Ancestral Roll and Chapter Roster* (1975, 1987)
- *Index to Miscellaneous Records* (1987)
- *A Brief History of the Maine Daughters of the American Revolution to March 1, 1925* (1925)
- *History of the Maine Society DAR* (1946)
- *Ancestral Roll, Maine DAR, and the List of Maine Soldiers at Valley Forge, 1777-1778* (1948)

Maryland (Maryland State Society Daughters of the American Revolution)
- *Directory of Maryland State Society Daughters of the American Revolution and Their Revolutionary War Ancestors 1892–1965* (1966)
- *Directory of Maryland State Society Daughters of the American Revolution and Their Revolutionary War Ancestors 1965–1980* (1979)
- *History of the Maryland State Society DAR 1892–1933; 1933–1943* (1933, 1943)

Massachusetts (Massachusetts Daughters of the American Revolution)
- *State History of the Massachusetts Daughters of the American Revolution* (1932)
- *State History of the Massachusetts Daughters of the American Revolution 1932–1941* (1941)
- *History of Massachusetts Daughters of the American Revolution 1932–1959* (1959)
- *Massachusetts Real Daughters* (1914)
- *Massachusetts State Directory of Members and Ancestors* (1974)

Michigan (Daughters of the American Revolution of Michigan)
- *Historical and Genealogical Record of the Michigan Daughters of the American Revolution*: Volume 1 and 2, 1893–1930 (1930); Volume 3, 1930–1940 (1940); Volume 4, 1940–1952 (1952); Volume 5, 1952–1964 (1964); Volume 6, 1964–1976 (1977); Volume 7, 1976–1988 (1990)

Minnesota (Minnesota Society, Daughters of the American Revolution)
- *Highlights in the History of the Minnesota State Society of the NSDAR, 1891–1991* (1994)
- *Centennial History, Minnesota State Society NSDAR, 1891-1991* (1994)
- *History of the DAR Chapters of Minnesota* (1928)

Mississippi (The Mississippi Society of the National Society of the Daughters of the American Revolution)
- *Mississippi Daughters and Their Ancestors* (1965, 1979)
- *Historical Directory of the DAR in Mississippi* (1933)
- *Chapters of the Mississippi Society, DAR* (1968)
- *A History of the Chapters of the Mississippi State Society of the National Society Daughters of the American Revolution* (1989)
- *History of the Mississippi State Society Daughters of the American Revolution, 1896-1996* (1996)
- *Mississippi: Her People, Places and Legends* (DAR history; 1977)

Missouri (Missouri State Society of the National Society, Daughters of the American Revolution)
- *Missouri State History of the DAR* (1929)
- *Missouri State History and Directory of the Daughters of the American Revolution, Bicentennial Edition* (1976)
- *Missouri State Society DAR Directory* (1986)
- *Revolutionary Soldiers Buried in Missouri* (1906)
- *Centennial Jubilee History of Missouri DAR Chapters* (1990)

Montana (Montana Society, Daughters of the American Revolution)
- *State Centennial History, Montana State Society DAR 1894–1994* (1994)

- *History of the DAR in Montana 1894–1940* (1940)
- *Montana Society DAR History 1940–1960* (1960)
- *State History Montana Society DAR 1960–1970; 1970–1980* (1970, 1980)

Nebraska (National Society Daughters of the American Revolution in Nebraska)
- *Nebraska State History of the Daughters of the American Revolution* (1928)
- *The Nebraska DAR-SAR Directory of Members and Ancestral Rolls* (1963)
- *DAR Nebraska Ancestor Index* (1994)
- *DAR Nebraska Ancestor Directory* (1994)
- *History of Nebraska Chapter Names* (1978)
- *The History of the Daughters of the American Revolution in Nebraska* (2000)

Nevada (Nevada State Society, Daughters of the American Revolution)
- No rosters or state history are in the DAR Library or the DAR Archives

New Hampshire (New Hampshire State Organization of the National Society of the Daughters of the American Revolution)
- *New Hampshire State History of the DAR* (1930)
- *Supplement to the New Hampshire History of the DAR 1930–1940* (1940)
- *Second Supplement to the New Hampshire History of the DAR 1940–1970* (1970)
- *A Brief History of the New Hampshire Society DAR* (1985)
- *New Hampshire Directory of Members and Ancestors* (1964)
- *New Hampshire Directory of Members and Ancestors, Supplement* (1976)
- *Living in the Lap of History* (2004)

New Jersey (New Jersey State Society of the National Society of the Daughters of the American Revolution)
- *State History of the New Jersey DAR* (1929)
- *New Jersey State Society History DAR 1891–1974* (1974)
- *Patriot Index, New Jersey State Society of the National Society Daughters of the American Revolution* (1997)
- *History of Chapter Names of the New Jersey State Society of the Daughters of the American Revolution 1891–1985* (1985)

New Mexico (New Mexico State Organization, Daughters of the American Revolution)
- *New Mexico DAR Lineage Book* (1976)
- *Members of the New Mexico State Organization NSDAR* (1995)
- *History of the New Mexico State Organization NSDAR*, 3 volumes, 1971, 1987.

New York (New York State Organization, National Society Daughters of the American Revolution)
- *History of the New York State Conference DAR: Its Officers and Chapters with National Officers from New York and Roster of Real Daughters [volume 1]* (1923)
- *History of the DAR of New York State 1923–1938, volume 2* (1938)
- *History of the DAR of New York State 1938–1953, volume 3* (1953)
- *History of the DAR of New York State 1953–1974, volume 4* (1974)
- *Historic Chapter Names 1890–1987* (1987)
- *Centennial History, New York State Organization, NSDAR, 1891-1991* (1991)

North Carolina (National Society Daughters of the American Revolution in North Carolina)
- *Genealogical Register Members and Revolutionary Ancestors 1890–1981* (1981)

- *Fifty Years of Service: History of the NSDAR of North Carolina* (1950)
- *North Carolina DAR Genealogical Register* (1947)

North Dakota (North Dakota State Society of the National Society Daughters of the American Revolution)
- *History of the North Dakota Daughters of the American Revolution 1915–1976* (1980)
- *Centennial History of the North Dakota Society, Daughters of the American Revolution, 1897-1997* (1997)

Ohio (The Ohio Society of the Daughters of the American Revolution)
- *Ohio State History of the DAR, volume 1* (1928)
- *Ohio State History of the DAR, volume 2* (1946)
- *Ohio State History of the DAR, volume 3* (1978
- *Master Index Ohio Society Daughters of the American Revolution, Genealogical and Historical Records, Volume 1* (1985)
- *Official Roster of the Soldiers of the American Revolution Who Lived in the State of Ohio*, 3 volumes (1959)

Oklahoma (Oklahoma State Society of the National Society Daughters of the American Revolution)
- *History of the Oklahoma Society DAR 1894–1939* (1939)
- *Oklahoma Society NSDAR Roster, 1909–1959 (1976)*

Oregon (Oregon State Society of the National Society Daughters of the American Revolution)
- *Oregon State Roster of Ancestors, Daughters of the American Revolution (1963)*
- *Oregon State Roster of Ancestors, Daughters of the American Revolution, First Supplement* (1978); *Second Supplement* (1993)
- *Oregon Daughters of the American Revolution* (1989)
- *History of the Oregon Society DAR* (1931)

Pennsylvania (The Pennsylvania State Society Daughters of the American Revolution)
- *The Pennsylvania Society of the DAR 1894–1930* (1930)
- *Pennsylvania State History of the DAR* (1947)
- *Pennsylvania State History of the DAR* (1976)
- *Pennsylvania State History of the DAR* (1990)

Rhode Island (Rhode Island State Society, Daughters of the American Revolution)
- *Revolutionary War Records and Biographical Sketches of the Ancestors of Rhode Island Daughters of the American Revolution*, 3 volumes (1964)
- *State History of the Rhode Island DAR* (1930)
- *State History of the Rhode Island DAR 1930–1938* (1938)

South Carolina (South Carolina State Society of the National Society of the Daughters of the American Revolution)

- *Membership Roster and Ancestral Index, 1954–1986* (1988)
- *Our Revolutionary Fathers, Volumes 1-2* (1942)
- *Roster and Ancestral Roll, South Carolina DAR* (1939, 1954)
- *History of the South Carolina DAR*, 4 volumes (1937, 1946, 1976, 1991)

South Dakota (South Dakota State Organization Daughters of the American Revolution)
- No rosters or state history are in the DAR Library or DAR Archives.

Tennessee (Tennessee Society Daughters of the American Revolution)
- *Membership Roster and Soldiers, The Tennessee Society of the Daughters of the American Revolution, 1894–1960, Volume 1* (1961)
- *Membership Roster and Soldiers, The Tennessee Society of the Daughters of the American Revolution, 1960–1970, Volume 2* (1970)
- *Membership Roster and Soldiers, The Tennessee Society of the Daughters of the American Revolution, 1970–1984, Volume 3* (1985)
- *Roster of Soldiers and Patriots of the American Revolution Buried in Tennessee* (1974)
- *History of the Tennessee Society DAR 1892–1990* (1990)
- *Tennessee State History DAR* (1930)

Texas (Texas Society National Society, Daughters of the American Revolution)
- *History of the Texas Society NSDAR* (1975)
- *The Roster of Texas Daughters' Revolutionary Ancestors* 4 volumes (1976)
- *Alamo Heroes and Their Revolutionary Ancestors* (1976)
- *Directory of the Texas Society of the NSDAR* (1990)
- *Texas State History of the DAR* (1929; reprint 1991)
- *History of the Texas Society NSDAR* (1976)

Utah (Utah Society Daughters of the American Revolution)
- *Who's Who in the Utah DAR* (1976)

Vermont (Vermont State Society Daughters of the American Revolution)
- *Vermont State Conference DAR 1892–1930* (1985)
- *Vermont DAR State History Book (1931–1985)* (1931, 1985)

Virginia (Virginia Daughters of the American Revolution)
- *Roster of the Virginia Daughters of the American Revolution (Revised) 1890–1958* (1959)
- *History of the Virginia State Society DAR, with Histories of the Chapters from 1892-1928 Inclusive* (1930)
- *History of the Virginia Daughters of the American Revolution 1891–1987* (1987)
- *History of Chapter Names, Virginia DAR* (1964), and *Supplement* (1967)

Washington (Washington State Society of the National Society, Daughters of the American Revolution)
- *History and Directory of the Washington State Society NSDAR*, 6 volumes (1924–1987)
- *Member Directory and Ancestor List of the Washington State Society of the National Society of the Daughters of the American Revolution* (1994)

- *Every Name Index to the Washington State Daughters of the American Revolution Genealogical Records Committee Collection Covering the Years 1927-2000.* 6 volumes (2003)

West Virginia (West Virginia Society, Daughters of the American Revolution)
- *West Virginia State History DAR* (1928)
- *West Virginia Daughters and Their Revolutionary Patriot Ancestors* (1981; 1997)
- *West Virginia State History DAR 1928–1982* (1982)

Wisconsin (Wisconsin Society Daughters of the American Revolution)
- *Wisconsin Society DAR in Review 1892–1971* (1971)
- *Wisconsin Society DAR in Review 1971–1989* (1989)
- *State History DAR Wisconsin 1892–1937* (1937)
- *Revolutionary War Ancestors, Members Numbers,* and *Supplements 1891–1964* (1965)

Wyoming (The Wyoming Society Daughters of the American Revolution)
- *Wyoming DAR Member and Ancestor Index* (1985)
- *Roster of Chapters and Members* (1975)
- *History of the DAR of Wyoming 1894–1946* (1946)

12.3
DAR CHAPTERS AND THEIR PUBLICATIONS

Many of the over 3,000 DAR chapters have published their own histories and rosters of members and their ancestors. These can be useful, once again, if a relative or direct forebear were a very active member of a chapter, biographical information may appear. Not all of these chapter histories are available in DAR collections.

12.4
UNITS OVERSEAS

Members of the DAR have long lived beyond the borders of the United States. During various periods in the past, DAR chapters have existed in such varied locations as Havana, Cuba; Shanghai, China; and Manila, Philippines. Today, Daughters have organized chapters in the United Kingdom, Bermuda, the Bahamas, France, Germany, Mexico, Australia, Japan, Italy, and Canada. Virginia C. Russell told the history of these foreign connections in the DAR publication, *Daughters Overseas: A History of Units Overseas.* Information on DAR members who were active in the older chapters overseas during the early twentieth century may also be found in articles in *The DAR Magazine* and in materials in the Office of the Historian General.

GUIDE TO SUBJECT RESEARCH IN DAR COLLECTIONS

Because of the varied and separated nature of many of the research collections at DAR, a subject approach to these sources beyond the department chapters is necessary. The broad categories of research in this chapter highlight the holdings of the DAR and how they relate to American genealogical research in general.

13.1
AFRICAN AMERICAN RESEARCH

During the past thirty years there has been an explosion of publishing in African American studies. Examinations of African American genealogical research have also increased in number. The DAR Library has developed a strong, growing collection of basic and detailed printed sources on this subject.

In the Library's General/African American section are many research manuals and guidebooks, histories of Americans of African descent, slavery and abolition studies, examinations of the "Great Migration" in the early twentieth century, and general reference materials. These offer researchers with a starting point and with ideas for further investigation. Burrough's *Black Roots: A Beginner's Guide to Tracing the African American Family Tree*, Blockson's *Black Genealogy*, Byers' *African American Genealogical Source Book*, Johnson and Cooper's *A Student's Guide to African American Genealogy*, and Streets' *Slave Genealogy: A Research Guide with Case Studies* are just a few of these items. *Roots* by Alex Haley, who undertook some of his research in the DAR Library, is also available in this section. Important periodicals, such as *The Journal of the Afro–American Historical and Genealogical Society, and The Journal of*

One of the great stimuli to the popularity of genealogical research in the late twentieth century was the publication in 1976 of Alex Haley's account of his family history, *Roots*. The subsequent televising in early 1977 of the miniseries reached an enormous audience. Coinciding with the Bicentennial of the Independence of the United States, these events combined to spark the imagination of the American public and to spur many into seeking their own family origins and the roles these ancestors played in the nation's development. The DAR Library recorded a fifty percent increase in visitors in 1976-77 over the previous year as a result. Interest has not waned in the past two decades.

In the mid-1960's and early 1970's Haley frequented the three major genealogical research centers in Washington, D.C. as he began his investigations. A few long-time staff members recall his visits to the DAR Library. In 1984, speaking to the DAR's Continental Congress, Haley remembered:

It was in the course of this that I would come to work at the DAR Library. There is one particular thing a lot of people don't realize and that is that the DAR Library is special in terms of black genealogical research.

Haley continued with a discussion of the presence of old plantation records and inventories which contain the names of many Southern slaves, and that if one is "blessed and lucky," their ancestors may appear in such records in the DAR Library.

Negro History/Journal of African American History offer much useful material.

At the beginning of the state sections are subsections for collected materials on each state for African American history and genealogy. One excellent example is Dr. Barnetta White's landmark publication *Somebody Knows My Name: Marriages of Freed People in North Carolina, County by County*. Within the county holdings researchers will find an increasing number of new publications such as published registers of free blacks in Virginia, Maryland, and the District of Columbia and community histories. African Americans appear throughout county histories and record abstracts, but researchers will be frustrated on occasion by older compilations of records which only list whites. Fortunately, recent abstractors are attempting to fill in these gaps. The Library's collection of District of Columbia marriage records is an example of such older and newer coverage.

Family histories, a significant portion of the Library's book collection, offer researchers of African American families many opportunities. Representative examples of studies specifically on black families include Fears' *Slave Ancestral Research: It's Something Else* and *Slave Ancestral Research in Seven Steps with in the Jackson–Moore Family History and Genealogy...*, Jupiter's *Agustina of Spanish West Florida and Her Descendants...*, Madden's *We Were Always Free, The Quander United Tricentennial Celebration, 1684–1984*, Redford's *Somerset Homecoming*, Sutton's *The Nickins Family, Non–Slave African American Patriots*, and Warner's *Free Men in an Age of Servitude: Three Generations of a Black Family*. Donations of African American family histories or notification of their publication are appreciated.

Family histories and genealogies of white families are also very important to African American researchers for the information they may reveal on the slave owners, their records, and their migrations. There are many such studies in the Library.

The Library's collection of census indices and the attendant microfilms in Seimes Technology Center are other useful sources. Among these indices are those for the 1850 and some 1860 slave schedules of the federal censuses. Although the actual schedules are only available locally at the National Archives and despite the fact that the indices only index the slave owner and not the slaves by name, these are important records. Some special compilations, such as Nitchman's *Blacks in Ohio, 1880* are based on census records.

An increasing number of excellent studies relating to the records of blacks in America's wars are natural inclusions for DAR collections, particularly those concerning the American Revolution. In addition to other studies on the latter subject, the DAR has had a project for many years to document minority service in the Revolution. This effort produced several booklets compiled by former Senior Genealogist, Elisabeth Whitman Schmidt. Rita Souther wrote the historical text for the Rhode Island volume, and Hazel Fuller Kreinheder penned the same for the New York, Maryland/Delaware/New Jersey, Pennsylvania/Ohio, Connecticut and Massachusetts booklets.

- *Minority Military Service, Connecticut, 1775–1783.* (1988)

- *Minority Military Service, Delaware, Maryland and New Jersey* (1998)
- *Minority Military Service, Maine, 1775–1783.* (1990)
- *Minority Military Service, Massachusetts, 1775–1783.* (1989)
- *Minority Military Service, New Hampshire/Vermont, 1775–1783.* (1991)
- *Minority Military Service, New York* (2001)
- *Minority Military Service, North Carolina, 1775–1783.* (1996)
- *Minority Military Service, Pennsylvania and Ohio* (2000)
- *Minority Military Service, Rhode Island, 1775–1783.* (1988)
- *Minority Military Service, South Carolina and Georgia, 1775–1783.* (1997)
- *Minority Military Service, Virginia, 1775–1783.* (1995)

In 2000 and into early 2001, Jean Davids Strahan, Researcher, DAR Library, and Eric G. Grundset, Library Director, undertook the task of updating and expanding the contents of the booklets and combining them into one volume using microfilm collections and publications not available when the original booklets were published. The result was the publication in 2001 of *African American and American Indian Patriots of the Revolutionary War*. This publication was followed by an exhibit in the DAR Museum and a symposium in January 2003, both entitled *Forgotten Patriots: African American and American Indian Patriots of the Revolutionary War*. A publication of the papers read at the symposium is planned for 2004 or 2005.

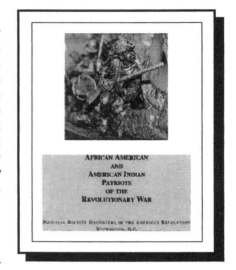

Green's *Black Courage*, Moebs' *Black Soldiers, Black Sailors, Black Ink: Research Guide on African–Americans in U.S. Military History*, Schubert's *On the Trail of the Buffalo Soldier: Biographies of African Americans in the U.S. Army, 1866–1917*, and Wilson's *Black Phalanx: African American Soldiers in the War of Independence, the War of 1812 and the Civil War* are examples of further military studies.

The Library's "Women's History" section also includes various historical studies and collected biographies of African American women and their roles in American history. In late 1995 and early 1996 the DAR Museum presented an exhibit "Talking Radicalism in a Greenhouse: Women Writers and Women's Rights." The exhibit contained much relating to women's rights and to the abolition movement. A descriptive checklist of the exhibit items is available from the DAR Museum Office.

13.2
BIBLES AND BIBLE RECORDS

Family births, marriages and deaths recorded in Bibles are the staple of genealogical research. DAR collections abound with Bible records from across the United States and from all periods.

Pages from the Hamner Family Bible, Buckingham County, Virginia, in possession of Eric G. Grundset.

The gathering of these essential sources has been and remains an important part of the DAR's commitment to the preservation of historical materials.

The Library welcomes donations of Bible records. Donors may make copies onto acid–free paper including the title page of the Bible. Details such as the Bible's publication date, current ownership, and other identifying facts linking the sources to a given family in a specific place are extremely important.

There are numerous Bibles in DAR collections. The DAR Museum and the Office of the Historian General collect Bibles for their artistic or imprint value, and the Library accepts donations of entire Bibles to insure preservation of the family register pages they include. Those that do contain family records receive a note to that effect in their cataloging records.

Researchers may search for Bible records in the following locations:

- throughout the Library's book collection accessible through the Analytical Index and the catalog in published family histories;

- in the GRC National Index online at the DAR's website: **www.dar.org**;

- in the Genealogical Records Committee reports, including the LDS microfilms of the pre–1972 reports in the Library's file collection under family surnames or names of Revolutionary War ancestors of DAR members;

- in the Library's manuscript collection under specific surnames;

- in the Historian General's Americana Collection; and,

- in indices to genealogical periodicals which contain innumerable Bible record transcriptions;

On a cautionary note, there are always problems with transcriptions of any kind, and those of Bible records are no exception. Illegibility of originals and improper corrections to original spellings and punctuation are common. In addition to casual mistakes, typographical errors, and inadvertent omissions, researchers may encounter the occasional serious problem. Falsified or altered records can appear, unfortunately. See the following article for an example of a questionable Bible record in a *Genealogical Record Committee Report:* Warren L. Forsythe, "Resolving conflict between records: a spurious Moseley Bible," *National Genealogical Society Quarterly*, 84:3 (September 1996), 182–199. Always take what is in print and seek to verify information with as many other sources as possible.

13.3
BIOGRAPHICAL RESEARCH

Genealogy is very closely related to biography, and many genealogists attempt to create accurate biographies of their ancestors as part of their research. Because of the closeness of these two studies, the Library maintains many biographical materials.

The Biography Special Collection contains numerous biographies, autobiographies, diaries, and collected papers of historically prominent Americans, particularly from the period of the American Revolution. Most biographies contain sections on the family and sometimes the genealogy of the subject. Genealogists would do well to consider the possibility that if their ancestor were a neighbor of a well–known individual, then that ancestor may have had contacts with that prominent neighbor and consequently appear in his or her papers. Important clues to one's own family history may appear in some unrelated person's papers, and if that person were Adams, Washington, or Jefferson, it makes the resulting genealogy even more interesting.

Collected biographies constitute an important part of the Library's biography collection. *The Genealogy and Biography Master Index* provides access to many lengthy and many brief biographies and related genealogical information. Biographical guides and indices direct researchers to still other potential sources. Standard sets such as *American National Biography* (1999), *The Dictionary of American Biography, The Encyclopedia of American Biography, volumes 1–54 (1917–1933)* and *The Encyclopedia of American Biography, New Series, volumes 1–40 (1934–1970)* offer considerable information. Large, but incomplete, runs of *Who's Who in America* and *Who Was Who in America* are familiar sources.

One major finding aid for both biography and genealogy is the Godfrey Memorial Library's monumental publication *The American Genealogical–Biographical Index to American Genealogical, Biographical, and Local History Materials.* In 205+ volumes (through early 2004) and nearly through the alphabet, the *AGBI* gives researchers access to hundreds of studies and sources. The Library owns the majority of the items indexed by this set.

Within each state section is a Biography subsection containing collected biographies and biographical dictionaries and encyclopedia. These vary in quality, reliability, age, and numbers. Many historical organizations are producing biographical dictionaries for their respective states, and the Library acquires these as they appear. Rosters of state legislators, governors, jurists, attorneys, and other prominent individuals are numerous. Biographies also constitute major portions of state, county and local histories produced during the nineteenth and twentieth centuries, sources that fill the shelves of the Library.

The Historical Research Library of the Office of the Historian General also contains some biographies of famous Americans. Refer to section 7.5.

13.4
CEMETERY RECORDS

Among the major materials represented throughout DAR collections are cemetery records. Cemetery surveys have been one of the DAR's primary volunteer activities from the early years of the National Society, and the resulting volumes of transcriptions number in the thousands. Most have entered the DAR Library through the Genealogical Records Committee, which collected many of them before urbanization and suburbanization began to obliterate smaller family cemeteries near cities in the second half of the twentieth century.

The DAR's survey of local cemeteries has varied in depth and coverage depending on the activities of individual members and local chapters. In some counties work has been extensive and long–term; in others, either spotty, short–term, or non–existent. Many surveys compiled years ago have never been updated and reviewed. Others have been brought up–to–date through the efforts of DAR members and chapters or local historical and genealogical societies. The Library has acquired thousands of volumes of cemetery records from these local groups around the country.

In the General/Cemeteries section are useful sources such as national directories of cemeteries and undertakers and studies on epitaphs, funeral customs, special symbols and inscriptions, and tombstone art, including the publications of the Association for Gravestone Studies.

Because of the many forms in which cemetery records appear, researchers must take a broad approach in their search in DAR collections and consider several areas of the building in their quest for these sources. In every instance (unless otherwise noted), check the names of counties, towns, villages, or churches where a cemetery may be located, the names of family cemeteries, and the names of specific cemeteries. Major sources at DAR for cemetery research include:

- The Library's online catalog and analytical index under the name of the cemetery, church, town, or county followed by "Cemetery records."
- The GRC National Index, online at the DAR's website, **www.dar.org**
- The Library's state file collection

- LDS microfilms of DAR materials (prior to 1972) and other sources using *The Cemetery Record Compendium....* See Chapter 5.
- The *Periodical Source Index* and *Genealogical Periodical Annual Index* listing hundreds of cemetery transcriptions in genealogical and historical periodicals and journals
- Seimes Technology Center, which has numerous cemetery records in microform.
- The Office of the Historian General's card indices to located and marked graves of Revolutionary soldiers, members, etc. See section 7.2.

13.5
CENSUS

DAR owns census records in various formats, but most are either in books or on microforms. These sources are located in several places.

13.5.1
FEDERAL CENSUS RECORDS

With the proximity of the National Archives and space considerations in mind, the Seimes Technology Center has not acquired all federal census records on microfilm. It does, however, hold a significant portion of these records, namely the 1790 through 1900 population schedules. DAR does not own the non–population or special census schedules with the exception of some mortality schedules (see section 13.5.4). In addition to these, the Center also owns the following microfilms:

1890: Indexes for the Special Census of Widows and Veterans are available for some states. An index for the few surviving population schedules is available in the Library, along with the microfilm for Kentucky through Wyoming.

1910: Only Florida, Maryland, Nevada, North Dakota, and Ohio are available. Consult the rest at the National Archives.

1920: Only Delaware, District of Columbia, Indiana, Maryland, and Virginia population schedules and index are available. Consult the rest at the National Archives.

1930: Only the 1930 North Dakota population schedules are available at DAR.

The 33rd Congress of the National Society ... adopted a Resolution requesting an appropriation by the Government for the restoration and preservation of the Early Census schedules of the population of the United States. This request has been granted so no further solicitation of the support of your Members of Congress for this particular measure is necessary.

The project was approved, funds were allocated for this purpose and work is now in progress covering all of the items requested—the restoration of the 19 damaged volumes, the photostating of the schedules of 1800, 1810 and 1820, for use in place of the originals which are to be withdrawn from further use.

Our special thanks are due President Roosevelt, the Civil Works Administration, and those of the Census Bureau whose approval made this result possible. The National Society Daughters of the American Revolution is to be congratulated upon their achievement of this project which is in conformity to the foundation principles of our Organization.

From Lue R. Spencer's article
"A D.A.R. Achievement,"
DAR Magazine, February 1934, p. 100

Most federal census records are also available online through the Library's subscriptions to the major subscription services.

13.5.2
INDICES FOR FEDERAL CENSUS RECORDS

The digitizing, indexing, and online availability of all federal census schedules, largely makes the traditional printed and microfilm census indexes of secondary research importance in the early twenty-first century. Researchers should be aware, however, of the fact that errors in data entry and typographical and transcription errors in these online sources can result in negative results in an online search. The traditional sources remain important backups for the newer search tools.

The Library owns printed indices to nearly all of the federal censuses for the years 1790 through 1870. All statewide indices are located in the Seimes Technology Center. Because of the varying quality of these indices, researchers are encouraged first to check an index, and if a name is not found but a county is known, read through the entire census for that county. Census takers did, however, miss many families and individuals, while some people avoided these government agents. All genealogical research guides offer sound advice on census research.

The Technology Center also owns a "national" census index produced on microfiche by Accelerated Indexing Systems (AIS) (1983 edition). AIS produced this index by merging and sorting the data from the state indices it had published into one large alphabet for the various census years. The index is comprised of several "searches" which focus in the following manner: Search 1 (Colonial & United States 1600–1819); Search 2 (1820–1829); Search 3 (1830–1839); Search 4 (1840–1849); Search 5 (Southern States 1850–1860); Search 6 (Northeastern and Northern States 1850); Search 7 (Midwestern and Western States 1850–1906); Search 7A (United States 1850–1906); Search 8 (United States Mortality Schedules, 1850–1885). Because of the production of many census indices since this edition appeared in 1983, this national index is more comprehensive for the earlier years covered than for the later ones. Many of the later years will only be covered by the printed indices available by state. Some early AIS census indices actually provide access to early tax and other lists and not census records specifically. These are included in this national census index. AIS provided a guide to this microfiche index entitled *American Genealogical Computer Catalogue (AGCC)* in 1983. Another helpful guide is the LDS–produced *Accelerated Indexing Systems, Inc. Microfiche Indexes*, which is its *Genealogical Library Instructional Materials, Series F, No. 1: Branch Genealogical Libraries: Instructional Materials*. Both offer insight into the use of this microfiche index.

13.5.3
TRANSCRIPTIONS OF FEDERAL CENSUS RECORDS

Scattered throughout the entire book collection in the DAR Library are transcriptions of federal census records for counties across the United States. These volumes will be located, for the most part, in the "State" section, then the county subsection. They will be available for some counties and not for others. Often if the Library's collection on a given county is weak, it will acquire these transcriptions to fill the gap. Some transcriptions of census records will also appear in genealogical periodicals and in the *Genealogical Records Committee Reports*. Indices to these types of publications must be consulted to locate this information. Often transcribers of census records have added annotations based on local genealogical sources to enhance the usefulness of the census information.

13.5.4
FEDERAL MORTALITY SCHEDULES AND POPULATION SCHEDULES
FORMERLY IN DAR CUSTODY

During the twentieth century, DAR has taken on the role of temporary custodian for a number of volumes of original records, once the property of the Bureau of the Census. In the years before the establishment of the National Archives, the Bureau distributed various schedules from several federal censuses to repositories in the appropriate states. On two occasions, the DAR accepted volumes for which the Bureau did not find homes.

From 1919 to 1930 DAR housed 134 volumes of agricultural, industrial, social, and manufacturing schedules for Colorado, the District of Columbia, Georgia, Kentucky, Louisiana, Montana, Nevada, Virginia, and Wyoming. Not every type of schedule was held for each state however. The Library transferred these volumes to Duke University, Durham, North Carolina in 1930. The records are listed in *Guide to the Cataloged Collections in the Manuscript Department of the William R. Perkins Library*, Duke University, edited by Richard C. Davis and Linda Angle Miller, pages 589–590.

In the late 1930s the Bureau of the Census deposited volumes of mortality schedules with the DAR, which maintained them until 1980 when they were transferred to the National Archives for preservation and microfilming. These records now constitute National Archives Microfilm Publication T655. The actual records involved were: Arizona, 1870, 1880; Colorado, 1870, 1880; District of Columbia, 1850, 1860, 1870, 1880; Georgia, 1850, 1860, 1870, 1880; Kentucky, 1850, 1860, 1870, 1880; Louisiana 1850, 1860, 1870, 1880; and Tennessee, 1850, 1860, 1870, 1880. The Library owns indices to all of these records except for Colorado and 1880 Tennessee. Various DAR members around the country prepared these indices.

The first edition of Val D. Greenwood's *Researcher's Guide to American Genealogy* (1973) correctly showed DAR as the custodian of these mortality schedules. The second edition (1990) of this volume notes the transfer to the National Archives. The Library still receives inquiries concerning these schedules as well as others that it never owned. Greenwood's list provides an accurate guide to the location of these and other mortality schedules.

The DAR again served as the temporary custodian for census records in 1956, but in this instance the volumes originated with the National Archives. After microfilming and attempting to find suitable locations in the states for the federal copy of the 1880 census population schedules, the Archives deposited 167 volumes with the DAR. These sources were maintained in the DAR Library until 1980. At that time the DAR decided to find repositories in each state involved to accept these deteriorating volumes. Although the records of this transfer are incomplete, the following list specifies the number of transferred books and their present locations:

- **ARIZONA** (1), Arizona Department of Library, Archives and Public Records, Phoenix.

- **CONNECTICUT** (10), Connecticut State Library, State Archives, Hartford.

- **IDAHO** (1), Idaho State Historical Society, Boise

- **IOWA** (33), State Historical Society of Iowa, Des Moines.

- **KANSAS** (21), Kansas DAR Library, 700 Avenue G, Box l03, Dodge City, KS 67801

- **MISSISSIPPI** (23), location not known. The Mississippi Department of Archives and History does not own these volumes.

- **MISSOURI** (45), Missouri State Archives, Jefferson City.

- **NEW HAMPSHIRE** (3), New Hampshire Archives, Concord.

- **NEBRASKA** (10), Edith Abbott Memorial Library, Grand Island.

- **NEW MEXICO** (3), location not known. The New Mexico Records Center and Archives states they do not own these volumes.

- **RHODE ISLAND** (6), Rhode Island Historical Society, Providence.

- **UTAH** (3), Utah State Archives and Records Services, Salt Lake City.

Although the 1880 population schedules are available online or on microfilm, the potential for illegible spots on the films makes the existence of the original volumes important. Several of the state agencies indicated that they also own the state copies of these schedules. Researchers may wish to compare the various versions with the two original copies, looking for discrepancies in transcriptions and perhaps omissions.

The 1980 transfers of the 1880 population schedules and the various mortality schedules mark the end of DAR's involvement in the retention and preservation of such federal records. The Library's Search Service will check the indices to the mortality schedules on written request. The Library does not, however, own many printed indices for the 1880 population schedules with the exception of those for a few states and some for individual counties.

Periodically, new indices to mortality schedules, which were never owned by the DAR, are published, and the Library adds these to the census index collection.

13.5.5
STATE CENSUS RECORDS

DAR owns a limited selection of State Census records and accompanying indices to a few of them. Most notable in book form are Ann Smith Lainhart's transcriptions of the 1855 and 1865 Massachusetts State Censuses for many towns; many counties' schedules for New York State Censuses (1825-1892) on microfilm and a few in printed volumes; the 1852 California State Census in book form; the 1855 Illinois State Census on microfilm; the 1865 Rhode Island State Census on microfilm; the Minnesota State Censuses for 1857, 1865, 1875, 1885, 1895 and 1905; the Wisconsin State Censuses for 1855, 1875, 1895, and 1905; the 1915 North Dakota State Census; and microfilm of surviving schedules for twenty–five Michigan counties for 1894. Examples of other published versions include the 1771 Vermont Census, the 1784–1787 North Carolina Census, and the 1885 Florida Census. There are also various books dubbed "State Censuses" which are, in fact, constructed from surviving tax lists. Examples of this include the 1740, 1760, 1782–1785 and 1787 "Censuses" for Virginia. More State Census records will be added in coming years.

13.6
CITY DIRECTORIES

In March 1987 the DAR Library received a donation of nearly 1,100 city directories from around the United States from the Bureau of the Census. These volumes are concentrated around the years 1910, 1920, 1930 and 1940, because they were once used by the Bureau to conduct age searches for individuals in the federal censuses for those years. Anyone who has conducted genealogical research in urban areas will testify to the value of city directories in helping to pinpoint the place of residence for individuals and families. They also frequently list occupations. The Library was fortunate to acquire these volumes because they added an additional dimension to the collection by providing sources for the twentieth century, a period lightly covered in the holdings.

THE

WASHINGTON DIRECTORY,

SHOWING THE

NAME, OCCUPATION, AND RESIDENCE

OF EACH

Head of a Family & Person in Business

TOGETHER WITH

OTHER USEFUL INFORMATION

CITY OF WASHINGTON

PRINTED AND PUBLISHED BY S. A. ELLIOT

Eleventh street w. near Pennsylvania Avenue

....

1827

THE

WASHINGTON DIRECTORY.

☞ *For explanation of abbreviations, see Preface.*

RESIDENTS.

ABBOT, John, clk in third auditor's office; dw Georgetown
Abbot, Joseph, hackman, n w corner Pn and 13w
Achman, Mrs. widow, Hn btw 19 and 20w
Acken, William, shipwright, corner 9e and Ms N Yard
Adams, John Quincy, President of the United States, at the President's mansion
Adams, Mrs. widow, 14e near Eastern Branch
Adams, Rebecca, widow, Bn btw 3 and 4e Capitol Hill
Adams, Margaret, widow, Ds btw 3 and 4e
Adams, Joseph, carpenter, 13½w btw C and Ds
Adams, Thomas, chairmaker, s side Pen av btw 12 and 13w
Adams, George, collector 6th and 6th wards, 8e btw K & Ls
Adams, George, police officer, corner 4e and Ls
Adams, John, bricklayer, Gn btw 17 and 18w
Addison, Thomas B. clk in general post office; dw George-town
Addison, W. D. clk in general post office; dw Pr. George's county, Md.
Agg, John, writer, Mrs. M'Cauley's, Pen av
Aiken, Prudence, widow, n side Cn btw 4½ and 6w
Alexander, Charles, upholsterer, n side Pen av btw 12 & 13w

The directories represent cities large and small across the country. They range in size from six–inch thick tomes covering New York, Chicago, Boston and Los Angeles to smaller compilations for such smaller urban areas as Grand Junction, Colorado (1912–13); Park Ridge, Illinois (1922–23); Columbia, Pennsylvania (1909), and Charlottesville, Virginia (1912–13). The condition of the volumes varies considerably. Some are very tattered and crumbling, and use is therefore restricted. Others are in excellent condition. Still others are bound photocopies of the original directory. All contain a wealth of information.

An important collection of Boston city directories from 1789 to 1868 is on microfiche in the Technology Center. A microfiche collection of pre-1860 directories for American cities is also housed in the center.

Many libraries own city directories for their locality and state, and some have holdings covering the entire United States. Researchers should investigate these important sources to learn more about their families and ancestors. The Library welcomes donations of city directories from anywhere in the United States for any time period.

13.7
COLONIAL RESEARCH SOURCES

Located on the east coast as it is, the Library naturally has excellent holdings of materials for the original colonies on the Atlantic seaboard. Additionally, because many DAR members also have belonged to the various "colonial" lineage societies, they had a heightened awareness of colonial publications and family histories. Consequently, many have contributed these materials to the DAR Library over the past century. Early in its history the Library assumed a focus beyond the Revolutionary period as a result of the broad interests of members.

Published and microfilmed colonial records and local histories combined with continuing acquisitions of recent publications for this period make the colonial research materials in the library extensive and extremely popular. Published collected sets of the records of colonial governments for most of the colonies provide valuable sources, and major microform collections of additional records offer further avenues for research. Various such state collections are beginning to appear on CD-ROM, such as the New Hampshire State Papers.

Immigration to the colonies during the seventeenth and eighteenth centuries has been the subject of numerous studies, many of which are discussed in greater detail in section 13.14. These represent a significant portion of the published passenger records in any library.

Colonial wars are the subjects of numerous publications in the Library's collections. Despite major record loss in some states for the colonial period, historians and genealogists have produced considerable literature to document these conflicts. Refer to section 13.20.1 for more information.

Many printed family histories and genealogies extend into the colonial period. The published lineage books and other compilations of some lineage societies with a colonial focus, such as the Colonial Dames of America, the National Society Daughters of the American Colonists, and the Society of Colonial Wars, are partially available for clues. Sources and publications related to the popular quest for descent from the first settlers in Virginia and Massachusetts are a surprising find for many researchers at DAR.

One point that is often forgotten, probably because it is so obvious, is that all Revolutionary War ancestors of DAR members were born in the colonial period and for this reason, the application papers themselves contain tens of thousands of connections to colonial families. Although not required and not encouraged, researchers will occasionally encounter lineages on older DAR membership applications extending a generation or two prior to the Revolutionary ancestor.

13.8
"DAUGHTERS" AS RESEARCH SUBJECTS

If an ancestor or relative were a member of the DAR, there will be some information on her at DAR Headquarters. The first step in researching a DAR member would be to obtain a copy of her membership application, any supplemental applications she may have filed, and any supporting proof for these papers.

Obtaining the member's national number is a crucial step in the research process. If you are visiting the building, request these in the reference desk in the DAR Library or at the reference desk in Seimes Technology Center. With the national number in hand, a visit to the Technology Center will enable researchers to view the application paper in digital form or microform (as a back-up copy). The surviving supporting documentation from applications is housed in the Library's file collection. All of these sources should provide some basic information on the member. Consult the staff on current procedures for obtaining copies of the applications.

DAR members who were national officers will likely have generated a variety of records or listings to help flesh out a biography. The Organizing Secretary General's Office maintains a file of information on national officers. Many national officers' photographs appear in issues of *The DAR Magazine* during their terms in office. Biographical sketches often accompany magazine entries during DAR election years. Photographs and other biographical information may appear also in various DAR publications in the Office of the Historian General. The magazine's published index would be the first place to check for names of prominent DAR members.

Information on state DAR officers may appear in various state publications such as state DAR histories and historical rosters, which often include biographical sketches of State Regents and officers. State yearbooks and other publications, if available, may also assist with this research. State Historians may also be able to help provide information on historic state officers.

The Office of the Historian General maintains records of marked graves of many deceased DAR members. Contact that office for details.

13.8.1
"REAL DAUGHTERS" AND "REAL GRANDDAUGHTERS"

Members of the DAR who were the actual daughters and granddaughters of Revolutionary War soldiers and patriots were known as "Real Daughters" and "Real Granddaughters." Besides their membership applications, which would only show a generation or two, a variety of information is available on these women who were "Real Daughters." The Office of the Historian General maintains several files of material on these women as well as a card file of marked graves of some Real Daughters. In the early years of the twentieth century, *The DAR Magazine* published biographical articles on Real Daughters, the magazine's index will lead researchers to them. A list of Real Daughters is available in the Office of the Historian General and the Library. Please see section 7.4 for more advice on researching Real Daughters.

13.9
FAMILY HISTORIES AND GENEALOGIES

About 40,000 volumes of published and unpublished family histories comprise a significant part of the collection. All are listed in the Library's online catalog. They cover all periods in American history and many have sections tracing the family back to its previous home across the ocean.

Genealogical compilations vary considerably in format and reliability. Some are detailed and well documented, while others are someone's rough notes and charts bound together with little proof included. The Library accepts all offers for these materials with the idea that every book or compilation may provide clues and proof of a lineage. Preservation of *any* genealogical information is another consideration. The Library receives new family histories daily from DAR members and non–members alike and welcomes all such donations. To donate a book to the Library, please contact the Acquisitions Librarian for procedures.

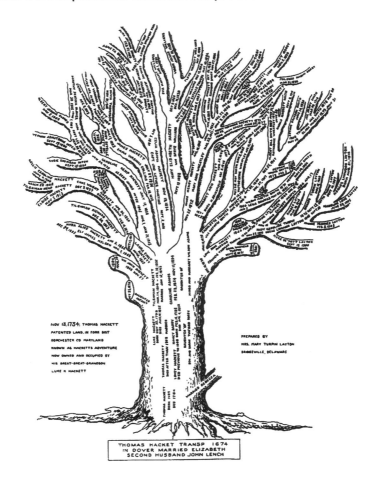

Collected family histories are a common format. Many include the words "encyclopedia" or "compendium." These are located in the General, State and Foreign sections of the book stacks depending on their subject focus. One such gathering is unique to the DAR Library: the "turquoise set." This includes numerous, brief genealogies and histories which were once housed in the Library's file collection because they would not wear well on open shelves. The staff removed them, arranged them alphabetically by surnames, and bound them into fifty–eight volumes. All are cataloged and accessible through the catalog.

An important and often difficult–to–locate source for genealogy is the family newsletter. Thousands must exist, but few find their way into libraries. The Library owns many historical and currently published family newsletters and journals. Many of these are bound and placed in the Family Section, but a large number reside unbound in files. The latest issues are in the files of the Serials section of the Library office. Associated with these newsletters are many family organizations. The Library has directories and lists of many of these to help researchers.

Biographies of prominent individuals usually contain considerable information on that person's family, descendants and ancestors. Researchers suspecting a connection to the well–known should consult biographies for clues.

Gaining access to family histories and genealogies is always a challenge. Many individual books do not have indices, a fact which greatly limits their usefulness. The Library catalogers will create multiple subject tracings for major surnames mentioned in each book they process. These tracings appear in the online catalog and provide considerable cross-referencing to hidden surnames. Aside from the Library catalog itself, various indices to family histories and genealogies guide researchers to the location of more hidden material. The Library's Analytical Index serves this purpose, along with such published guides as *The American Genealogical–Biographical Index* and *The Periodical Source Index*.

Most family compilations are printed in limited quantities. The Library is fortunate to have so many of these. Researchers frequently request ordering information, which is often not available. The Library maintains information on out–of–print and rare book dealers and on some companies specializing in photocopy reprints of old genealogies. A long standing policy, based on concern for copyright protection and on limited staffing, prevents the Library from making copies of entire books.

Frequently overlooked sources for details of family history are architectural histories, pictorial books of houses and buildings in states or counties, and similar publications. After all, families lived in houses, and the history of those families is part of the history of the house. These compilations of architectural information may be found in several locations in the DAR Library. "Architecture" books are near the beginning of most state sections. There are many studies of historic buildings in the county sections as well and in the Museum Reference Library.

In addition to books, the Library's files contain innumerable brief typescript studies and pamphlets. Many of these are unavailable elsewhere. A collection of a few hundred genealogical charts and "family trees" is also available. In Seimes Technology Center, researchers will discover nearly 600 reels of microfilm containing copies of family genealogies and histories. Some of these are duplicates of volumes in the Library; others are not. All microforms are cataloged.

13.10
FEDERAL GOVERNMENT RECORDS

<table>
<tr>
<td>

What Might Have Been

DAR began a campaign shortly after the turn of the century urging its members to contact their elected officials in the United States Congress for the purpose of gaining support for the creation of a national archives. During the course of this effort, which lasted off and on until the late 1920's, various sites were considered by the federal government for the proposed building. One was in the block between E and F, 18th and 19th Streets, N.W., the present location of the General Services Administration. If only this site had been selected—it is a short two-blocks from DAR Headquarters! The actual site of the National Archives is now eight long blocks by foot from DAR—"you can't get there from here" by public transportation very easily.

</td>
<td>

Census, passenger lists, land registers, pension records and other federal records that have been published are plentiful in DAR collections. These sources are discussed in other sections of this chapter.

Numerous published finding aids to the holdings of the National Archives point the way to research just eight blocks down Consititution Avenue at Archives I or in College Park, Maryland, at Archives II. Less obvious are valuable materials available in the Library such as *The Territorial Papers of the United States* in twenty-six volumes concerning the governments of the territories that became states and *The Official Records of the War of the Rebellion* examining the Civil War.

</td>
</tr>
</table>

13.10.1
THE U.S. SERIAL SET

Another very useful publication that opens the door to voluminous federal sources is *The U.S. Serial Set Index,* which is a finding aid to federal government publications since the 1780s. The Library owns this index through 1889 and portions of the *American State Papers* series. Although the entire Serial Set is not available at DAR, the Department of the Interior's Natural Resources Library next door to DAR owns a largely complete collection. This library is open to the public with presentation of a photo ID and makes the Serial Set easily accessible.

13.10.2
W.P.A. PUBLICATIONS

The DAR Library owns about 1,000 volumes of the publications of the Historical Records Survey of the Works Progress Administration (later the Work Projects Administration). Because of the DAR's involvement at the local level in supporting the work of the W.P.A. during its lifetime from 1935 to 1942, the W.P.A. donated many of its publications to the DAR Library. In the Washington area, only the National Archive's Library has a larger collection of W.P.A publications.

The majority of the published volumes is in the series "Inventory of the County Archives," These inventories of county records list local records found in courthouses in the states at the time the survey was completed. Not all counties in every state have a published inventory. Even if a county of interest is not available, researchers may wish to review an inventory for another county as a representative example of the types of records that should be in any county in that state. Many of the publications have useful introductions and discussions of records and record–keeping practices.

Portions of other W.P.A series are available in the Library's special "W.P.A. Collection." These include inventories of federal records in the states, calendars of manuscript collections, guides to the records of religious bodies, and indices to a few newspapers. All are of potential value to genealogists and should not be overlooked.

Separate from the special collection of W.P.A materials, researchers will also encounter many transcriptions of records at the county level prepared by the W.P.A.'s Historical Records Survey. Several state sections—particularly Florida, Michigan, Tennessee, and West Virginia—include numerous such volumes. Once again, because of the DAR's local support for W.P.A projects, the DAR Library received many of these transcriptions, which are very similar to the DAR's own Genealogical Records Committee reports.

In the Historical Research Library, maintained by the Office of the Historian General, is a set of the Federal Works Agency of the Work Projects Administration's series of state guides in the "American Guide Series." See section 7.5 for more information.

13.11
FOREIGN RESEARCH

DAR collections focus largely on American sources and families, but because research often takes genealogists beyond American shores the Library maintains a basic selection of research guidebooks, dictionaries, atlases, indices, and historical sources designed to lead researchers to other materials and research centers. As new guides are published for different countries, the Library acquires them. The Library does not collect books on twentieth-century European or world conflicts, local history, or other similar materials.

Among the holdings in this section are materials on the following countries and regions:

Africa — Basic histories of West African kingdoms, nations and peoples, particularly Liberia and Sierra Leone, combined with the African American research materials (see section 13.1) offer introductory sources for researchers of African descent.

Australia — Basic information sources are available.

Bermuda — Important record abstracts from the seventeenth to nineteenth centuries are available and reveal many contacts with mainland families.

Canada — In terms of organization, the Canadian section of the DAR Library follows the pattern of the United States section. The bulk of the Canadian collection is arranged by "province" and by county or other subdivision within the province.

Because the United States has a history of relations with eastern Canada dating back to colonial days, the heaviest concentration of books is for the eastern provinces such as Ontario, Quebec, Prince Edward Island, Nova Scotia, and New Brunswick. At the end of the Revolution, a number of American Loyalists settled in these eastern provinces of Canada and the Library has a number of books on the topic (see section 13.20.4.15). All Canadian provinces are represented in the collection, however.

Highlighting the Canadian section is an extremely useful series of books published by the Genealogical Research Library of Toronto. These books are *The Atlantic Canadians 1600–1900, The Central Canadians 1600–1900, The Western Canadians 1600–1900* and *The French Canadians 1600–1900*. Each title contains three volumes listing over 500,000 names. The books provide the user with an alphabetical list of every adult male and single female householder known to be living in Canada between those years. A variety of sources were consulted to compile these books including land records, city and town directories, early Canadian census records, marriage records and cemetery records. Additional information for the entries includes place of residence and occupation.

In addition to *The French Canadians 1600–1900*, the Library has several specialized works on French Canadian families. These include the *Dictionnaire Généalogique des Familles du Quebec des Origines a 1730*, and Tanguay's multivolume *Dictionnaire Généalogique des Familles Canadiennes*, both of which lists individuals alphabetically by surname and include such details as birthdate, marriages and children. The serial publications *Lost in Canada?* and *Our French–Canadian Ancestors* have lengthy narrative articles on lives of individual ancestors with citations to sources.

England — A mixed collection of English materials is owned by the Library. Research manuals, collected family studies, and archival guides predominate. A largely complete set of the *Publications of the Harleian Society*, containing many abstracts from church registers, is a source which adds some depth generally not found in the Library's foreign books.

The 1983 edition of the *Domesday Book* is also available. This multivolume compilation of the 1086 Norman census of England's population and property is a unique resource for medieval England.

A few genealogical periodicals, notably *The Genealogist, The Genealogist's Magazine*, and *Family Tree Magazine*, have been donated to the Library in recent years and provide useful articles on English methodology, sources, and specific families. Some of the standard works on English royal and noble lineages are also available, including some editions of *Burke's Landed Gentry* and related publications.

Emigration from England during the colonial era is the subject of numerous volumes in the "General/Emigration & Immigration" section. The work of Peter Wilson Coldham, such as *The Complete Book of Emigrants* and *The Complete Book of Emigrants in Bondage*, document English migrants to the American colonies and are popular, standard studies. Many others offer similar lists and histories of this crucial influx of settlers. Published materials for the post–Revolution period are limited for English immigrant research however.

Innumerable American family histories and genealogies and compiled studies carry lineages back to England, and these are plentiful in the Library's collections. Many works on the Chesapeake and New England colonies examine English connections and family origins of those American "cradle" regions. In the Library's section on the American Revolution, researchers will find a growing literature on the English involvement in the war with the rebellious colonies.

France — Basic information sources for French research are available. Specific studies on French Huguenot immigrants to the American colonies highlight this well–known group, particularly sources for Huguenots in Virginia and South Carolina. Records and histories for Acadian immigration, for French refugees from Santo Domingo, and for French Canadian research round out the French–related holdings in the Library. See also the discussion of French military involvement in the American Revolution in section 13.20.4.11. The donation of the National Huguenot Society Collection in 2003 added numerous French-related publications.

Germany — Sources for German and German–American research pervade the DAR Library. Standard published historical sources for immigrants into the American colonies and the resulting records of their settlements, churches, and families in Pennsylvania and other middle colonies/states abound. More recent publications by Burgert, Jones and others on the origins and settlements of German immigrants offer valuable information. The popular series *Germans to America* lists passenger arrivals after 1850.

A copy of Siebmacher's *Wappenbuch* is available. This is a multi–volume study of heraldry and names with a history of publication dating to the seventeenth century.

Genealogical periodicals *German Genealogical Digest, Publications of the Pennsylvania German Society, The Germanna Record, The Report of the Society for the History of Germans in Maryland, Der Kurier*, and *The Palatine Immigrant* expand the Library's coverage.

For information on the Hessians during the American Revolution refer to section 13.20.4.14.

Ireland — Irish immigrants to America during the colonial period are often hidden by the similarities of their names to those of other migrants from the British Isles, but they were here. While some studies such as *Emigrants from Ireland to America, 1735-1743*, examine these early arrivals much of the most recent material for Irish immigration focuses on the Great Famine of the 1840s. The Library offers various histories and published passenger lists for this period including Glazier and Tepper's *The Famine Immigrants 1846-1851* (7 volumes) and Harris and O'Keefe's *The Search for Missing Friends: Irish Immigrant Advertisements Placed in the Boston Pilot* (1831-1876; 8 volumes; one CD-ROM). Other works examine the effect of the Famine on specific areas such as *Ireland to North America: Emigrants from West Cork* by Joseph A. King. Collected family histories and research manuals for Ireland provide additional opportunities for understanding the Irish research process.

Italy — Basic information sources for Italian research in the Library include the series *Italians to America*, the journal *POINT: Pursuing Our Italian Names Together*, and various local studies.

Latin America — A number of new guides to Hispanic genealogical research have appeared in recent years, and the DAR Library has acquired these to give proper referral to researchers. Among the more recent titles are: Byers' *Hispanic American Genealogical Sourcebook*; Platt's *Hispanic Surnames and Family History*; and Ryskamp's *Tracing Your Hispanic Heritage*.

There are also numerous sources on Hispanic families in the Southwestern states, Louisiana, and Florida in the appropriate state section. These range from collected genealogies, histories, and record abstracts. Spanish Land Grants in Florida are available on microfilm in the Seimes Microfilm Center. Spanish participation in support of the American Revolution is also the subject of various studies in the Library. See also the discussion of Spanish involvement in the Revolution in section 13.20.4.12.

Netherlands — Basic Dutch information sources, major nineteenth–century immigration indices, and considerable materials in New Netherland, New York, and New Jersey sections of the Library comprise the majority of the resources relating to the Dutch in North America in DAR collections.

Poland — Basic information sources are available along with some local sources on major Polish–American communities.

Russia — Basic information sources are available for nineteenth and early twentieth century Russian immigration to the United States. Some sources on the history of Russian America are in the West Region section of the Library.

Scandinavia — Very basic Scandinavian research guides cover the Nordic countries. Information on specific groups of immigrants or individuals to North American is more extensive and may be found in county and community histories for areas where they settled.

Sweden is best represented in the Library's collections primarily because of its size and the centuries-old connections with North American settlement. Among the major sources for Swedish research are the *Swedish American Genealogist*, printed immigration indices, and histories and sources relating to Swedish and Finnish settlers of New Sweden in the mid–seventeenth century.

Scotland — Scots immigrants have come to America since the seventeenth century but are often difficult to trace because of Anglicized names, names similar to English ones, and poor to non-existent migration records. Various researchers have worked to illuminate the role of the Scots in early America, and the Library maintains a good collection on this subject. The work of David Dobson has been significant in filling in gaps in the historical record and includes such titles as *Directory of Scottish Settlers* (7 volumes), *Directory of Scots Banished to the American Colonies 1650–1775*, *Scots on the Chesapeake 1607–1830*, and *Scots in the Carolinas*. Others have produced similar studies, and there are several which focus specifically on Scottish settlers in specific states, such as Haw's *Scots in the Old Dominion*, Meyer's *Highland Scots of North Carolina 1732–1776*, and Steen's *New Aberdeen or the Scotch Settlement of Monmouth County, New Jersey*. Research manuals focusing on genealogical study in Scotland, specific family histories, collected family works, and general histories round out the Scottish materials in the Library.

Scots–Irish (Ulster Scots) — Millions of Americans have ancestors from the Scottish settlement of northern Ireland and the major migrations to the colonies in the eighteenth century. Library holdings include many local, state and general studies on these immigrants. Most are historical accounts, but some contain genealogical information. One basic guide is Reintjes' *Scotch–Irish: Sources for Research* and many articles in genealogical periodicals offer additional advice.

Switzerland — Basic information sources on Swiss research and Swiss names are available.

Wales — Basic information sources for research in Wales are available.

West Indies — Important record abstracts from the seventeenth and eighteenth centuries offer researchers information on families that first settled in the Caribbean and later migrated to the mainland colonies. Abstracts of Barbados wills and vital records, the classic journal *Caribbeana* (v. 1, 2, 4–6), and other scattered sources provide useful coverage for this region. Grannum's *Tracing Your West Indian Ancestors: Sources in the Public Record Office* is an excellent source for British possessions in the area. Such current periodicals as *Généalogie et Histoire de la Caraïbe, The Newsletter of the Saint–Domingue Special Interest Group,* and *Caribbean Historical and Genealogical Journal* (published 1993 to 1998) are very helpful.

13.12
GENEALOGICAL DIRECTORIES

Many directories are in print to help researchers locate various types of current information. They list family associations and their publications, genealogical researchers, genealogical and historical societies, research centers and libraries, and book publishers. Others provide addresses for county courts, federal courts, and cemeteries and funeral homes.

13.13
HERALDRY

The DAR Library has a small collection of basic books on heraldry and coats of arms including Siebmacher's *Wappenbuch*. During the 1920s and 1930s, *The DAR Magazine* ran a column "A Page in Heraldry," which offered coats of arms on specific surnames and commentary. This is not a subject in which the Library specializes. In Washington, the Library of Congress has a large number of books on heraldry and related topics.

An early view of Boston.

13.14
IMMIGRATION AND NATURALIZATION RESEARCH

Many sources to assist with immigration research are available in the Library. While the DAR does not own all National Archives microfilm of passenger arrivals at U.S. ports, records for most major eastern and Gulf ports are available with the exception of the late nineteenth-century records for the port of New York.

The *Passenger and Immigration Lists Index*, edited by P. William Filby with Mary K. Meyer, is the standard source for gaining access to many **published** records of immigrants into the American colonies and the United States. The Library owns this multi–volume index along with the majority of sources therein referenced. Researchers should consult this set to determine if an ancestor appears in a **published** passenger list found in books and journals. As the editors locate new materials, they include these references in the next annual supplement to the set.

РУКОВОДСТВО Д.А.Р.
ДЛЯ ПРИНИМАЮЩИХ ГРАЖДАНСТВО

Russian Edition

Издано
НАЦИОНАЛЬНЫМ ОБЩЕСТВОМ
ДОЧЕРЕЙ АМЕРИКАНСКОЙ РЕВОЛЮЦИИ

New publications of immigration records appear frequently. Some cover the colonial period and others the nineteenth and twentieth centuries. The DAR Library's holdings are not limited to any one period or to only a few national groups. While significant materials list immigrants from the British Isles, major indices also cover Czech, Dutch, German, Greek, Italian, Russian, and Swedish newcomers. Those sources for the British Isles concentrate on the colonial period movements of English, Scottish, Scots–Irish, and Irish to America, and on the Irish migrations relating to the Great Famine. Those for the rest of Europe concentrate on French Huguenot and German colonial migrations and nineteenth–century departures from across the continent. The series *Germans to America* (1850-1897) is one of the Library's most popular sets.

In 1910 the Connecticut DAR began a program to publish manuals to assist recent immigrants to the United States with their citizenship tests. These manuals were in the native language of several groups. By the early 1920's, the expense and popularity of the program made the Connecticut DAR enlist the involvement of the National Society. For the next three decades or so the DAR published many other manuals in numerous foreign languages of Europe, Asia and Latin America. Since the 1950's the manuals have been available only in English at the request of the federal government.

Example above right:
-Russian manual (1947)

These materials can be found for the most part in the Library's General section under "Emigration." There are significant holdings however, in many state sections, which contain studies and sources relating specifically to migrations into a specific state from Europe or other parts of North America. Examples include materials on German Palatine immigrants into New York, Germans into Pennsylvania, Dutch and Scandinavians in New Sweden and New Netherland, Spanish and French into Louisiana, Spanish into Florida, German Salzburgers into Georgia, and French Huguenots into Virginia and South Carolina. The variety of immigrants into this country over the centuries leads to the publication of new studies that examine the settlement and lives of immigrant groups on specific communities and counties. All shed light on the evolving American population.

One less obvious source for immigration information is DAR membership applications. Because many Revolutionary War soldiers and patriots were themselves immigrants to North America, researchers will often discover a

European place of origin for a family through the vital information these sources provide on the ancestor of a DAR member. Because documentation of colonial immigration is so difficult, this information could be crucial in developing a search strategy across the Atlantic.

Naturalization records are among the most difficult–to–locate, decentralized, and least frequently published of sources. Still, as these become available in print, the Library acquires them to provide clues for immigration research and the origins of families and individuals. Generally, abstracts of naturalization records will be located in the catalog under the name of the county or city in which the records were created.

13.15
JEWISH RESEARCH

A basic collection of materials for Jewish research is available at DAR. The Library's General/Religion section has various sources such as collected family genealogies, research guides, histories of Judaism in the United States, and major genealogical and historical journals. For the latter, the Library owns a largely complete set from volumes 1 (1905) to 82 (1994) of the periodical *Publications of the American Jewish Historical Society/American Jewish Historical Quarterly/American Jewish History* (with indices), as well as an incomplete run of *American Jewish Archives* between volumes 6 (1954) and 47 (1995). In other sections of the Library, researchers will encounter studies of Jewish participation in the American Revolution and on Jewish communities around the United States, particularly those that date from the colonial period. Histories of Jewish settlements in specific states are also available. In the General/Names section are several recent and important volumes on the origins of Jewish family names.

In the Seimes Technology Center is a collection of Jewish research sources on microfiche. These include "Jewish Applicants for Emergency Passports (1915–1924)," "Burials in the Old Section of the Washington Hebrew Congregation's Cemetery," "Jewish Genealogical Consolidated Surname Index," "Jewish Genealogical Societies Publications," "Gazetteers of Eastern Europe," and other sources relating to Holocaust Research. The Library does not, however, collect books on Jewish history in Europe because of the huge volume of material available on this topic and the availability of much of it in the library of the National Holocaust Museum on the other side of the Mall.

13.16
LAND RECORDS

Land records are a fundamental source for genealogists. Abstracts, indices and guides concerning land abound thoughout DAR collections. From original deeds in the Americana Collection to deed abstracts and CD–ROMs containing indices of federal land records, researchers will find much to investigate. Histories of land policies and ownership in the United States, guides to use and interpretation of land records, and studies on surveying offer background information for genealogists. *The American State Papers: Public Lands Series* [1789–1837] is a ten–volume set including the index *Grassroots of America* and offers much detail on the development of early federal land policies as well as the names of thousands of Americans involved with public land sales and purchases.

Throughout the state sections, researchers will find land materials specific to each state, especially records of colonial land patents. These include publications with a state–wide coverage or approach, studies interpreting the development of land ownership in some states, and important indices to land records. In many of the public land states, volumes examine and sometimes index the sales of public lands by the federal land offices in each state.

County deed abstracts from around the country fill the shelves in the Library. Most are from the seventeenth to the nineteenth centuries. Some counties have had extensive abstracting, while others only minimal. These volumes are among those that the Library collects as crucial sources. Microfilms of selected county deed books are in the Technology Center.

13.17
LAW SOURCES

General material to assist genealogists with interpretation of historical legal documents and sources are part of the Library collection. Legal dictionaries, citation guides, encyclopedia, and manuals are available along with historical analyses of such subjects as marriage, divorce, and common law. In the various state sections, researchers may also find legal materials specific to their state of interest such as legislative acts, codes or historical studies. *The U.S. Statutes at Large* 1789–1881 are available on microfiche. The massive quantity of law materials useful to genealogists and the unavailability of most historical legal publications preclude the DAR Library from collecting heavily in this area.

13.18
LINEAGE SOCIETY PUBLICATIONS

As a lineage society itself, the DAR has received many publications from other such organizations during the twentieth century. These are not always complete or current, but they may provide useful clues for further investigations. DAR does not have copies of application papers for these organizations with the exception of the General Society of the War of 1812 for which a partial collection is available on fifteen microfilm reels covering approximately 1914 to 1976.

Various lineage societies with similar membership requirements and objectives as the DAR are often confused with the latter organization. Several of these are listed below for general reference. Please note that although the DAR Library owns some of the publication of many of these societies, all are completely separate organizations from DAR. Each maintains its own files, application papers, and libraries. Additional information on these and other lineage societies may be found online at the websites of these organizations.

National Society, Children of the American Revolution (C.A.R.)
C.A.R. was established in 1895 by the DAR and subsequently incorporated as a separate organization. Anyone under age 21 who can trace their direct ancestry to a person who "rendered aid to the cause of American Independence" may join on invitation from members of a local society. Although C.A.R.'s offices are located in DAR's Constitution Hall, it is

completely separate and maintains its own application papers and files. All correspondence should be sent to N.S.C.A.R., 1776 D St., N.W., Washington, D.C. 20006–5303.

National Society, Sons of the American Revolution (SAR)

The SAR formed in 1889 and maintained its national headquarters in Washington, D.C. until 1979, when they moved to Louisville, Kentucky. Its membership is comprised of men over age 18 who are direct lineal descendants of "an ancestor who was at all times unfailingly loyal to, and rendered active service in, the cause of American Independence..." [NSSAR pamphlet, *General Information and Application Requirements*] The DAR does not own any SAR applications or files. SAR maintains an important genealogical library at its headquarters at 1000 South Fourth Street, Louisville, KY 40203. Telephone: 502–589–1776; **www.sar.org**. The DAR Library has some SAR national and state publications.

National Society, Daughters of the Revolution of 1776 (DR)

This society formed in 1891 after a policy rift with the DAR. It disbanded several years ago. The papers of the DR were donated to the Suffolk County Historical Society, 300 W. Main Street, Riverhead, NY 11901; telephone, 516–727–2881. The Suffolk County Historical Society will check the records of the Daughters of the Revolution in reply to written inquiries. Researchers frequently confuse the DR with the DAR for obvious reasons, and the latter receives inquiries that may relate to DR members. The DAR Library has some older DR publications.

General Society, Sons of the Revolution (SR)

Founded in 1876, this society is headquartered at Fraunces Tavern, 54 Pearl Street, New York, NY 10004. It is composed of male lineal descendants over 21 of one who "assisted in the establishment of American Independence by services rendered during the War of the Revolution..." [Hereditary Register (1986), p. 50.] The DAR Library has some older SR publications.

Society of the Cincinnati

The Society is located at 2118 Massachusetts Avenue, N.W., Washington, D.C. 20008; telephone: 202-785-2040. It maintains a library of 35,000 volumes. Contact the Society for additional information on research and membership. The DAR Library owns some Society of the Cincinnati publications.

The Library's collection of publications of other lineage societies includes some material for these major groups and a limited number of publications for other smaller groups. These publications may include lineage books, rosters, directories, yearbooks and histories. Check the catalog for listings. More recent information that updates listings in these publications may be available from each organization.

- National Society Daughters of Colonial Wars

- Colonial Daughters of the XVII Century

- Colonial Dames of America

- National Society U.S. Daughters of 1812

- General Society of the War of 1812

- National Society Daughters of the American Colonists

- National Society Daughters of Colonial Wars

- National Society Daughters of Founders and Patriots of America

- Order of Founders and Patriots of America

- The Society of Colonial Wars

- National Society of the Sons and Daughters of the Pilgrims

- United Daughters of the Confederacy

- Women Descendants of the Ancient and Honorable Artillery Company

13.19
MAPS, ATLASES AND GAZETTEERS

The Library has an eclectic map collection. Some are actual folded or rolled maps in the expected format. Others from are books and journals, removed by the staff years ago for reasons not entirely clear today. Retrospective cataloging of the maps is a slow, ongoing process.

Atlases represent an important source for genealogical study. The Library's collection ranges from modern state road and topographical atlases, to early property atlases and historical atlases. The series, *Atlas of Historic County Boundary Changes*, is a major addition to the literature and is published in state or regional volumes. Similar studies detailing the minute evolution of important jurisdictional lines, offer researchers crucial information for record location and ancestral residences.

Place names are essential clues in research and historical and contemporary gazetteers help locate forgotten, extinct, and current places. These guides may be found with atlases in the "Geography" subsections within the state and regional sections as well as the General section of the Library.

13.20
MILITARY RECORDS RESEARCH

Sources for research in the military records of the United States and the states are a significant part of DAR collections. Consequently any discussion of these sources must be within a broad historical context. Publications, microforms and manuscript materials for most of the nation's historical conflicts abound. Coverage for the American Revolution is naturally a major component of this material, but the War of 1812 and the Civil War also receive strong attention.

Each section on a specific war or on particular military records in this discussion highlights general and specific sources in DAR collections. References are also given as illustrations of the types of publications and records available.

The inclusion of a book or a source in this guide does not imply that it is an acceptable source for DAR Revolutionary War service. Consult *Is That Lineage Right?* for listings of what is acceptable.

13.20.1
EARLY COLONIAL WARS

The first English colonists to Virginia established Jamestown in the territory of the Powhatan Indians. Relations between the two cultures were tense at times, but relatively peaceful. Peace was shattered in 1622 and again in 1644 when Powhatans led by Opechancanough unsuccessfully attempted to annihilate the colonists. The story of the Anglo–Powhatan wars is included in general works on Virginia history. Some documents relating to Virginia's early Indian wars may be found in *The Records of the Virginia Company of London*.

After some thirty years of peace in Virginia, war erupted again in 1675, this time against the Susquehannocks, a tribe previously friendly to the colonists. When the Virginia government did not respond to the crisis, a Provincial Council member named Nathaniel Bacon led two expeditions against the Indians and later unsuccessfully attempted to seize control of the government. Documents relating to the upheaval can be found in *Bacon's Rebellion: Abstracts of Materials in the Colonial Records Project.*

New England colonists were no more successful in dealing with the Indians. A 1636 war between the Massachusetts Bay Colony and the Pequots and one from 1675–1676 against the Wampanoag and their chief King Philip resulted in English victories and near destruction of the tribes. General histories of the period with emphasis on the Pequot War and King Philip's War are available in the Library. An especially interesting source on the two wars is *The History of the Indian Wars in New England from the First Settlement to the Termination of the War with King Philip, in 1677* written by Rev. William Hubbard and originally published in 1677. Researchers interested in military records of the period should examine Bodge's *Soldiers in King Philip's War,* which includes lists of Massachusetts soldiers involved, biographical sketches of the officers and documents related to the war. Additional official materials on the Pequot War and King Philip's War may be found in *Records of the Governor and Company of the Massachusetts Bay in New England, The Public Records of the Colony of Connecticut* and *Rhode Island Colonial Records.*

Heightened competition between England, France, Spain and the Netherlands led increasingly to armed conflict. The colonists found themselves pitted against an alliance of French and Indians in King William's War and Queen Anne's War, against the Spanish in the War of Jenkin's Ear and opposite both the Spanish and the French in King George's War. Between 1652 and 1674 the British fought three wars against the Netherlands. The Second Anglo–Dutch War (1664–1667) resulted in the British capture of New Amsterdam, now New York. Accounts of the surrender of New Amsterdam may be found in *Narratives of New Netherland 1609–1664* and *Documents Relating to the Colonial History of New York*.

Colonial participation in these wars varied. Rosters of the soldiers who served from the colonies are found in several sources including *Colonial Delaware Soldiers and Sailors, Virginia's Colonial Soldiers, The Military History of the State of New Hampshire 1623–1861* and *A List of Rhode Island Soldiers & Sailors in King George's War 1740–1748*. Massachusetts took a particularly active role in these conflicts. Rosters of Massachusetts men in the colonial wars include *Massachusetts Officers and Soldiers in the Seventeenth Century Conflicts, Massachusetts Officers and Soldiers 1702–1722, Massachusetts Officers and Soldiers 1723–1743* and *Massachusetts Soldiers in the French and Indian Wars 1744–1755*. Additional material on colonial involvement in these wars may be found in official records such as *Journals of the House of Representatives of Massachusetts*. Several general histories of these early colonial wars, as well as histories of specific tribes, are available in the Library.

13.20.2
THE FRENCH AND INDIAN WAR

In May 1754 a young Major George Washington of the Virginia militia, and a small group of soldiers under his command skirmished with French soldiers near what is now Uniontown, Pennsylvania. This engagement and Washington's subsequent surrender to the French after a month long siege in a hastily constructed fort was the beginning of the French and Indian War. Within a year, regular British troops were dispatched to North America under General Edward Braddock who found defeat and death at the hands of the French. The conflict expanded until it included most of the nations in Europe where it was known as the Seven Years War. Battles were fought around the globe. After initially suffering a number of defeats, the British army in North American successfully invaded Canada and captured Quebec. When the war was over, the British dominated North America and French influence was at an end.

The full story of the French and Indian War is recounted in a number of works including Schwartz's *The French and Indian War 1754–1763: The Imperial Struggle for North America*, Jennings' *Empire of Fortune*, Gipson's *The British Empire Before the American Revolution*, and Parkman's classic study *Montcalm and Wolfe*. Specific campaigns of the war are explored in Older's *The Braddock Expedition and Fox's Gap in Maryland*, Kopperman's *Braddock at the Monongahela*, Steele's *Betrayals: Fort William Henry and the "Massacre"* and Dunnigan's *Siege–1759: The Campaign Against Niagara*. The experience of the French soldiers is portrayed in Gallup and Shaffer's *La Marine: The French Colonial Soldier in Canada 1745–1761* and in Bonin's *Memoir of a French and Indian War Soldier*. Hargreaves' *The Bloodybacks* depicts the life of the British enlisted man during this period and Ford's *British Officers Serving in America 1754–1774* lists individuals by name with rank, regiment and date of commission.

The French and Indian War saw the first extensive use of American troops to supplement British regulars. Some of these American units were highly specialized such as Rogers

Rangers whose story is told in *Reminiscences of the French War with Robert Rogers' Journal and a Memoir of General Stark* and Loescher's *Genesis: Rogers Rangers, The First Green Berets*. Most Americans who served however, did so in "provincial" units of infantry like those examined in Anderson's *A People's Army: Massachusetts Soldiers and Society in the Seven Years' War*. A remarkable number of muster rolls have survived from this period. Examples of these rolls include Bockstruck's *Virginia's Colonial Soldiers*, De Lancey's *Muster Rolls of New York Provincial Troops 1755–1764*, Bradshaw's *Pennsylvania Soldiers in the Provincial Service 1746–1759*, *Massachusetts Officers and Soldiers in the French and Indian Wars 1755–1756* and *Massachusetts Officers in the French and Indian Wars 1748–1763*. Additional lists of provincial soldiers can be found in the *Pennsylvania Archives* and the *Delaware Archives, Military*. Each of these lists is useful for establishing military service during the war, but the rolls do not include information on the soldiers' spouses or descendants.

13.20.3
DUNMORE'S WAR AND THE BATTLE OF POINT PLEASANT

The frontier conflict in 1774 in the Ohio Valley known as Dunmore's War is viewed by some as the last colonial war and by others as the beginning of the American Revolution. The Library has materials on this conflict in general and on the Battle of Point Pleasant. The DAR accepts service in this battle in a limited way. Please contact the Genealogy Department for clarification. The best-known source on this war is Thwaites' *Documentary History of Dunmore's War*.

13.20.4
Part 1
THE AMERICAN REVOLUTION

Some of the most enduring images of American popular culture come from the Revolution. Paul Revere's ride, the "Minute Men" of Concord and Lexington, the defense of Bunker Hill, Washington crossing the Delaware, the winter at Valley Forge and Betsy Ross are the subjects of statutes, paintings and books. All of these images are based on the actions of real people although they are now legendary. Equally important are the contributions of the American officers and men who did not achieve fame, yet performed countless acts of heroism and sacrifice in the cause of the Revolution. Because of their celebrity, it is easy to find accounts on the service of George Washington, Paul Revere or Israel Putnam. Finding specific information on the common soldier is an altogether different prospect. This has always been a primary objective for the DAR.

A number of obstacles face any researcher interested in a Revolutionary soldier. The passage of time takes its toll on documents. Records are destroyed or deteriorate. Then too, the military establishments of the eighteenth century were not as well organized or as exact in their record keeping as the modern army. As a result, the researcher should not expect to find the minutiae of a modern military personnel record for a Revolutionary War soldier. Finally, while the Continental Army was the national army during the Revolution, it was not the only organized body of American soldiers. Throughout the war, state and town militia units under the authority of the state governments supplemented and supported the Continental Army. Consequently, not one, but several different government bodies kept records on the American troops.

13.20.4.1
The Continental Line and the Militia

When they arrived in the New World, the English colonists brought with them the concept of militia, a military force for defense formed from the male population. In more densely populated New England one finds town militia, while in the South, militias included all the men in a county or an even wider area. Militiamen elected their own officers, practiced military drill and kept weapons in their homes. They served as a military unit only in times of crisis. By the time of the Revolution, the militia was an established feature of American colonial life. Militiamen stood on the green of Lexington and plagued the British retreat back to Boston the same day. Following the events in Lexington and Concord, the Massachusetts Provincial Congress called for the establishment of a New England army. Several colonies, including Massachusetts responded by forming regiments that were dispatched to Boston. In June 1775, the Continental Congress called for Pennsylvania, Maryland and Virginia to form companies of riflemen which, when added to the troops outside Boston, would form the nucleus of the Continental Army. Later Congress would expand the call for enlistments to include all of the colonies.

Large standing armies were not a feature of eighteenth century American life. In order to pursue the cause of independence it was necessary for the Congress to create the Continental Army from the only trained military force at its disposal: the existing state militia units. This was only a stopgap measure and a matter of some concern to the army's new commander, George Washington. The militiamen were nonprofessional soldiers and their enlistment was limited to a matter of months. It was not until late 1776 that Congress authorized enlistment periods in the Continental Army for a period of no less than three years or the duration of the war. At the same time, Congress asked that each state form a specific number of regiments for service in the Continental Army. The extended enlistment period gave Washington the opportunity to form the professional army he desired, but the army never grew to the point it could without the support offered by the militia. Throughout the war, whenever the Continental Army was on campaign, it was joined by local militia that would assemble in time for the battle then leave once the shooting stopped.

A good one-volume history of the army during the Revolution is Wright's *The Continental Army* published by the U.S. Army Center of Military History. Included in the book is a list of Continental Army units with an organizational history for each and a list of each regiment's engagements. Berg's *The Encyclopedia of Continental Army Units* has a brief history of every unit that served in the Continental army and selected militia units with appendices on the organization of the Army, the size of the army and a list of the units at Valley Forge.

Individual histories of Revolutionary War regiments are relatively rare. Most state units are studied as a group in works such as *The North Carolina Continentals, The Pennsylvania Line: Regimental Organization and Operations, 1776–1783, The Virginia Continental Line.* E.M. Sanchez–Saavedra's *A Guide to Virginia Military Organizations in the American Revolution, 1774–1787* includes a description of every Virginia unit including the state navy, and identifies the officers in each unit. These books are available in the Library in the state sections.

For the most part these broader studies do not include the names of common soldiers. Exceptions to this rule are *The Commander–in–Chief's Guard, Revolutionary War* by Carlos E. Godfrey, *History of the First New Hampshire Regiment in the War of the Revolution* by Frederic Kidder and *The German Regiment of Maryland and Pennsylvania in the Continental Army* by Henry J. Retzer, which contain rosters. *Pierce's Register* preserves the names of officers and men of the Continental Army who received back pay from Paymaster General John Pierce in the form of certificates in 1783. A full listing of the officers in the Continental Army is available in Francis B. Heitman's *Historical Register of Officers of the Continental Army During the War of the Revolution*. Fortunately, records for the enlisted men of the Continental Army were preserved by the U.S. War Department, although not without some difficulty.

The Continental Line and the Continental Army are one and the same. The term "Line" is derived from the most common battlefield formation of the day. In battle infantry regiments advanced in long lines facing the enemy. The two opposing lines would then blaze away at each other until one side or the other retired from the field ending the battle. Any maneuvering on the battlefield was performed by Light Infantry or other auxiliary units, whose efforts contributed little to the outcome of any engagement. Ultimately it was the Line regiments that determined the course of the battle. It was a matter of pride to be part of a "Line" regiment as it indicated the soldier was a professional.

13.20.4.2
Compiled Service Records

Accidental fires in 1800 and 1801 and a deliberate one set by the British in 1814 destroyed a number of federal records relating to Revolutionary War soldiers. No effort was made to replace these documents until the late nineteenth century, when the United States War Department acquired records from other federal departments or duplicated materials owned by the state governments. Using these sources, the War Department recreated service records for Revolutionary War soldiers. The compilations resulting from these efforts were later microfilmed by the National Archives and made available to the public under the title *Compiled Service Records of Soldiers Who Served in the American Army During the Revolutionary War*. The original documents are now permanently housed at the National Archives. All 1,096 rolls of this microfilm publication are available for use in the Seimes Technology Center. The service records are arranged first by state, then by regiment, and within the regiment alphabetically by the individual soldier's surname.

An index to the *Compiled Service Records* is also available on microfilm in the Microfilm Center. This index is the basis for a four-volume publication by Virgil White entitled *Index to Revolutionary War Service Records*. Arranged after the style of its microfilm parent, White's work lists soldiers alphabetically and gives the regiment and rank for each soldier. In the *Compiled Service Records*, one finds the name and rank of the soldier, his known period of service, rate of pay, and notations of significant events during the service of the soldier.

Supplementing the *Compiled Service Records* is *Miscellaneous Numbered Records in the War Department Collection of Revolutionary War Records, 1775–1790's*. This microfilm series, also available in Seimes Technology Center, is a collection of documents primarily concerned with the administration of the Continental Army. As such, the materials include official correspondence, records of supplies, receipts, court martial proceedings, council minutes and payrolls. A *Special Index to the Numbered Records in the War Department Collection of Revolutionary Records* is also available on microfilm.

The *Compiled Service Records* and the *Miscellaneous Numbered Records* include the names of those soldiers who served in the Continental Army or in militia units that served with the Continental Army but were not incorporated into it. Militia units that did not participate in campaigns of the Continental Army are not listed in the *Compiled Service Records*.

13.20.4.3
Naval Records of the Revolution

The American Revolution was not restricted to land, yet the struggle at sea is one of the lesser-known stories of the conflict. At the time of the Revolution, Great Britain had the most powerful fleet in the world. The Continental Navy never grew large enough to seriously contest the Royal Navy in large-scale fleet actions. The single best-known naval battle of the Revolution was the clash between the *Bonhomme Richard* commanded by John Paul Jones and the British *Serapis*. Yet there is more to the story of the war at sea than this single combat. Between them, the captains of the Continental Navy and American privateers amassed an impressive record. Several Continental Navy captains, most notably John Paul Jones, emerged victorious from engagements with British ships. Working in conjunction with the Navy, Continental Marines staged amphibious operations in the Bahamas and in Great Britain.

Commissioned by Congress specifically to seize British merchantmen in return for prize money, American privateers proved to be a constant annoyance to the Royal Navy and a menace to the merchant fleet. While none of these events proved to be decisive turning points in the Revolution, by the end of the war there was a well-established American presence at sea. Two narrative histories, Miller's *Sea of Glory* and Allen's two-volume *A Naval History of the American Revolution* tell the full story of American naval efforts during the Revolution.

The Continental Navy and Marines

The importance of the sea and the need for American ships was obvious from the first. Not long after he assumed command of the army, George Washington observed that the besieged British garrison in Boston was unlikely to suffer much hardship as long as supplies arrived by sea. Clearly, an American navy could hinder British shipping. Washington took matters into his own hands by creating a small "fleet" of eight vessels for the purpose of harassing British supply ships. *George Washington's Schooners: The First American Navy* contains a great deal of information on the officers and men of Washington's private navy. In October 1775, the Continental Congress established the Continental Navy partly in response to Washington's concerns and partly due to raids on Rhode Island by the Royal Navy. Congress established a Continental Marine Corps less than one month later on November 10, 1775.

Official papers dealing with Washington's navy and the establishment of the Continental Navy and Marines are found in *Naval Documents of the American Revolution*, a multivolume set that includes many contemporary materials dealing with naval operations. Because relatively few records of the Continental Navy still exist, *Naval Documents* draws from a wide range of sources including official correspondence from America, Great Britain and France, extracts from the journals of Parliament and the Continental Congress and reprints of contemporary newspaper articles. The full text of Congressional documents regarding the Continental Navy and American privateers is also found in *Journals of the Continental Congress*. Existing records of individual service for American mariners are available in the microfilm publication *Compiled Service Records of American Naval Personnel and Members of the Departments of the Quartermaster General and the Commissary General of Military Stores Who Served During the Revolutionary War*. These service records and a name index to the series are available in Seimes Microfilm Center.

Many of the commanders in the new Continental Navy had some experience in sea warfare, but were not professional military men. Of the captains, John Paul Jones is the best known, yet even he served only on merchantmen before the war. In spite of their varied backgrounds, all of these men would make a mark on the Continental Navy, beginning with Esek Hopkins who led a daring raid on the Bahamas in March 1776. *Naval Officers of the American Revolution: A Concise Biographical Dictionary* has a brief biographical sketch of Hopkins and the other officers of the Continental Navy and Continental Marines while *Mariners of the American Revolution* includes the names of both officers and common seamen. A full biography of Hopkins and several biographies of John Paul Jones are available in the Library including Ellsbery's *Captain John Paul* and Morison's *John Paul Jones*.

No less important to the war at sea were the Continental Marines who served as the shock troops of the Navy. *Biographies of Continental Marine Officers* contains 130 biographical sketches with particular attention paid to service during the Revolution. In addition to the full story of Marine involvement, *Marines in the Revolution: A History of the Continental Marines in the American Revolution 1775–1783* has an appendix of Marine officer biographies and a ship–by–ship roster of Marines including officers, non–commissioned officers and privates.

Privateers

Much of the damage to British shipping came not from the Continental Navy, but from privateers. These were enterprising individuals who were commissioned by the Continental Congress, or its representatives to prey on British vessels. A list of the ships and their captains is found in *Naval Records of the American Revolution 1775–1788*. These ships and men were not amalgamated into the Continental Navy, the ownership of a privateering vessel remaining in private hands. Although armed, privateers rarely met the Royal Navy in open combat, preferring to seize merchant vessels. Maclay's *A History of American Privateers* gives a general overview of American privateers in the Revolution and the War of 1812 focusing on the more renowned ships and captains.

Typically privateers devoted all their energies to the capture of ships, but on occasion privateers were called on for other duties. While he was in France, Benjamin Franklin commissioned three privateers for the duty of rescuing American prisoners of war. An account of this episode is Clark's *Ben Franklin's Privateers,* which identifies the captains of these vessels and names a number of seamen.

A more extensive study of the privateers is McManemin's *Captains of the Privateers During the Revolutionary War*. This study focuses on the careers of over sixty of the most successful privateering captains. Sanchez–Saavedra's *A Guide to Virginia Military Organizations in the American Revolution, 1774–1778* lists Virginia's privateering vessels with the names of the owners and captains. Additional information on privateers, both the ships and the men who sailed them, is found in Eastman's *Some Famous Privateers of New England* and Middlebrook's *Maritime Connecticut During the Revolution*.

State Navies

With so much of the population concentrated along the coastline it is no surprise that nearly every state was able to launch its own navy. Most of these navies were defensive in nature. Consequently, the duties of the state navies bound the ships to the coastline and the interior waterways. Some of the New England states however, particularly Massachusetts, ranged as far as the English Channel. It was not uncommon during these long voyages for the line between privateer and state navy to blur somewhat. Frequently, the defense of the coastline was an aggressive one. In the largest naval engagement of the war, excluding French operations, the Massachusetts Navy assaulted the British ships and garrison stationed at Penobscot. A history of this fiasco, which resulted in the near destruction of the Massachusetts Navy, is Cayford's *The Penobscot Expedition*.

The Library has several studies of these state navies including McManemin's *Revolution on the High Seas: A History of Maritime Massachusetts During the Revolutionary War,* Jackson's *The Pennsylvania Navy, 1775–1781*, Still's *North Carolina's Revolutionary War Navy* and Stewart's *Virginia's Navy of the Revolution*, which includes a roster of men who served in the Virginia Navy. Sanchez–Saavedra's *A Guide to Virginia Military Organizations in the American Revolution, 1774–1778* includes a list of Virginia State Navy vessels by type and by name and identifies the officers for each ship. As the name suggests, *Massachusetts Soldiers and Sailors of the Revolutionary War* identifies men of the Massachusetts Navy, and the *Pennsylvania Archives* names the mariners of the Pennsylvania Navy. In *Captains of the State Navies During the Revolutionary War*, McManemin details the lives and careers of 29 captains from various states. Also included is a brief description outlining the activities of each state navy.

13.20.4.4
State Records and Rosters

Many militia units never came within sight of the Continental Army but still performed valuable service during the Revolution both in battle and in more mundane tasks such as guard duty. Information on these militia men as well as muster rolls for state regiments that did serve with the Continental Army appear in a number of publications including many compiled and published by individual state governments.

State published rosters for the Revolution are as many and varied as the states themselves. Some of these publications such as *Georgia's Roster of the Revolution* are nothing more than lists of names. *Massachusetts Soldiers and Sailors of the Revolutionary War* arranges the names alphabetically and provides a brief description of service for each. Most of the entries in this seventeen-volume set include the individual's place of residence at the time of the Revolution and some entries contain a physical description of the soldier or sailor. A supplement to this set that has names not included in the original seventeen volumes is available in the Seimes Technology Center. *Rolls of the Soldiers in the Revolutionary War 1775 to 1783* from the state of Vermont consists primarily of payrolls, showing rank, regiment and length of service. Roberts' *New York in the Revolution* lists officers and men of the Continental Line regiments from New York as well as county militia. Another source for New York soldiers is Fernow's *New York in the Revolution,* which includes listings for every New York military unit during the war. Eckenrode's *Virginia Soldiers of the American Revolution* published by the Commonwealth of Virginia in 1912 is more of an index, with citations to other sources of information. *Official Register of the Officers and Men of New Jersey in the Revolutionary War* groups soldiers by rank and provides a brief description of military service for each. The *Delaware Archives, Military* devotes three volumes to the Revolution, lists soldiers by unit and includes rank, amount of pay, period of service and any significant events in the enlistment of the individual soldier. These lists and others are in the state sections of the Library.

In some cases muster rolls are included as a part of a larger compilation of state records such as the *Pennsylvania Archives* and the *Maryland Archives.* The *Pennsylvania Archives* is a 128-volume compilation of early Pennsylvania documents. Revolutionary War records are scattered over four series in several volumes. These volumes include not only muster rolls, but can include official correspondence and even officers' journals. Like the *Pennsylvania Archives,* the *Archives of Maryland* is a large multivolume set that includes documents written before, during and after the Revolution. Maryland soldiers are identified in volume 18 of the *Archives of Maryland,* which carries the title *Muster Rolls and Other Records of Service of Maryland Troops in the American Revolution.*

Supplementing the official state publications are those rosters compiled by individual authors. Like the official ones, these rosters contain varying amounts of information depending on the intent of the compiler. John Gwathmey compiled a *Historical Register of Virginians in the Revolution* from a variety of sources to produce a list of names in alphabetical order with rank and unit of service for each individual and place of residence for most. Wright's *Maryland Revolutionary Records* uses pension applications and marriage records as sources for his list of soldiers. The Fishers' *Soldiers, Sailors and Patriots of the Revolutionary War—Vermont* and *Soldiers, Sailors, and Patriots of the Revolutionary War—Maine* lists individuals alphabetically by surname and include whatever genealogical information may be available such as marriages, children and place of burial. Bobby Gilmer Moss has compiled two works relating to the Revolution in South Carolina: *Roster of South Carolina Patriots in the American Revolution* and *The Patriots at Kings Mountain.* To compile the rosters in both books, Moss carefully consulted a variety of sources. As a result, while Moss' lists are as near to comprehensive as possible, the entries for each man do not have the same level of detail. Moss includes a description of service for every soldier, but for some entries he has information on post–Revolution activities and even some genealogical information such as birth and death dates, spouse and children. The emphasis is on genealogy in Burgess' *Virginia Soldiers of 1776.* Through the use of documents in the Virginia State Library, the Virginia State Archives, the Virginia Land Office and "other reliable sources" Burgess compiled not only service records for a number of Virginia veterans, but information on their families as well. Peden's *Revolutionary Patriots of Delaware 1775–1783* includes the names of both soldiers and women who contributed to the Revolution and genealogical information for some entries. In addition, information on individual soldiers and their families may be available in the Library's documentation files.

13.20.4.5
Patriotic and Civil Service

Not everyone who contributed to the Revolution served in the military. A number of individuals assisted the cause through patriotic and civil service. The *DAR Patriot Index* classifies civil service as "the holding of a Civil office such as: Constable; Jailor; Juror; Justice of Peace; Moderator; Ordinary; Selectman; Sheriff; Surveyor of Highways; Tax Collector; Town Clerk; Town Treasurer, etc." Patriotic service as defined by the DAR encompasses many occupations. According to the *DAR Patriot Index* patriotic service during the Revolution includes:

> An Associator; Collector of Provisions; Defender of Fort or Frontier; Delegate to a Continental Congress or to a Provincial Congress; Express Rider; Fence Viewer; Furnishing a substitute; Gunsmith who gave his services; Inspector of provisions; Legislator; Member of the Boston Tea Party, or the Cherokee Expedition, or the Galvez Expedition, or the Kaskaskia Campaign; Member of a Committee made necessary by the War; Minister who made patriotic sermons; Munitions maker; Nurse; Taking an Oath of Allegiance; Patroller; Prisoner of War or of the Indians; Ranger; Refugee; Rendering aid to the wounded; Rendering material aid; Signer of a petition or a non–importation agreement; Surgeon; Wheelwright.

Information is readily available on ranking politicians such as members of the Continental Congress in sources such as the *Papers of the Continental Congress*. Two sources for identifying local officials including selectmen, committeemen, grand jurors, town clerks, fence viewers, surveyors and others are *Massachusetts Town Officials 1775–1783* and *Non–Military Service in the Revolutionary War from Extracts Connecticut Town Council Minutes 1774–1784*. A similar source for Maine is *Town Officers, Members of Wartime Committees, Preachers of Patriotic Sermons, Contributors of Material Aid 1774–1784*. All three works were compiled through the efforts of G.R.C. committees. Other sources for this type of service include state and county records for the period.

Another means of showing support to the Revolution was by taking an "Oath of Allegiance" to the Revolutionary governments in the individual states. Some of these oaths have been compiled and are available in a number of sources in the Library. Examples of these lists include *Delaware Signers of the Oath of Allegiance* and *New Jersey Oaths of Allegiance 1777–1778* both compiled by DAR chapters and such state records such as *The Pennsylvania Archives* and the *New Hampshire State Records* series.

Sources that are useful for identifying suppliers to the army and government are financial records or claims against the state. *Certificates and Receipts of Revolutionary New Jersey* is one such source that lists payments by the state to individuals for services rendered to the army or the government. Other examples of these records include the transcriptions of *Stub Entries to Indents Issued in Payment of Claims Against South Carolina Growing Out of the Revolution, Virginia Revolutionary Publick Claims*, which contains many but not all of the Virginia claims, and *North Carolina Revolutionary Army Public Accounts*. Each of these sources indicates the name of the claimant, the type of goods provided, and the amount of the claim. These sources are also available in Seimes Technology Center.

GROUPS IN THE AMERICAN REVOLUTION

13.20.4.6
The Continental Congress

During the Revolution, the Continental Congress functioned as the national government. The documents of the Congress have been published in *Journals of the Continental Congress, Letters of Delegates to Congress, 1774–1789*, and Burnett's *Letters of Members of the Continental Congress. Index: Papers of the Continental Congress 1774–1789* provides subject and name access to the documents of the Congress except for the *Journals*, which has its own index. *The Papers of the Continental Congress*, a microfilm series from the National Archives is in the Seimes Technology Center.

The members of the Continental Congress are the subjects of many books. Collected biographies of these men and general histories regarding the Congress and the signing of the Declaration of Independence are in the Library. A representative sample of works on the Congressional delegates includes Ferris and Morris' *The Signers of the Declaration of Independence*, Wilson's *The Book of the Founding Fathers* and Thomson's *One Hundred Famous Founders*, which includes biographies of the signers of the Constitution as well. Of genealogical interest is Frederick Pyne's *Descendants of the Signers of the Declaration of Independence*.

Most of these books contain portraits of the Congressional Delegates and some brief information on their families. Heathcote's *The Signers of the Declaration of Independence* is unique in that it includes of photographs of the graves of the Signers. Fairhurst's *Homes of the Signers of the Declaration* presents photographs of the houses still standing that were owned by these men.

The Library owns several older works on the signers. These include Dwight's *Signers of the Declaration of Independence* published in 1895; the 1832, 1834 and 1844 editions of Goodrich's *Lives of the Signers to the Declaration of Independence;* and *Biography of the Signers to the Declaration of Independence* published in 1827. These volumes contain some information on the families of the members of Congress. Ancestral information on the delegates is available in *Lineage Lines of the Fifty–six Signers of the Declaration of Independence* from the New York DAR G.R.C.

Some of the delegates to the Continental Congress went on to serve in the Constitutional Convention. The Library has a number of works dealing with the signers of the Constitution. These include the collected biographies found in Coleman's *The Constitution and Its Framers;* Charleton, Ferris and Ryan's *Framers of the Constitution;* Bradford's *Founding Fathers;* and Meister's *The Founding Fathers,* which includes information on the families of the signers. General histories on the events surrounding the signing of the Constitution are available in the Library as well.

13.20.4.7
Prisoners of War

Neither side in the Revolution was prepared to deal with prisoners of war. In many cases, prisoners were housed in whatever facilities were available where overcrowding and poor sanitation became common problems. To alleviate these conditions in New York City, the British hit upon the expedient of housing American prisoners aboard prison ships where thousands died. Dandridge's *American Prisoners of the Revolution* includes the names of many American prisoners in the text and lists the names of eight thousand men known to have been held on the notorious prison ship "Jersey". This particular ship is the subject of two memoirs: Greene's *Recollections of the Jersey Prison–Ship* based on the manuscripts of Captain Thomas Dring and Andros' *The Old Jersey Captive*.

A listing of American prisoners held in Canada is found in McHenry's *Rebel Prisoners at Quebec 1778–1783*. Many captured American privateers and sailors were held in England. Their plight, and some prisoners' names are in Cohen's *Yankee Sailors in British Gaols*. A first person account of the experience is found in *The Prisoners of 1776; A Relic of the Revolution*, the journals of Charles Herbert, a Massachusetts sailor held in Old Mill Prison, Plymouth, England. Peterson's *Known Military Dead During the American Revolutionary War, 1775–1783* includes the names of some of the Americans who died in captivity. Rather than deal with the harsh conditions on prison ships, some of the Americans captured at Charleston enlisted in the British army. A transcript listing the names of these men is in *Continental Prisoners in His Majesty's Service, 1781*.

The largest single group of prisoners captured by the Americans was those British and German troops taken at Saratoga. Known as the "Convention Army" for the surrender convention between Gates and Bourgoyne, these men, and in some cases their dependents, were moved from one camp to another from Massachusetts to Virginia. Sampson's *Escape in America: The British Convention Prisoners 1777–1783* tells the story of these prisoners and includes the names of men who escaped or made the attempt. German troops who were prisoners are identified in Smith's *Muster Rolls and Prisoner–of–War Lists in American Archival Collections Pertaining to the German Mercenary Troops Who Served with the British Forces During the American Revolution*.

13.20.4.8
Women

Throughout the colonies women contributed to the Revolution in many ways. Their efforts have not gone unrecognized. The Library maintains a file of articles and references to women in the Revolution, and the Library Director is compiling a bibliography of these studies for publication in 2005. DAR also published Somerville's *Women in the American Revolution* in 1974, but this largely anecdotal review contains no documentation and is out of print.

A number of women are listed in *The DAR Patriot Index* as patriots and a few as soldiers. The third volume of the earlier edition of *The DAR Patriot Index* is an index to the spouses of soldiers and patriots. Naturally, this is overwhelmingly a list of the wives, and although there have been many corrections since this book was published in 1986, it remains a useful listing of thousands of American women alive during the Revolutionary period.

Many works on women in the Revolution are available in the Library. General overviews include Hoffman and Albert's *Women in the Age of the American Revolution* and Norton's *Liberty's Daughters*. Abstracts from diaries and journals of women from the Revolution are found in Evans' *Weathering the Storm*. Collected biographies of specific female patriots include Kelley and Feinstone's *Courage and Candlelight*, Laska's *"Remember the Ladies"*, Ellet's *The Women of the American Revolution*, Claghorn's *Women Patriots of the American Revolution: A Biographical Dictionary* and *Petticoat Patriots of the American Revolution*. Some of these accounts border on the legendary, while others are more scholarly. Full-length biographies of individual women include Young's *Masquerade: The Life and Times of Deborah Sampson, Continental Soldier,* and Seller's *Patience Wright: American Artist and Spy in George III's London*.

13.20.4.9
Minority Service

People from all walks of life and many ethnic groups served in the Revolution. African Americans and American Indians in particular made significant contributions to the Revolution. Several general works in the Library on the contributions of the African American to the Revolution including Quarles' *The Negro in the American Revolution*, Kaplan's *The Black Presence in the Era of the American Revolution* and Nash's *Race and Revolution*.

DAR promotes the Revolutionary War military service of African Americans and Native Americans in its book *African American and American Indian Patriots of the Revolutionary War*. This 200-page book was produced by a cooperative effort between Library staff and current and former staff members of the Genealogy Department to identify minority participants in the Revolution. The original basis for the book was a series of works published by the DAR under the collective title of *Minority Military Service, 1775-1783* by several DAR employees. For each state, the book lists the names of African Americans and Native Americans. In terms of organization, *African American and American Indian Patriots of the Revolutionary War* follows the arrangement of the *Minority Military Service* booklets. Each state chapter begins with a brief account of minority participation in that state as well as the effects of the war on African Americans and Native Americans in that state. This introduction is followed by a list of the minority participants from that state with referenced sources. Robert Greene's *Black Courage,1775-1783*, also published by the DAR, includes brief biographies of selected servicemen as well as a compiled list of African American pensioners. Nell's *Colored Patriots of the American Revolution* written in 1855, and the Kaplans' *The Black Presence in the Era of the American Revolution* examine the Revolutionary War careers and lives of selected African Americans in depth.

State–specific works on African Americans and Native Americans in the Revolution include Walling's *Men of Color at the Battle of Monmouth June 28, 1778* and White's *Connecticut's Black Soldiers, 1775–1783*. Both of these works include the names of African American soldiers and their regiments, but Walling's book includes the names of Native Americans as well. Other sources that identify African American and Native American troops include Moss' *Roster of South Carolina Patriots in the American Revolution*, Jackson's *Virginia Negro Soldiers and*

Seamen in the Revolutionary War, *Massachusetts Soldiers and Sailors of the Revolutionary War*, Stryker's *Official Register of the Officers and Men of New Jersey in the Revolutionary War* and Newman's *List of Black Servicemen Compiled From the War Department Collection of Revolutionary War Records*.

13.20.4.10
George Rogers Clark

Through a series of daring campaigns in 1778 and 1779, Virginian George Rogers Clark and a small band of soldiers occupied what Virginia then considered its Illinois County and pushed out the British. The story of Clark's campaign is in several works including *George Rogers Clark Papers 1771–1781*, *The George Rogers Clark Adventure in the Illinois* and *George Rogers Clark and the Revolution in Illinois 1763–1787*. Muster rolls and payrolls for Clark's men are transcribed in Harding's *George Rogers Clark and His Men: Military Records, 1778–1784*. Also refer to section 13.20.4.17 for further information.

13.20.4.11
French Military Records

In spite of their traditional antagonism against Great Britain, the French did not immediately and openly ally themselves with the American patriots. Even more than Great Britain, France was left battered by the French and Indian War having lost not only her North American possessions, but a great deal of money in the process. Then too, the French government was not willing to commit to open war with Great Britain when the success of the Revolution was still very much in doubt. Thus, while individuals such as Lafayette did rally to the American cause, France was unwilling to support the Revolution until after the American victory at Saratoga. France recognized American independence in December 1777 and formally concluded an alliance one month later. A French fleet under Admiral d'Estaing was dispatched in the spring of 1778, but failed to achieve any success against the British. It was not until the arrival of a French army under Comte de Rochambeau in July 1780 that the French effectively contributed to the American cause. With Rochambeau's army and the addition of a French fleet under Comte de Grasse, Washington bottled up the army of Cornwallis at Yorktown and won a victory ensuring American independence.

The story of the negotiations that led to the French recognition of the American independence is told in *Yankees at the Court, French Policy and the American Alliance of 1778* and *New Materials for the History of the American Revolution*. General histories of French participation in the Revolution include *The French in American During the War of Independence of the United States, 1777–1783*, *France and North America: The Revolutionary Experience* and *The French Forces in America, 1780–1783*. *The French Army in the American War of Independence* has a brief history of the French military presence during the Revolution and includes full color illustration of French uniforms. In addition, the Library has an interesting memoir by Count William de Deux–Ponts, *My Campaigns in America* that covers French activities from 1780–1781.

The Library has two reference works that identify officers of the French army. Bodinier's *Les Officiers de L'Armeé Royale* includes a great deal of information of the organization of the

French army and the opinions of the officers with regards to the Revolution and Americans in general. Also by Bodinier is *Dictionnaire des Officiers de L'Armée Royale qui ont Combattu aux Etats–Unis Pendant la Guerre d'Indépendance* which arranges the officers in alphabetical order by surname and includes a brief biography for each. Full length biographies of Rochambeau and de Grasse in English are also available. *Les Combattants Français de la Guerre Américaine* published by the French Ministère des Affaires Étrangères in 1905 identifies soldiers and mariners of all ranks who served in America although some regiments list only the officers. The arrangement of the book is by regiment and then by rank within the regiment. An every name index aids the researcher in locating individual soldiers.

13.20.4.12
The Gálvez Expeditions and Spanish Involvement

Like France, the Spanish government viewed the American Revolution as an opportunity to regain territories lost to Great Britain in previous wars, particularly Gibraltar and the Floridas. After Great Britain rebuffed Spanish attempts at negotiations, Spain formally allied herself with France in April 1779. A Spanish declaration of war against Great Britain followed two months later. At the time Bernardo de Gálvez, a young professional soldier, was the governor of Spanish Louisiana. In the two years prior to Spain's declaration of war, Gálvez used every means at his disposal to weaken British influence in the area, including financial assistance to Oliver Pollock, a patriot and a supplier for George Rogers Clark.

Although Spain declined to participate in the French North American campaigns, Gálvez did not remain idle and launched his own offensive. With an army of professional Spanish soldiers and Louisiana militia Gálvez captured Manchac, Baton Rouge and Natchez from the British in 1779. The following year Gálvez seized Mobile and in 1781 captured Pensacola. Biographies of this interesting figure in American and Louisiana history include LaFarelle's *Bernado de Gálvez, Hero of the American Revolution* and *Bernardo de Gálvez in Louisiana 1776-1783* by John Walton Caughey.

General histories of the Gálvez campaigns are available in the Louisiana and Florida sections of the Library as well as the General section of the Library devoted to the Revolution. Gálvez's own observations are published in *Yo Solo: the Battle Journal of Bernardo de Gálvez During the American Revolution* edited by Bernardo de Gálvez. Rosters of the officers and men who served with Gálvez are available in *Spanish Records: List of Men Under General Don Bernardo de Gálvez in his Campaigns Against the British; Officers Spanish and Natives of Louisiana Serving Under Gen. Don Bernardo de Gálvez;* and *General Archives of the Indies, Seville, Spain*. All three works are transcripts compiled from official documents by C. Robert Churchill. Other rosters include Schmidt's *Louisiana Patriots 1776–1783*, DeVille's *Louisiana Soldiers in the American Revolution,* the Houghs' *Spain's Louisiana Patriots in its 1779-1783 War with England During the American Revolution* and Holmes' *Honor and Fidelity: The Louisiana Infantry Regiments and the Louisiana Militia Companies 1766–1821*. Official transcripts of original Spanish documents on the American Revolution are compiled in the multivolume set *Documentos Relativos a la Independencia de Norteamérica Existentes en Archivos Españoles*.

13.20.4.13
British Forces

At the time of the American Revolution, Great Britain possessed one of the best armies in the world. The Royal Navy was probably the strongest fleet on the face of the earth. Yet British leadership was ill equipped to win the war. Although they won engagements, the generals consistently underestimated the resolve of the Americans, making victories such as Bunker Hill costly. Ultimately, the blunders of the British generals contributed to American independence. Several studies in the Library examine the failure of the British military during the war including Bowler's *Logistics and the Failure of the British Army in America, 1775-1783*, Seymour's *The Price of Folly* and Gruber's *The Howe Brothers & the American Revolution*.

A number of diaries, journals and memoirs by British soldiers have survived from the Revolution. Reprints of these person accounts are available in the Library including *The Journal of Thomas Sullivan, A Soldier in the 49th Regiment of Foot in America*. This narrative is unusual in that while officers penned most of the surviving journals, Sullivan was an enlisted man who participated in the Battle of Bunker Hill. Other sources include *The American Journals of Lt. John Enys*; *The Journal of Stephen Kemble, Lieutenant Colonel 60th Regiment of Foot*; *The Lost War: Letters from British Officers During the American Revolution* and *The Twilight of British Rule in Revolutionary America: The New York Letter Book of General James Robertson*.

Complimenting the memoirs, journals and letters by British military personnel are a number of works that examine every facet of the war as experience by Great Britain. The British view of the war is explored by Hibbert's *Redcoats and Rebels* and by Clark's *British Opinion and the American Revolution*. Alan Kemp's *The British Army in the American Revolution* and Reid and Hook's *British Redcoat 1740-1793* study uniforms, equipment and tactics of the army. Even literature gets a thorough examination in Kallich's two-volume work *British Poetry and the American Revolution*. A useful guide for researchers interested in the British Army is *In Search of the "Forlorn Hope": A Comprehensive Guide to Locating British Regiments and Their Records (1640-WWI)*. This guide includes a complete listing of British regiments, the battles in which they fought by year and the official number and nickname of the regiment.

Considering the power and reputation of the British fleet, the Royal Navy played a nearly negligible role in the Revolution. The Royal Navy suffered major defeats at Charleston, South Carolina in 1776 and at Yorktown in 1781. Although the Navy did capture a number of privateers and bested some American ships in combat, privateers continued to operate throughout the Revolution and single combat between ships had no great impact on the war. General histories of the Royal Navy during the Revolution are in the Library including Syrett's *The Royal Navy in American Waters, 1775-1783* and Graham's *The Royal Navy in the War of American Independence*. A list of *The Commissioned Sea Officers of the Royal Navy 1660–1815* includes the names of officers who served in American waters during the war.

13.20.4.14
The Hessians

No group of Revolutionary War soldiers is more infamous than the Hessians. These German auxiliaries of the British army were hard professional soldiers accustomed to a harsh life of war and discipline. Their language and their manner were foreign. They had a reputation for cruelty.

Initially feared and despised by the Americans, the Hessians' vulnerability became apparent when they surrendered to Americans at Trenton and Saratoga. That the Hessians were in the colonies at all was not a matter of their own choosing, but the result of an agreement between princes.

At the beginning of the Revolution Great Britain had a small professional army, not enough to combat the colonies in rebellion and protect British interests around the world. In order to press the war in America, the British were faced with the choice of enlarging their own army by recruiting from a largely unenthusiastic population or by hiring auxiliary troops from another source. Because the ancestors of George III were German, the Crown contracted with several German principalities for troops. Approximately 30,000 Germans served with the British army during the Revolution. The full story of the German involvement in the war is recounted in *The Hessians and the Other German Auxiliaries of Great Britain in the Revolutionary War* by Edward J. Lowell, *German Mercenaries in Canada* by J.P. Wilhelmy, and *The German Allied Troops in the North American War of Independence 1776–1783* by Max Von Eelking. A list of officers from ensign and above for each regiment that served in America is in the latter book.

The best list of individual German soldiers, officers, noncommissioned officers and enlisted men, is a multivolume set originally published in Germany entitled *Hessiche Truppen im Amerikanischen Unabhängigheitskreig* or the "HETRINA" for short. The HETRINA includes the names of all soldiers who served from the regiments of the principalities of Hesse–Cassel and Waldeck. The information for each soldier includes name, rank, regiment, date of birth, place of origin and remarks on the soldier's service. A brief history of the Hessian involvement in the war and an explanation of the list is included in both German and English. Another source on the Germans, derived in part from the HETRINA is Burgoyne's *Waldeck Soldiers of the American Revolutionary War*. This list is limited to the soldiers of the Third English–Waldeck Regiment and includes a timeline of significant events in the history of the regiment's American service and brief biographical sketches of the soldiers.

One of the most important sources of information on the Germans is *Hessian Documents of the American Revolution 1776–1783: Transcripts and Translations from the Lidgerwood Collection at Morristown National Historical Park, Morristown New Jersey*. This collection of 362 microfiche is in Seimes Technology Center. The Lidgerwood Collection of Hessian documents on microfiche consists of over 20,000 pages of original documents and 10,000 pages of translations detailing the service of Germans in America. Most of the information is taken from official journals, reports, order books and correspondence by the German officers involved. A guide to the collection is in the Library.

In addition to the observations recorded in the Lidgerwood Collection, the Library has a number of published journals and diaries by German troops. These include *A Hessian Officer's Diary of the American Revolution* by Johann Ernst Prechtel, *A Hessian Diary of the American Revolution* by Johann Conrad Dohla, *The American Revolution, Garrison Life in French Canada and New York* translated by Helga Doblin and a collection of diaries and memoirs in *Hessian Journals: Unpublished Documents of the American Revolution*.

In spite of the method of their introduction to the American colonies many German soldiers elected to stay in America. Some deserted, others were prisoners of war who remained with their former captors and still others simply settled in the colonies at the expiration of their term of service. A list of Hessian prisoners is in *Muster Rolls and Prisoner of War Lists in American Archival Collections Pertaining to the German Mercenary Troops Who Served With the British Forces During the American Revolution* by Clifford Neal Smith. While imprisoned, many of these Germans were employed by the local population as laborers or in more skilled tasks. *Muster rolls and Prisoner of War Lists* shows if a prisoner was employed, the name of his employer and the soldier's trade before enlistment. Another source for tracing these soldiers is *Notes on Hessian Soldiers Who Remained in Canada and the United States After the American Revolution, 1775–1783* also by Smith. *Notes on Hessian Soldiers* is divided into three parts to provide the genealogists with different points of access: "Place of Origin", "Regiment and Company" and "Date of Defection".

A list of some German soldiers who remained in Canada after the war is *The Hessians of Nova Scotia* by Johannes Helmut Merz, which includes some information of the descendants of these soldiers. Other works on the same topic by Merz include *He was a Hessian, Register of German Military Men*, and *Er War Ein Hesse! The Register of German Military Men* is a list of over 4000 soldiers known to have stayed in Canada after the Revolution. Each entry in the *Register* includes such information as the soldier's name, his regiment, last known place of residence in Canada and some brief notation regarding marriage or children. One of the sources used by Merz to compile the *Register* was *German Military Settlers in Canada After the American Revolution* by Virginia DeMarce. This work lists soldiers by surname and contains a great deal of genealogical information.

Some descendants of the Germans who remained after the war formed the Johannes Schwalm Historical Association in the late 1970s. Initially a society of descendants from Johannes Schwalm, a German soldier of the Revolution, the Association's interest expanded to include the study of all German auxiliaries and descendants. Their publication, *The Journal of the Johannes Schwalm Historical Association, Inc.* is an excellent source for genealogists and historians interested in the German auxiliaries.

The term "Hessian" is derived from the principalities of Hesse–Cassel and Hesse–Hanau. Although the Hessians constituted the largest group of German soldiers, other principalities supplied troops as well. These principalities were Brunswick, Waldeck, Ansbach–Bayreuth and Anhalt–Zerbst. Under the customs of the day, these Germans were considered "auxiliaries" rather than mercenaries, the distinction being that a mercenary hired himself to a foreign army while the auxiliaries were loaned out as a group. Their monarch received payment from the British crown while the soldiers remained on the payroll of their principalities.

13.20.4.15
Loyalists

In many respects, the Revolution was the first American civil war. A number of colonists were not eager for independence from the British crown. In fact, a number of American colonists actively opposed the Revolution and went so far as to form their own military units to resist the "rebel" armies in the field. These American opponents of the Revolution were termed "Tories" or "Loyalists". Some estimates put the total number of Loyalists as high as one–third of the population in the colonies.

The saga of the Loyalists is well represented in the DAR Library. One of the most comprehensive treatments is *The Loyalists of America and Their Times* (1880) by Egerton Ryerson, which covers the development of revolutionary sentiment from 1620 forward and the experience of loyal Americans during the Revolution and the War of 1812. A more focused study is *Royal Raiders: The Tories of the American Revolution* by North Callahan, a narrative history of the Loyalist military and political experience during the Revolution. *The Loyalist Perception and Other Essays* concentrates on Loyalist opinions regarding the Revolution while *The Price of Loyalty* allows these people to speak for themselves through a collection of letters and other writings by loyal Americans. Loyalists lived in every colony during the Revolution, but two of the colonies with the highest Tory population were New York and Massachusetts. The story of Loyalists in these colonies is recounted in Potter's *The Liberty We Seek*. Loyalism in other colonies including East and West Florida receive attention through a series of essays in *Loyalists and Community in North America*. All of these works and others are in the DAR Library.

State Histories

Although strongest in New York, Massachusetts and the South, Loyalism was pervasive throughout the colonies. For nearly every one of the state sections that constitute the original thirteen colonies, the Library has a study or a list of Loyalists. While some of these books are not as comprehensive as others, each is useful in its own way. In the Virginia section one finds two concise studies on Loyalists with two different approaches. *Loyalism in Virginia* concentrates on the economic aspects of the conflict between the patriots and loyal Americans, while the emphasis of *Loyalism in Revolutionary Virginia* is on civil war among Virginians in the areas of Norfolk and the Eastern Shore. *A State Divided: Opposition in Pennsylvania to the American Revolution* by Anne Ousterhout and *The Loyalists of Revolutionary Delaware* by Harold B. Hancock, both of which examine Loyalism colony–wide during the Revolution, use a broader approach. Neither book however, provides the user with a comprehensive list of Loyalists within those colonies. *Loyalists of New Jersey* on the other hand, lists Loyalists by name and gives a brief biographical entry for each. Loyalist biographical information is also found in *The Loyalists of Massachusetts* and *Divided Hearts: Massachusetts Loyalists 1765–1790 A Biographical Directory*.

Records of Confiscation

As supporters of the crown, the Loyalists were singled out for special treatment by the Patriots. Throughout the colonies, Loyalists saw their homes looted and burned and their property confiscated. While marauding bands accomplished much of the destruction, most of the confiscated property was later sold by the states as official policy. Fortunately for genealogists, many states kept records of these seizures and the later disposal of the property. *Connecticut Loyalists* lists Loyalist landowners in Greenwich, Stamford and Norwalk, describes the confiscated property and names the purchaser. Similar lists are found in *The Loyalists in North Carolina During the Revolution; Sequestrations, Confiscations and Sale of Estates, State Papers of Vermont; Loyalism in New York During the Revolution* and *The Disposition of Loyalist Estates in the Southern District of the State of New York*.

A great deal of information on the land confiscations and the Loyalists themselves appear in state records. In the *Pennsylvania Archives*, 3rd series, v.10, one finds proclamations by the

Supreme Executive Council of Pennsylvania to seize the property of loyal Americans. The names of these Loyalists are included in the proclamations. The disposition and sale of their former property is described in detail in the *Pennsylvania Archives*, 6th series, volumes 12 and 13. A similar list of names and sales of confiscated property is found in *The Revolutionary Records of the State of Georgia*, volume 1 and a list of disenfranchised Loyalists of New Hampshire is included in *State Papers. Documents and Records Relating to the State of New Hampshire*, volume 8.

Military Records

In response to the deprivations and assaults they suffered at the hands of the patriots, and in defense of the Crown, Loyalists armed themselves and organized into military units. Particularly in New York and in the South regular regiments of Loyalists fought in conjunction with the British or operated independently. Relatively few records exist for these Loyalist groups. The single best source in the Library for these soldiers is *Loyalists in the Southern Campaign of the Revolutionary War* by Murtie June Clark. This three volume set includes muster rolls for regiments formed in 1777 and after. Although all of the units listed served only in the Southern campaigns, the soldiers listed did not come exclusively from the South. The set does not have any biographical information on the soldiers, but it does include a complete roster of each regiment, the name and rank of the individuals in the regiment, and the period of service. One of the best known Loyalist formations was a brigade of three battalions formed in New York under the command of Brigadier General Oliver DeLancey. From its formation in 1776 until 1778 the DeLancey Brigade operated on Long Island and the area around New York City. After 1778 the First and Second Battalions were sent south. A reprint of the *Orderly Book of the DeLancey Brigade* for the period September 1776 to June 1778 is available in the Library. The DeLancey Brigade served the Loyalist cause until the end of the war and disbanded in Nova Scotia, Canada in 1783.

The Loyalists in Canada

In the wake of the British defeat at Yorktown and the subsequent Treaty of Paris, many Loyalists chose to leave the colonies and to start anew in the eastern provinces of Canada. These American exiles settled in New Brunswick, Nova Scotia and what became the province of Ontario. An overview of this exodus and the initial stages of settlement is found in the Mikas' *United Empire Loyalists: Pioneers of Upper Canada.* The thoughts and feelings of the Loyalists are found in *Eleven Exiles: Accounts of Loyalists of the American Revolution* and *Loyalist Narratives From Upper Canada* both of which focus on the lives and experiences of specific Loyal Americans.

With these Loyalists were over 3,000 Black Loyalists, some former slaves, who took refuge in New York during the War. Many of these African Americans settled in Nova Scotia although over 1,000 returned to Africa. A list of all the African Americans who departed from New York is found in The *Black Loyalist Directory* edited by Graham Russell Hodges. Included on the list are such details as age, sex, place of origin and name of former owner if previously a slave.

The sudden influx of American expatriates gave the British government the opportunity to move colonists into unsettled areas of Canada. As an added plus, many of the Loyalist settlers were veterans of the Loyalist regiments. Men with experience in warfare could only help to solidify

British control of Canada. The land grants awarded to the Loyalists serve as the basis for several lists in the DAR Library. *Loyalist Lists* by E. Keith Fitzgerald records the arrival of three Loyalist regiments for settlement: Rogers' Rangers, Jessup's Rangers and the 1st Battalion of the King's Royal Regiment of New York. Also included is a list of nonmilitary exiles. Three of the four lists include not only the name of the head of the household and his original occupation, but also the number of women and children and the family's place of origin. The Jessup's Rangers list does not include any information on women and children. None of the lists indicate where these people settled. *Loyalists and Land Settlement in Nova Scotia* compiled by Marion Gilroy does indicate the acreage and general location of individual land grants, but includes only the land holder's name, former rank or place of origin.

The Claims Commission

In 1783, the British government established an American Claims Commission designed to financially compensate Loyalists for their losses. Initially, the Commission set a deadline of March 1784 to receive claims. Because this proved to be an unreasonable time frame for many claimants, the deadline was later extended to 1786. The commissioners held hearings for each claim. A transcript of the testimony for many of these hearings is in Fraser's *Second Report of the Bureau of Archives for the Province of Ontario*. Transcripts missing from the earlier report are included in *Loyalist Settlements 1783–1789* published by the Archives of Ontario. The records of these hearings serve as the basis for several lists in the DAR Library.

One of the earliest lists of Loyalists is *Biographical Sketches of Loyalists of the American Revolution* (1864), a two-volume set by Lorenzo Sabine. In these books, Sabine gives an overview of the Loyalist experience with emphasis on the political scene of the Revolution and after. This essay is followed by brief biographical entries on individual Loyalists. The content for these sketches varies considerably. Sabine includes such information as where the Tory lived before the Revolution, occupation and experience during and after the war. Although Sabine did not have access to the records of the commission, much of the information included in his sketches is based on papers used at the hearings and retained by the descendants of the original claimants.

Both *Biographical Sketches of Loyalists of the American Revolution* by Gregory Palmer and *American Loyalist Claims* and *American Migrations, 1765-1799*, by Peter Wilson Coldham, base their information on English sources. Palmer's book is essentially an updating of Sabine's work. Palmer does not have a historical essay on the plight of the Loyalists, but spends a good deal of time speculating on Sabine's sources in the earlier work. Using the records of the commission, Palmer is able to verify much of Sabine's information and add additional names to the list. In style, both Coldham and Palmer follow Sabine for the biographical sketches, but include a source for every entry.

Perhaps the most complete list of loyal Americans is *The New Loyalist Index* by Paul J. Bunnell. To compile this list, Bunnell used a variety of sources including land grant records muster rolls and the Claims Commission records as abstracted by Coldham. Bunnell is also the author of *Research Guide to Loyalists* that lists the availability of primary and secondary source material in the United States and Canada.

United Empire Loyalists

On November 9, 1789 Lord Dorchester, then Governor General of Canada conferred the title of United Empire Loyalist on the American Loyalists who fought for the crown. This was a hereditary title to be passed down from generation to generation. Descendants of the original U.E. Loyalists perpetuate the memory of the early settlers in the United Empire Loyalists' Association. Among the publications of this society is the three-volume *Loyalist Lineages of Canada*, a list of Loyal American settlers and their descendants and the periodical *The Loyalist Gazette*, a source of good general articles on Loyalists and the American Revolution.

13.20.4
Part 4
POST–REVOLUTION SOURCES ON THE WAR

13.20.4.16
First Person Accounts

Filling in the details of an ancestor's life is an important part of genealogical research, and a fortunate few genealogists will benefit from diaries and journals kept by some individuals.

In the process of applying for pensions veterans supplied proof of their service either in testimony or with documentary evidence. This was a necessary part of the application process and is often the only written information on an individual's participation. Such manuscripts also mention many other persons with whom the author had contact, and consequently assume an importance to many researchers.

Most soldiers of the Revolution had neither the time nor the inclination to record their experiences or thoughts about the war. Nonetheless, several first person accounts by both officers and enlisted men have survived, and some examples are owned by the Library. March to Quebec is a compilation of journals written by participants of Benedict Arnold's campaign in Canada. Personal accounts by officers include *The Revolutionary Journal of Col. Jeduthan Baldwin, The Journal and Order Book of Captain Robert Kirkwood of the Delaware Regiment of the Continental Line, The New–York Diary of Lieutenant Jabez Fitch* and the *Memoirs of Captain Lemuel Roberts*. The experiences of the enlisted soldier are recorded in *Diary of a Common Soldier in the American Revolution, 1775–1783* [by Jeremiah Greenman], *The 1777 Journal of Robert Treat of Orange, Connecticut*, and the *Memoirs of the Life of John Adlum in the Revolutionary War*. A number of journals and diaries of the period can also be found in the series *Eyewitness Accounts of the Revolution*. While none of these accounts contain a great deal of genealogical information, they are extremely useful in illustrating eighteenth century military life and the experience of the Revolutionary soldier.

13.20.4.17
Pension and Bounty Land Records

It was a common practice before the Revolution for provincial governments to offer pensions for disability as a result of military service. On August 26, 1776 the Continental Congress passed a law allowing for half pay to disabled officers and men. The very early pensions awarded to invalid soldiers are found in *Abstract of Semi–Annual Payments to Invalid Pensioners of the Revolutionary War March 4, 1801 Through September 5, 1815* compiled by the Thomas Marshall Chapter, DAR. Congress continued to expand the pension program during the Revolution and after. Eventually the Federal government assumed responsibility for pensions issued by the state governments for Revolutionary service. The full text of the pension and land acts is contained in *Army and Navy Pension Laws and Bounty Land Laws of the United States* (1861).

In order to secure a pension, an applicant appeared in a court of record with proof of his military service. This proof could take the form of documents or witnesses. Widows who applied for pensions also needed documentary evidence to support their claims. The court certified the evidence then passed the documentation on to the Pension Office for final approval. Because the pension laws were restrictive, at least initially, the Pension Office rejected a number of applicants. A list of *Rejected and Suspended Applications for Revolutionary War Pensions* shows that lack of proof was the primary cause for rejection. Beyond name and place of residence, relatively little information on applicants is available from this list or from *Pensioners of Revolutionary War Struck Off the Roll* although the latter volume does indicate in many cases the regiment of the applicant. As time passed Congress modified the pension laws to include more individuals. The last pension law relating to the Revolution passed on March 9, 1878 and allowed widows to receive pensions if the veteran served at least two weeks.

In addition to pensions, the Continental Congress attempted to encourage enlistments by the offer of free land to veterans. Congress passed the first bounty land act on September 16, 1776. This act granted land to officers and soldiers who were engaged in military service and served to the end of the war and to representatives of veterans who were killed during the war. Enlisted men and non–commissioned officers were granted 100 acres by the act; an ensign up to 150 acres; a lieutenant was granted up to 200 acres; other officers up to colonel could receive 500 acres. Considering the first pension law offered half pay only if one was wounded or maimed in battle to the point of disability, the offer of free land was a much more attractive inducement for enlistment. Later acts expanded the eligibility requirements for bounty lands to include the widows and children of veterans.

Many men took full advantage of the bounty land offer. A number of lists in the DAR Library preserve the names of these individuals with varying degrees of additional information. *Kentucky Land Warrants, for the French, Indian, & Revolutionary Wars* gives the name of the Revolutionary War veteran, his rank, regiment of service, term of enlistment, date of land grant and amount of land. On the other hand *Ohio Military Land Warrants 1789–1801* lists only the names of recipients and the date of the grant. Patrick Wardell used land grants in part to produce his multivolume *Virginia/West Virginia Genealogical Data From Revolutionary War Pension and Bounty Land Warrant Records* and William Lindsay Hopkins was able to discover a great deal of military service information using rejected *Virginia Revolutionary War Land Grant Claims 1783–1850*.

State governments also made such awards of land to veterans. The names of state land grant recipients are found in *Revolutionary War Bounty Land Grants Awarded by State Governments* compiled by Lloyd DeWitt Bockstruck. *Georgia Revolutionary Bounty Land Records 1783–1785* lists the names of soldiers and refugees entitled to bounty lands in that state. Georgia veterans with three years of residence in the state were also entitled to land from a statewide lottery in 1827. *Authentic List of All Land Lottery Grants Made to Veterans of the Revolutionary War by the State of Georgia* preserves the names of these veterans. Microfilm copies of original land grants and warrants from North Carolina are available in the Seimes Technology Center under the titles *Revolutionary Pay Vouchers, Land Grants, Wills, Tax Lists and Other Records from the North Carolina State Archives* and *North Carolina Warrants and Surveys, Western Territory, 1778–1791* [Tennessee].

Because proof was required for the approval of a pension or a bounty land warrant, the application files of Revolutionary veterans and their widows is an important source of information. A pension file contains not only proof of the veterans service, including testimony, affidavits, and documentary evidence, but frequently information on the veteran's family. All of the pension and bounty land files have been microfilmed and compiled by the National Archives under the title *Revolutionary War Pension and Bounty Land Warrant Application Files, 1800–1900*. These pension files are available in Seimes Microfilm Center. All of the files are arranged alphabetically by the surname of the veteran. The *Index of Revolutionary War Pension Applications in the National Archives* is available in the Library. Virgil White has abstracted all of the pension files and published them in a four-volume set entitled *Genealogical Abstracts of Revolutionary War Pension Files*. As the title suggests, the main emphasis in White's work is on genealogy, not military records, but he does include the branch of service, if not the regiment or rank, and the individual's pension application number. Entries are arranged alphabetically by the applicant's surname and include date of application, family names and some detail on the life of the veteran or his widow.

The DAR abstracted selected pension files in two series entitled *Pension Papers* (233 vols.) and *New Hampshire Pension Records* (101 vols.). More emphasis is placed on military service in these abstracts than in White's work however, with particular attention placed on testimonies of experiences during the war. Both sets are indexed by a special card index in the Library, which will be digitized and placed on the DAR's website. Grace M. Pierce compiled and abstracted *Rhode Island Pension Records* in six volumes and followed the format of the *Pension Papers*. These and other pension abstracts, including a five-volume set of transcripts by Mabel Van Dyke Baer, are located in the DAR Library. Additional lists of pensioners compiled by the DAR or others are located in the state sections including *Pension Records of Soldiers of the Revolution Who Removed to Florida* by Jessie Fritot for the Jacksonville Chapter, DAR; Quisenberry's *Revolutionary Soldiers in Kentucky* and *Some Tennessee Heroes of the Revolution*.

During the course of their work DAR staff genealogists assembled a large collection of photocopies of federal pension applications either by extracting them from the documentation from DAR membership application or by ordering copies. Several years ago, after the Seimes Technology Center acquired the National Archives microfilm of these pensions, the Library received these paper copies. The Library staff placed these alphabetically arranged files in the manuscript collection. There are eighty–three boxes of these copies. Some have copies of the final pension payment papers attached. All are available to researchers.

On a periodic basis during the nineteenth century, the Federal government published lists of all living pensioners. These lists are not as informative as the pension application file but are useful in determining the pensioner's name, rank, or in the case of a widow her husband's rank, and place of residence. In *Revolutionary Pensioners: A Transcript of the Pension List of the United States for 1813* pensioners are listed in alphabetical order within their state of residence with their former rank and the amount of their pension. *The Pension List of 1820* adds place of residence during the Revolution to the information on the 1813 list. Copies of original pension payment records are available to the public on microfilm under the title *Ledgers of Payments to U.S. Pensioners Under Acts of 1818 Through 1858* in the Seimes Technology Center.

In 1840 a census was taken of surviving Revolutionary War pensioners. This census was published in 1841 under the title *A Census of Pensioners for Revolutionary or Military Services*. It includes the name, age, and place of residence for the pensioner along with the names of individuals with whom the pensioner resided in 1840. The source has been reprinted several times.

Most pensioners received their stipend through the application process, but it was not uncommon for individuals to petition Congress for a pension. These petitions were referred to the House Committee on Revolutionary Pensions. Some of these petitions are compiled in *Revolutionary Pensioners 1827–1831*, a bound copy of original house reports relating to pensions. Although these reports are confined to only a four year span, they contain a great deal of information relating to pensioners and to the petitioners in particular. Several petitions relate the military service of the veteran in great detail. *Revolutionary Pensioners 1827–1831* does not have an index, but the *CIS US Serial Set Index Part I, American State Papers and the 15th–34th Congress* provides limited access to these and other Congressional documents of the period.

13.20.4.18
The Draper Manuscript Collection

Fascinated by the George Rogers Clark story and the experience of the settlers across the Alleghany Mountains, historian Lyman C. Draper spent much of the nineteenth century compiling a massive amount of material on the frontier during Revolutionary period. When Draper died in 1891, possession of his compiled manuscripts passed to the State Historical Society of Wisconsin. These manuscripts include diaries, journals, maps, muster rolls and other original documents concerning the early history of a number of states including Georgia, Illinois, Ohio, Kentucky and Tennessee and the western parts of Virginia and the Carolinas. In addition, Draper conducted interviews or corresponded with participants in the events of the frontier and their descendants.

The papers cover events from the 1740's until after the War of 1812 including incidents from the Revolution such as the battle of King's Mountain (the subject of Draper's only book *King's Mountain and its Heroes*), the George Rogers Clark expedition and Indian warfare on the frontier. The manuscripts include information on the famous, such as the "George Rogers Clark Papers," as well as the contributions of enlisted soldiers, women and minorities. This invaluable collection is available on microfilm in the Seimes Technology Center. Several subject guides to the manuscripts and an overall *Guide to the Draper Manuscripts* by Josephine Harper are in the Library.

13.20.4.19
Death and Burial Records

By modern standards the battle casualties of the Revolution seem relatively light, but at the time it was very shocking and left a major imprint on post–war society. It was not uncommon for the dead and wounded to number in the hundreds rather than in the thousands as was the case in the Civil War and later American wars. Before it was common for soldiers to wear identification, many of the fallen remained unknown. This was the case in the Revolution. After years of research, Clarence Stewart Peterson compiled a list of *Known Military Dead During the American Revolutionary War 1775–1783*. Stewart includes the names of those Americans killed in action or who died while in service. For those named in the book, Stewart includes rank, whether or not the soldier was killed or died of other unspecified causes and the date and place of death if known. His study is not, however, comprehensive.

Most of the men who served in the Revolution survived the war. Many followed the western movement of emigrants living to old age in a state far from their starting point. A special project of the DAR has been the marking of the graves of known Revolutionary War veterans and patriots. Many chapters have reported grave marking ceremonies in *The DAR Magazine* throughout the twentieth century. The Office of the Historian General maintains card files on reported located and marked graves. See Chapter 7 for further information.

One outgrowth of this activity is the large number of cemetery books and transcripts in the Library from DAR chapters around the country. In most cases several volumes have been issued for a state over a number of years such as *Graves of Revolutionary Soldiers in New Jersey* originally transcribed in 1926, *Revolutionary War Patriots Buried in New Jersey* and *Alphabetical Listing of Located Graves in New Jersey of Revolutionary War Patriots*. Most of these volumes are unique typescripts, but some such as *Roster of Soldiers and Patriots of the American Revolution Buried in Indiana* were commercially published and bound. The amount of information contained in each volume varies. *Graves of Revolutionary Soldiers, Located and Marked by the Peoria Chapter, NSDAR* contains photos of headstones, abstracts from pension applications and newspaper articles. *The Golden Book: Revolutionary Soldiers' Graves Pennsylvania* lists only the name, dates, location of cemetery and occasionally the veteran's regiment.

Researchers must be aware, however, that there are errors in these indices and publications. Use these sources for clues. Do not accept information in print without additional proof.

13.20.4.20
Lineage Societies

A number of lineage societies have been formed in the United States based on ancestral service in the Revolution. The DAR is the largest lineage society based on descent from a participant in the American Revolution. In addition to the *DAR Patriot Index*, the Library has a variety of state and national rosters for these societies. The rosters in the DAR Library include those of the National Society of the Sons of the American Revolution, the Society of the Cincinnati and the Sons of the Revolution. Information on Revolutionary War service may also be found in the *Order of Washington Lineage Book* and in the application papers of the Order of

Lafayette (1917–1930) bound in book form. See section 13.18 for additional information on these groups.

13.20.4.21
DAR Rosters

Many state sections contain Revolutionary War rosters compiled by the DAR. Although a variety of information appears in these rosters, the changing nature of historical study and the number of individuals and styles involved in compiling these volumes, the researcher should not accept the evidence in total without first verifying the information from other sources. There are many unverified and erroneous listings in these books, and the staff genealogists do not accept them as proof of Revolutionary War service.

One of the largest such rosters is *Histories of Revolutionary Soldiers*, a set of over forty volumes compiled and transcribed by various chapters of the Georgia DAR from 1967 to 1987. The Georgia *Histories* lists the soldiers and patriots in alphabetical order within each volume, describes service, indicates where the individual is buried and lists family members. Every entry in the book includes a list of sources for the information. An index is available for the Georgia series. *Roster of Revolutionary Soldiers and Patriots in Alabama* compiled by Louise Milam Julich for the Alabama DAR follows an arrangement identical to that of the Georgia *Histories*.

The Rachel Caldwell Chapter of the DAR in Greensboro, North Carolina produced ten volumes of *Biographical Sketches of Soldiers and Patriots in the Battle of Guilford Courthouse, March 15, 1781* (1958–1971). Each entry includes service information and genealogical information if any was available. There is no comprehensive index for the set, but each volume is indexed separately and all the books are arranged alphabetically by the surname of the soldier or patriot. A state–wide *Roster of Soldiers from North Carolina in the American Revolution* was published by the North Carolina DAR in 1932. *The Official Roster of the Soldiers of the American Revolution Who Lived in the State of Ohio* published by the Ohio DAR uses a "*Who's Who*" style entry with a heavy use of abbreviations. The information in the three volumes of Ohio rosters is derived from a variety of sources; not all of these sources are verifiable. All of these DAR rosters and others are located in the state sections of the DAR Library.

THE WAR OF 1812

For researchers interested in a general history of the War of 1812, the Library has a number of books available. These range from Lossing's classic *The Pictorial Field–Book of the War of 1812* (1868) to Cobbert's rare *The Late War Between Great Britain and the United States* (1815). More recent works on the war include Hickey's *The War of 1812: A Forgotten Conflict* and Stagg's *Mr. Madison's War*. Works on specific battles are found throughout the collection including Lord's *The Dawn's Early Light* on the 1814 Washington/Baltimore campaign and Whitehorne's *While Washington Burned: The Battle for Fort Erie*. Books on the Battle of New Orleans such as Albright's *New Orleans: The Battle of the Bayous* and Arthur's *The Story of the Battle of New Orleans* are found in the Louisiana section. Also in the state sections are works on the contributions of individual states during the war such as Quisenberry's *Kentucky in the War of 1812*. Among these general histories is coverage on the early invasion of Canada by the United States, an event often forgotten or ignored by American texts. Not surprisingly, the Canadians have not forgotten American incursion onto their soil and have published a number of books on the conflict including Zaslow's *The Defended Border: Upper Canada and the War of 1812*, Berton's *The Invasion of Canada* and *Flames Across the Border* and Gray's *Soldiers of the King: Upper Canadian Militia, 1812-1815*.

When President Madison asked for a declaration of war, the United States had only a small standing army. As it did during the Revolution, the government turned to the state militias to supplement and support the national army. Despite early opposition to the war in some parts of the country, every state responded to the call. The names of these volunteers are preserved in both official state publications and commercially published rosters. Muster rolls for the War of 1812 available in the Library include *Pennsylvania Archives; the Delaware Archives, Military; Roster of Soldiers in the War of 1812–14* [Vermont]; *Roster of Ohio Soldiers in the War of 1812;* and *Muster Rolls of the Soldiers of the War of 1812 Detached from the Militia of North Carolina in 1812 and 1814*. All of these state publications are useful in determining the regiment and rank of individual soldiers and some such as the Vermont roster include additional details on individual service, but these books do not include genealogical information.

The naval side to the War of 1812 is well represented by general works such as *War on the Great Lakes* and Shomette's *Flotilla: Battle for the Patuxent*. As was the case during the Revolution, licensed privateers preyed on British merchantmen or engaged British ships of war. Some of these privateers are identified in Cranwell and Crane's *Men of Marque: A History of Private Armed Vessels Out of Baltimore*

British troops burning books in the Library of Congress

During the War of 1812, Eastman's *Some Famous Privateers of New England* and Murphy's *Letters of Marque and British Aliens in the U.S. During the War of 1812* from official records. Compiled naval correspondence, reports and other official documents can be found in *The Naval War of 1812: A Documentary History,* which includes a name index for located individuals in the Navy. *Deep Water Sailors, Shallow Water Soldiers* identifies sailors, marines and soldiers who participated in the Lake Erie campaign. Brief biographical entries for soldiers and marines drawn primarily from pension records are included in an appendix. Dixon and Eberly's *Index to Seamen's Protection Certificate Applications: Port of Philadelphia 1796–1823* identifies mariners from the War of 1812 period. The information on each applicant includes name, age, ethnic group, and state or country of birth.

Like the soldiers and sailors of the Revolution, veterans of the War of 1812 were eligible for pensions and bounty land grants. Veterans' and widows application files are housed at the National Archives and available for research on microfilm. The names of both veterans and widows appear in the government publication *List of Pensioners on the Roll January 1, 1883* and White's *Index to Old Wars Pension Files 1815–1926.* Researchers are more likely to find widows in the *List of Pensioners* than veterans, because the list was published nearly seventy years after the end of the war. The *List of Pensioners* does not have an index and the arrangement is by state, then county, then by individuals listed in no particular order. White includes pensions from a much longer period of time and arranges the names in alphabetical order.

Abstracts for these pension applications appear in several different forms throughout the Library collection and contain much useful information for the genealogist. White's *Index to War of 1812 Pension Files* contains very brief entries that can include the name of the veteran, his regiment, place of residence and his wife's name. Longer abstracts appear in *Major Index to Pension List of the War of 1812* and Baer's *War of 1812 Bounty Lands and Pension Applications.* Entries in the latter work, a typed manuscript, run a page in length or more. State–specific works based on pension and bounty land lists in the collection include Gandrud's multivolume *Alabama Soldiers, Revolution, War of 1812, and Indian Wars,* Walker's *Illinois Pensioners List of the Revolution, 1812 & Indian Wars,* Wright's *Maryland Militia War of 1812* and Lontz's *Pennsylvania War of 1812 Pensioners.*

American battlefield casualties in this conflict were relatively light in comparison with later wars. Peterson's list of *Known Military Dead During the War of 1812* includes deaths in battle and by other causes. The names are arranged in alphabetical order and includes rank, regiment and date of death. Most of the soldiers survived the war and died of natural causes. The known burial sites of 1812 veterans can be found in several books throughout the collection including *An Index of Veterans of Connecticut During the Years 1812, 1813, 1814, 1815, 1816* and *Index to the Grave Records of Servicemen of the War of 1812 State of Ohio,* both compiled by the National Society of the United States Daughters of War of 1812.

The *1812 Ancestor Index* of the National Society of the United States Daughters of 1812 is available in two volumes in the Library. This index lists the names of the individuals recognized by the society as having served in some capacity during the War of 1812. Names are alphabetical and entries include rank and state, birth and death dates, and spouses and children. Additional lineage information on 1812 veterans can be found in volumes 13–39 of the applications of the General Society of the War of 1812. Microfilm copies of these applications are in the Seimes Technology Center. Indices to members and ancestors are found at the front of the reels.

13.20.6
THE MEXICAN WAR

Although it is now largely a forgotten conflict, the Mexican War had important consequences for the United States. In the Treaty of Guadalupe–Hidalgo that ended the war, Mexico ceded to the United States what became the states of New Mexico, Arizona, California, Nevada and Utah. It was the first foreign war of the United States to the extent that all of the battles were waged on Mexican soil. The DAR Library has several excellent histories of the Mexican War including Bauer's *The Mexican War 1846–1848*, Hamry's *The Story of the Mexican War,* Eisenhower's *So Far from God* and one of the first accounts of the war *A Complete History of the Mexican War 1846–1848* (1849) by Nathan Covington Brooks.

On the American side the Mexican War was fought by a combination of United States Army regulars and volunteer units from the states, particularly from the South. *North Carolina in the Mexican War 1846–1848* recounts that state's involvement in the war until the departure of North Carolina troops from Mexico in 1848. South Carolina sent the Palmetto Regiment to Mexico where it served with distinction from the landing at Vera Cruz to the assault on Mexico City. *South Carolina in the Mexican War* tells the story of the Palmetto Regiment and includes a roster and some photographs of its members. The *Military History of Mississippi 1803–1898* includes a section on the Mexican War with lists of casualties. In *Maryland and District of Columbia Volunteers in the Mexican War*, Charles J. Wells lists all of the soldiers in alphabetical order with rank, date of enlistment, age at time of enlistment and any remarks from the soldier's record. A separate section shows the muster rolls for the Baltimore and District of Columbia Battalion and the Maryland and District of Columbia Regiment. *Official Roster of the Soldiers of the State of Ohio in the War With Mexico, 1846–1848* offers a brief history for each Ohio regiment in the war, with a company–by–company roster of each regiment. The rosters include the name of each soldier, his age, rank, period of enlistment and remarks on his service.

MAP
TO ILLUSTRATE THE
MEXICAN WAR.

In order to pursue the war, the United States was forced to wage campaigns on three fronts: Mexico, California and New Mexico. These were alien landscapes to most of the American soldiers with a largely unfriendly climate. Supplies for the army were poor and disease a constant companion. *Army of Manifest Destiny* tells the story of this force and its hardships interspersing the narrative with first person accounts by the soldiers. The experiences of the army in California were recorded in letters by Napoleon Jackson Tecumseh Dana, a lieutenant with the U.S. Army. Dana's letters are compiled and transcribed in *Monterey Is Ours! The Mexican War Letters of Lt. Dana*. Graphically illustrating the American experience in the war is *Eyewitness to War: Prints and Daguerreotypes of the Mexican War, 1846–1848* which contains the first photographs of American soldiers on campaign and contemporary prints of the battles. The names of at least some of these soldiers are preserved in *Index to the Dispatches and to the Names of United States Soldiers Who Fought in the Final Battles of the Mexican War* compiled by Mary Emily Smith Witt. Through a careful reading of military correspondence, Witt produced a list of both enlisted men and officers who served during the assault on Mexico City. Abstracts of the dispatches are included as well.

When the shooting stopped, the ordeal was not over for many American troops. In California and New Mexico, especially around Santa Fe, a United States occupation force was necessary. The native Mexican citizens of these territories did not welcome the Americans. It was many years before tensions eased and the native New Mexicans and Californians accepted the American presence. The story of the first days of American occupation in New Mexico is told by *Seeds of Discord* and *Turmoil in New Mexico,* and in California by *California Conquered* and *General M.G. Vallejo and the Advent of the Americans.*

Many of the soldiers who survived the war and the peace later received a pension from the federal government. From 1886 to 1926 the government accepted pension applications from Mexican War veterans and their widows. These applications are indexed by Wolfe's *Mexican War Pension Applications*, Troxel and Warner's multivolume set *Mexican War Index to Pension Files 1886–1926*, and White's *Index to Mexican War Pension Files*. Each of these works differs slightly from the others in terms of arrangement and information. White's compilation includes the soldier's name, pension number, date of application and regiment of service. Troxel and Warner include the same information as White, but add the soldier's date of death or dates during which the soldier or widow received a pension, if known. Wolfe's transcription does not include the rank or regiment of the soldier.

The memory of the soldiers is kept alive by the lineage society Descendants of Mexican War Veterans. A roster of members and their ancestors is located in the Library. The ancestor list is arranged alphabetically by surname, and includes the rank and regiment for each man.

13.20.7
THE CIVIL WAR

Most libraries have a number of books on the American Civil War consisting largely of biographies and battle histories. These books concentrate on the broad canvas of the war, and the dominating personalities who made policy and planned the strategy. In such studies, the common soldier, if mentioned by name at all, serves only to provide color to the narrative, to describe their feelings in battle, on campaign or in camp. For the genealogical researcher, such works provide the background, but not the detail of what the war did to a family. At the DAR Library the emphasis is on how the Civil War affected the community, the family and the individual.

Over three million men served in the armies of the Confederacy and the Union during the Civil War. Each one of these men left behind some record of service. The basic problem for the genealogist is pairing the name of an individual with a military unit. Until recently, this was something of a daunting task. While a researcher may know the state where an ancestor lived before the war, this information does not translate easily into proof of service during the war. For this proof one must turn to published regimental rosters.

Not long after the smoke cleared from the battlefields, the United States War Department produced the *Official Army Register of the Volunteer Force of the United States Army*. While useful, this set is not quite the genealogical bonanza suggested by the title, for the text lists only officers. Except for the U.S. Colored Infantry regiments and specialized units such as the U.S. Sharpshooters and the Veteran and Reserve units, regular U.S. Army officers are not included in the list. Arrangement in the books is by state, then by regimental number. Because the set has a name index, the researcher does not need to know a regimental number to find an individual soldier. Information on each man in the *Official Army Register* includes date of rank and whether or not the officer was promoted, discharged or killed in action. Naturally, the *Register* contains information only on Union officers. For similar information on Confederate soldiers, one must consult the state sections of the Library.

13.20.7.1
General History

One of the primary sources on the war is *War of the Rebellion: Official Records of the Union and Confederate Armies,* originally in book form and now on CD-ROM. In the aftermath of the Civil War, the United States War Department collected and compiled the official papers of both the Union and the Confederacy. Wars generate records and the Civil War is no exception. The Civil War armies routinely used reams of paper to issue orders, send messages and describe troop movements. Commanders on every level wrote post–battle reports indicating the contributions of individuals and the accomplishments or failures of divisions, brigades and regiments. These records comprise the 128 volumes of the *Official Records*. The Library owns a copy of this set and the index.

For studies of the major battles of the Civil War turn to the state sections of the DAR Library. Several accounts of the Battle of Gettysburg are in the Pennsylvania section. Researchers interested in the Shiloh campaign or the battle for Chattanooga will find these studies in the Tennessee section. Similarly, overall accounts of how a state fared during the war are in the state sections such as William R. Trotter's three volume study *North Carolina in the Civil War*. Burton's *The Siege of Charleston 1861–1865*, Morris and Foutz's *Lynchburg in the Civil War* and similar works on specific cities or counties are located in the state sections with other books on the counties.

13.20.7.2
Research Guides

While researchers will find considerably more material available at the DAR Library than they might have expected, the collection is limited to published sources. There are several guides, however, to the larger repositories of Civil War records. The National Archives and Records Administration is custodian for the records of the Union and most of the national records for the Confederacy. Henry Putney Beers' *The Confederacy: A Guide to the Archives of the Government of the Confederate States of American* and a companion volume *The Union: A Guide to Federal Archives Relating to the Civil War* by Beers and Kenneth W. Munden describe the National Archives collection of Civil War documents. The records of service for individual soldiers are available on microfilm at the National Archives. A description and index of these records is provided by *Military Service Records: A Select Catalog of National Archives Microfilm Publications.* The Library of Congress owns a number of Civil War papers and related material, which are cataloged in *Civil War Manuscripts: A Guide to Collections in the Manuscript Division of the Library of Congress.* These and other guides are found in the Library.

It is one thing to know where a source is located, it is quite another to know how to use that source effectively. Neagles' *U.S. Military Records* describes what records are available to researchers at the federal and local level for American soldiers from 1776 to the present and how to access these records. Other works in the DAR Library concentrate solely on using Civil War materials from general overviews to narrower ones. Two basic guides, Schweitzer's *Civil War Genealogy* and Groene's *Tracing Your Civil War Ancestor* are available. In addition, one finds *Confederate Research Sources*, an earlier work by Neagles, and Secret's *Guide to Tracing Your African Ameripean* [sic] *Civil War Ancestor*, both designed for specific research audiences. Those researchers interested in tracing a Civil War ancestor may also wish to consult the selected publications the Library has available from the United Daughters of the Confederacy.

Even for the DAR Library, the study of genealogy does not begin and end with the American Revolution. More books have been published on the American Civil War than on any other war in the nation's history. The official records left behind are more complete than any of the previous American wars. Because so many men saw duty, the Civil War is boon to genealogists. The DAR Library's collection on the Civil War is designed to help the researcher find their ancestor among the three million men who served, and to offer some picture of what life was like for the common soldier.

13.20.7.3
State and National Rosters

To recognize the contributions of their citizens to the war, a number of state governments, North and South, published rosters of the veterans. Some of these books, such as *Roster and Record of Iowa Soldiers in the War of the Rebellion*, were printed within the lifetime of many veterans while others like *North Carolina Troops, 1861–1865, A Roster* were completed recently or are pending completion. The Library also owns many other rosters including those of Pennsylvania and Michigan. These lists are invaluable to the researcher, but the organization and content of the rosters vary considerably. The most common arrangement is by regiment, then by company and within the company alphabetically by surname as in *Rosters of the Confederate Soldiers of Georgia, 1861–1865*. Of the state rosters *Tennesseans in the Civil War* and *Records of Louisiana Confederate Soldiers and Commands*, use a purely alphabetical scheme listing all the soldiers by name followed by unit designation, as does Hartzler's *Marylanders in the Confederacy*. Following the lead of the *Official Army Register, New York in the War of the Rebellion 1861–1865* and *The Official and Statistical Register of the State of Mississippi* include only the names of officers from the company level up. Many of the omissions and idiosyncrasies of the state rosters are corrected by *The Roster of Confederate Soldiers 1861–1865* and *The Roster of Union Soldiers 1861–1865*. These multivolume sets list in alphabetical order all of the soldiers for whom the National Archives has a service record. Both of these sets are located in the Library.

13.20.7.4
Regimental Histories

Because not all state histories include specific information on individuals, the researcher should turn to regimental histories for details from service records. Most recent regimental histories use these service records as a starting point. Unlike the state rosters, the regimental histories are more detailed, dedicating an entire book to the history of one regiment. One of the best examples of this genre is the *Virginia Regimental History Series*. Each of the eighty volumes in the series contains a complete roster of the regiment, abstracts of individual service records and a narrative of all the important actions of the regiment. The Library also owns individual regimental histories written by veterans such as Kirk's *History of the Fifteenth Pennsylvania Volunteer Cavalry* (1906) or more recent studies like Nikazy's *Forgotten Soldiers: History of the 4th Tennessee Volunteer Infantry Regiment (USA) 1863–1865* (1995). These and other regimental histories are in the state sections of the Library and *Ohio Civil War Regimental Histories and Reunions* is available in the Seimes Microfilm Center.

13.20.7.5
Veterans' Memoirs

Beyond the information found in secondary sources and that compiled by the federal and state governments, are the personal experiences of the soldiers themselves. Proud of their accomplishments, Union and Confederate veterans published their own accounts of the war. In the DAR Library, one finds a variety of memoirs spanning the spectrum of the Civil War experience. Some of these memoirs have been in print for over one hundred years, while others were published only recently. Reed's *Hardtack and Coffee* (1887) and *The Civil War Reminiscences of Major Silas T. Grisamore, C.S.A.*, originally printed from 1867 to 1871, were written and published during the lifetime of the authors. Private David Holt's *A Mississippi Rebel in the Army of Northern Virginia*, on the other hand, was edited and published long after Holt's death.

Confederate veterans in general were far from reluctant to reminisce and refight the war in print. Two journals of the late nineteenth century, the *Confederate Veteran* and the *Southern Historical Society Papers*, provided retired Confederates with a forum to air their views. Although obviously partisan, both periodicals contain a number of interesting war accounts as well as reprints of official Confederate records. As the publication of the United Confederate Veterans Association, the *Confederate Veteran* regularly featured articles on individual veterans, living and dead, and published a great number of obituaries for its membership.

13.20.7.6
Diaries and Letters

From general to private, Civil War literature is rich with diaries and letters. Both North and South sent a large number of literate men to the war, men who recorded their thoughts for their families and for the future. Quite a few diaries and letter collections have been published commercially, particularly in recent years. The library has a number of these including *All for the Union: The Civil War Diary and Letters of Elisha Hunt Rhodes* edited by Robert Hunt Rhodes and *The Diary of John K. Benefiel for the Year 1864: A Civil War Soldier, 46th Reg. Indiana Volunteers*. In addition, under the auspices of the DAR's G.R.C. several members have compiled letters and diaries written by Civil War ancestors such as *Copy of a Diary Written Through the Civil War* by Capt. James Gibson copied by Mrs. Meta Russell for the Alamo Chapter, DAR; *The Civil War Journal of J.C. Wandling, Washington, N.J.* compiled by Alma Jackson Chambers and Esther W. Berner for the Jemima Cundict Chapter, DAR and *Civil War Diary of Peter F. Smith* compiled by Shirley Garmon for the General Robert Irwin Chapter, North Carolina DAR. These diaries and letters are located throughout the collection.

While it is unlikely the average researcher will come to the Library and find his or her ancestor's letters or diaries neatly compiled and waiting on the shelf, these thoughts recorded over a century ago are useful even if one's ancestor does not pen them. Diaries and letters often mention the names of other individuals in the regiment. Moreover, these letters and journals chronicle the day–to–day existence of the soldier. Pieces of information take an ancestor from being a grim two-dimensional figure staring from a faded photograph, to a living, breathing being.

13.20.7.7
Pension Lists and the 1890 Union Veterans' Census

On the instructions of the United States Senate, the Pension Bureau published a five-volume list of all living pensioners in 1883. Although not identified as such, a large number of those listed were Union veterans; some were from earlier conflicts. The federal government, of course, did not pension Confederate veterans. The arrangement of the list is by state, county and town. Pensioners living abroad are included in volume 5 of the set. Names are not arranged in any particular fashion within the town and addenda of additional names are inserted at will. The lack of organization is due in large part to the Senate's insistence to have the list produced in less than one month. Despite its flaws, *The List of Pensioners on the Roll, January 1, 1883* contains a great deal of useful information. Each entry includes the pension number, the name of the pensioner, the reason for the pension, the amount of the pension, the date the pension was granted and where the pensioner was living at the time.

Less than seven years after the publication of the 1883 list, a special census enumerated Union veterans and widows of veterans. Had it remained intact, this census would have been an excellent resource for genealogists. Unfortunately, most of the schedules for Alabama through Kansas and the District of Columbia are missing. The Library has the existing census on microfilm with indices on microfiche for Kentucky through Wyoming. In addition, the Library has several published volumes of these censuses both by states such as the *1890 Civil War Veterans Census: Tennessee* and the *Missouri 1890 Special Federal Census of Union Veterans and Widows of Veterans of the Civil War* and by locality including *1890 Laurel County Kentucky Special Federal Census* and *1890 Yancey Co., NC Veteran's Census*.

The purpose of the 1890 veteran's census was to identify potential pensioners from the Union army. Consequently, the census takers excluded Confederate veterans, although the West

Virginia schedules of this special census include former soldiers from both sides with the Confederate veterans crossed out.

The states of the former Confederacy offered pensions to their own aging veterans. The Library owns the indices to many of these state pension applications including *Tennessee Confederate Widows and Their Families, Mississippi Confederate Pension Applications* and *Register of Florida CSA Pension Applications*. Information contained in these indices varies from book to book, but all include the name of the pensioner, the regiment of service, the date of application and the home county of the applicant. Copies of a number of Virginia's printed pension lists for veterans and their widows in the early twentieth century are in the Library's collection.

13.20.7.8
Burial Records

After the war many veterans returned to the town of their birth to live out the rest of their days. Others moved in all directions of the compass, finding their final resting place hundreds of miles from where they were born. The DAR Library has a number of cemetery listings for Civil War veterans. For the most part, these listings are located in the county sections of the collection such as *839 Confederate Soldiers Buried in Clay, Cleborne and Randolph Counties, Ala.*, although the Florida section boasts a statewide directory of deceased veterans. Union war dead and place of interment are listed in *The Roll of Honor*, a publication of the United States Army Quartermaster Corps. *The Roll of Honor* has a name index. See also section 13.4.

13.20.7.9
County Histories

The period between the end of the Civil War and the turn of the century saw a boom in the publication of county histories, most of which are in the Library. Because nearly every county sent some men off to fight, the Civil War was an important part of these histories. When these men went as a regiment, the names of every man in the regiment were recorded in the county history. Individual entries often include a brief description of service and on occasion, some biographical information. *The History of Essex County, New Jersey*, (1884), examines the county's service during the war, describes the service of each regiment from the county and lists by name all ranks in the regiment. If the author of the history was a veteran however, considerably more information is available. Writing in 1913, Union veteran W. L. Curry devoted three–quarters of *History of Jerome Township, Union County, Ohio to the Civil War*, including photos of veterans, regimental rosters and histories and full individual service records. A number of more recent publications by local historians concentrate exclusively on the Civil War at the county level. *For Home and Honor* offers the service records of Madison County, Virginia veterans and describes how the county was affected by the war. As the title suggests, *Civil War Veterans of Athens County, Ohio: Biographical Sketches* includes biographical and genealogical information in addition to war experiences. These and similar histories are in the Library's state sections.

13.20.8
THE INDIAN WARS

From the formation of the Republic until 1890 the United States was almost constantly at war with one Native American tribe or another. A selection of studies on the individual wars and the tribes involved is available in the American Indian Collection. For more information on the soldiers involved, researchers should consult the abstracts of pension reports in the Library including *Index to Volunteer Soldiers 1784–1811, Index to Volunteer Soldiers in Indian Wars and Disturbances, 1815–1858, Index to Old Wars Pension Files 1815–1926* and *Index to Indian Wars Pension Files, 1892–1926*. State militia took an active role in the wars prior to 1861. Information on these soldiers is available in the state section in sources such as *Alabama Soldiers: Revolution, War of 1812, and Indian Wars; Abstracts of Pensions, Soldiers of the Revolution, 1812 & Indian Wars Who Settled on the Kentucky Side of the Ohio River;* and *The Battle of Tippecanoe*. A recently published three volume set *Eyewitnesses to the Indian Wars, 1865-1890* edited by Peter Cozzens contains a number of useful and interesting first person accounts of the Indian Wars.

13.20.9
THE SPANISH AMERICAN WAR

America's "splendid little war" with Spain in 1898 was the first major conflict following the organization of the DAR in 1890. Naturally, the young, patriotic group supported the war effort against the aging Spanish Empire. The National Society's enthusiasm for the war is reflected in surviving publications from the period. One DAR activity, in particular, produced materials of potential genealogical value.

The DAR established a "Hospital Corps," and certified and sent out nearly 1,000 nurses for the United States Army. The DAR's first Librarian General and first Surgeon General, Dr. Anita Newcomb McGee, was very instrumental in this effort. For researchers with a Spanish American War nurse in their family "List of United States Army Nurses Appointed on Recommendation of the Daughters of the American Revolution Hospital Corps," *American Monthly Magazine* v. 15 (September 1899), 360–422, will be of interest. A roster of women nurses enlisted for the war by the DAR Hospital Corps also appears in the *DAR Report to the Secretary of the Smithsonian Institution*, v.2, 1897-1898 (1900). The Historian General's Office has some additional material on the DAR's participation in support of this war effort, including a rearranged list of the nurses in the above article sorted by state. Subsequent to the war many of the nurses were involved in the Spanish–American War Nurses Association.

Researchers at DAR will also find the occasional book listing the participants from a particular state in the Spanish American War. Examples of these include Riley's *Roster of the Soldiers and Sailors Who Served in Organizations from Maryland during the Spanish–American War* and

The Official Roster of Ohio Soldiers in the War with Spain 1898–1899. Some county histories also contain rosters of local soldiers in this conflict.

13.20.10
WORLD WAR I

Genealogically, not much has been published on World War I, although Schaefer's *The Great War: A Guide to the Service Records of All the World's Fighting Men and Volunteers* (1998) is a good place to start. The DAR Library does not own a collection of general histories of this war. There are, however, a number of sources available at DAR of interest to those researching ancestors involved in "The Great War," some of which are unique.

Scattered throughout the Library collection, one will encounter various state or local rosters and histories describing the activities of that state or locality during the war. Some examples include Fraser's *Roster of Men and Women Who Served in the Army or Naval Service of the United States or Its Allies from the State of North Dakota*, Davis's *Virginians of Distinguished Service in the World War*, and *Indiana World War Records: Gold Star Honor Roll, 1914–1918*. These and others provide some coverage for the first major war of the twentieth century. Researchers will find rosters of local soldiers and sailors in some county histories. If the Library does not own such studies or listings for a particular state or locality, researchers will likely find works like those mentioned above in other libraries.

Ashley K. Nuckols' *Deaths: American Expeditionary Force, 1917, 1918* is a good beginning source on World War I service. This is a multivolume set arranged by state, that provides listings of individual soldiers, and some copies of photographs of those who died during the war. Each volume is indexed. A recently published guide *Uncle, We are Ready : Registering America's Men, 1917-1918* explores the records generated by the draft and the information contained therein.

The DAR's stated purpose to promote patriotic endeavor naturally resulted in involvement of DAR members in the country's war efforts. World War I was the second war in which the United States participated after the DAR's founding in 1890. Support for the war effort by DAR members took many forms, and one project in particular resulted in materials of genealogical significance.

AU COMITE D. ....
DES
"FATHERLESS·CHILDREN·OF·FRANCE·INC."
LA FRANCE RECONNAISSANTE

Certificate sent by the French Government, and signed by the President of France, to show that country's gratitude to the National Society Daughters of the American Revolution, for adopting over 5,000 French war orphans. The certificate was received by the Treasurer General, NSDAR, through the Headquarters of the Fatherless Children of France.

Towards the end of the war and in the years immediately following it, the DAR urged its members to complete four–page, printed forms detailing the lives and service of men and women in their families who were in the military during the conflict. Some submissions are from DAR members, who were themselves involved. The result of this effort to preserve historical information and to honor war participants was a collection of 117 volumes of *War Service*

Records for World War I. The set is divided into state volumes. Within each state's volumes, the forms are arranged in alphabetical order **by the submitting DAR chapters**. Then the forms themselves are in alphabetical order by the names of the subject of each brief report. Among the information requested (not all forms are filled in completely) are name, date of birth, place of birth, relationship of the submitter to the subject of the report, marriage, names of parents, names of children, education, fraternal orders, military service, and discharge information. Some of the submissions include excellent photographs of the subjects.

The *War Service Records* are in the custody of the Office of the Historian General. Depending on the condition of the paper and photographs, one may be able to obtain photocopies from these registers. Researchers interested in knowing of the availability of a volume for their state of interest and particulars relating to their use should contact the Archivist, Office of the Historian General **prior to making a visit**.

The collected questionnaires are not indexed, and they are by no means a complete listing of either all American participants in World War I or of all the relatives of DAR members who served. They do, however, illustrate the type of work the DAR has often performed. They are an interesting and unknown collection of information that DAR members gathered for posterity. Until a few years ago, the staff was unaware of their existence, until a locked storage cabinet needed relocation in the Library's storage area. The key emerged after some searching, and the contents revealed. The Library transferred the collection to the Historian General for preservation and safekeeping. A similar set of completed questionnaires for World War II already in the latter office's custody provided an excellent complement.

13.20.11
WORLD WAR II

The literature on World War II is enormous and is readily available in libraries nationwide. The DAR Library does not collect general studies on this war. There are various publications, however, similar to those for World War I mentioned previously, which detail the activities and military participants from states and localities during the conflict. Examples of these are Lutz's *Richmond in World War II*, Parlier's *Pursuits of War: The People of Charlottesville and Albemarle County, Virginia in the Second World War*, and Lindvahl's study for Effingham County, Illinois, *They Served With Honor*. Some recent county histories include sections on their military personnel who participated in World War II.

> We wish we had the space to give you the detailed information from the reports of the state librarians. They show contributions from states of many thousands of books and magazines to U.S.O. centers, Army and Navy hospitals and military camps, as well as many books sent to our approved schools and to local libraries. All states have sent books to their adopted ships. Delaware sent a victrola to their adopted ship.
>
> Mabel J. Smith, Librarian General, In her April 1945 Board Report in *National Historical Magazine*, June 1945, p. 407.

As it had during the First World War, the DAR developed a project asking members to complete printed forms detailing the basic biographical and service information of their relatives involved in the war effort. The result of this attempt to preserve historical information was a collection of ninety–four volumes of questionnaires, generally labeled *World War II Honor Roll* or *World War II War Service Records*. These are arranged by state, then by donating chapter, and then alphabetically by subject. Unlike their World War I predecessors, these questionnaires are one page long and contain much less information. Few photographs appear. The collection does not appear to be complete and several states are not represented. The Office of the Historian General maintains this set and the same conditions for use apply to it as with the World War I *War Service Records*. Similarly, not all members completed submissions for their relatives, and there is no index. In 2000, the DAR published a multivolume set entitled *World War II Book of Remembrance*. This set is a list of individuals who served in the war and were honored by individual members of the DAR for their service. In addition to the name, each entry includes where the honoree lived, their branch of service, and in many cases their rank. There is also an increasing body of literature on how local communities were affected by the war such as *The Pursuits of War: the People of Charlottesville and Albemarle County... in the Second World War* by Gertrude Dana Parlier and others, and *Alamance : a county at war* by Don Bolden.

13.20.12
THE KOREAN WAR AND THE VIETNAM WAR

While histories of these conflicts are increasing in number, the DAR Library does not collect general military histories for them. An occasional county history will include a roster of local participants, and some cemetery transcriptions list burials of Korean War and Vietnam War military personnel such as *Van Wert County, Ohio Veteran's Memorial* by Helen L. White Prill which includes veterans from every conflict or *Register of Vietnam War Casualties from Kentucky* edited by Julia D. Rather and Jeffrey Michael Duff which focuses specifically on the Vietnam War.

13.21
NAMES

Names are, of course, crucial to genealogical inquiry. The recently published three volume *Dictionary of American Family Names* edited by Patrick Hanks examines the most common surnames in the United States and gives the country of origin for the family name. Patrons using this source will discover the name Macon is French in origin, while the origins of Leatherbury are in Lancashire, England and the Gleason name is from Munster in Ireland. In all, the work examines over 70,000 surnames tracing their origin, their meaning, and for many entries, gives the most commonly associated first names. The Library houses a number of additional books on given names, surname origins, nicknames, occupational names, naming patterns, and general studies of the subject useful to genealogists. Many of these volumes examine names from specific national or ethnic groups such as *Swiss Surnames, a Complete Register* edited by Emil Meier or *Jewish Family Names and their Origins: an Etymological Dictionary* by Heinrich W. Guggenheimer and Eva H. Guggenheimer.

13.22
NATIVE AMERICAN RESEARCH

The DAR has long had an interest in Native Americans, and its American Indians Committee established in 1936 "provides financial assistance and educational aid to native American youth" through support of several schools and with a scholarship program. With this activity as background, the DAR Library established a special collection designed to assist with Native American research in 1987 using existing holdings and newly donated materials. It has continued to expand since its inception. Now numbering some 1,200 volumes, the American Indian Collection provides historical and genealogical information for first peoples across the United States.

While the focus of this collection is general history and culture, genealogical studies and guidebooks are becoming more numerous. Researchers will find histories of specific Native American nations, state studies, and materials on interactions with European settlers. There are five shelves concerning the Cherokee alone. In addition to the special collection itself, much information on Native Americans can be found throughout the collection under the states and their counties.

Many records maintained by the federal and state governments relating to Native Americans are now being published, republished, or indexed. The Library attempts to acquire these. Researchers in Washington will find much to consult on this subject at the National Archives, the Department of the Interior Library, and the Library of Congress. The DAR Library offers this general collection as a supplement to its outstanding materials on Americans of European descent.

Guides for Native American research include Byers' *Native American Genealogical Sourcebook,* Kavasch's *A Student's Guide to Native American Genealogy* and Gormley's *Cherokee Connections: An Introduction to Genealogical Sources Pertaining to Cherokee Ancestors.*

13.23
NEWSPAPERS

DAR does not maintain a newspaper collection per se. Certain genealogical compilations such as those containing query columns from *The Boston Transcript* (1924–1933 only) and *The Hartford Times* (1934–1964; also on microfiche) are available however. More commonly discovered in the stacks are compilations from local newspapers of vital and genealogically significant news. Obituary indices for newspapers as large as *The New York Times* and as small as *The Martinsburg Gazette* are among these publications. Announcements in religious newspapers covering entire states or regions are the subjects of frequent new publications. Directories showing what newspapers were published in specific towns and cities are also available. Microfilms of some colonial newspapers are available in the Seimes Technology Center.

13.24
PERIODICALS

Numbering nearly 1,200 subscriptions, state and local genealogical and historical periodicals are a significant portion of the Library's holdings. Some of the longer runs of these publications have been relocated to conserve shelf space, but they are available to researchers. Coverage tends to be strongest for the eastern states. Family newsletters and journals, both historical and current, are also owned and are located in the Family section. Many of the Library's periodical holdings are not available elsewhere in the Washington area.

Many genealogists tend to overlook the important work historians have published in national, state and local historical journals. Conversely, historians often overlook the contents of genealogical publications. Both groups would benefit from the use of each other's materials. For genealogists, historical journals contain background on many events in the past that had a direct bearing on the lives of our ancestors. Frequently, a historical article will shed light on the interpretation of court records or a military engagement. Such studies may be the only place one will find such clarification. Proper historical context is crucial to correct application of the sources used in genealogical study.

Indices to periodicals include *The Periodical Source Index, the Genealogical Periodical Annual Index,* and *the Combined Retrospective Index to Journals in History 1838–1974.* In addition, many journals have their own cumulative indices.

13.25
PRESIDENTS AND THEIR FAMILIES

The Library has a focused collection of books on the Presidency, the Presidents, and the First Ladies. Sources on their families, ancestors, and descendants are included along with biographies and some collected papers of individual Presidents. Major books include Brogan and Mosley's *Burke's American Presidential Families*, Quinn–Musgrove and Kanter's *America's Royalty: All the Presidents' Children*, and Roberts' *Ancestors of American Presidents*. Studies on the ancestors or descendants of specific Presidents are also available, such as McLean's *The English Ancestry of Thomas Jefferson*. Considerable published material on George Washington is in the Library's biography collection and in the Historical Research Library of the Office of the Historian General. The DAR Library is the repository for the documentation papers of the Presidential Families of America society. The papers and publications of the society are kept in the Library's office suite.

13.26
RELIGIOUS/CHURCH RECORDS AND HISTORIES

The Library maintains basic histories and guides to the records for many Christian denominations and Jewish congregations in the United States. Histories of specific churches and abstracts of many historic church records populate the shelves in the state sections in large numbers, however. Burials in churchyards and associated cemeteries appear in the many cemetery transcriptions throughout the collection. Some church records are available in the Historian General's Americana Collection and in microform.

13.27
STATE AND REGIONAL RESEARCH

State records and histories offer sources and background not available in federal and local materials. The quantity of records for the fifty states is staggering and most are not published. The Library owns many state records which are in book form, and the Seimes Technology Center houses major microfilmed state government sources. The emphasis there is to offer materials not available in other research centers in the Washington area.

County, town, and community histories constitute a large portion of the Library's state sections. Not only are most late nineteenth and early twentieth century "mug books" and subscription histories for counties across the country available, many more recent histories sparked by the Bicentennial, county and town anniversaries, and other historic events are as well. Recent county histories containing family sketches written by local residents are also plentiful.

The explosion in genealogical publishing in the past three decades centers in large part on record abstracts and transcriptions. These types of publications represent sources that the Library collects aggressively and nationwide. Marriages, deeds, wills, court minutes, tax lists, town minutes, militia lists, church records and cemetery transcriptions from Virginia to Oregon and Louisiana to Minnesota are collectively one of the Library's strengths. More arrive daily and are shelved shortly thereafter.

Copies of individual documents from these many sources are common types of documentation with DAR membership applications and are found in the Library's file collection. They will be portions of lineage proof and therefore in files under the names of Revolutionary War ancestors of DAR members.

When original deeds, wills, and similar items were found in these files, the staff photocopied them and placed the originals in the Americana Collection. This section within the Historian General's Office preserves many original pre–1860 documents mostly from donors and occasionally from transfers within the building. A card index to genealogical materials in the Americana Collection provides access to much of this information.

The following list highlights the major components of each state and regional section in the DAR Library and the Seimes Technology Center. These sections are not limited to the sources listed below, however. Selected State DAR bookplates also appear throughout this section.

Alabama

The Gandrud collection of county record abstracts provides the basis of Alabama materials, but many other abstracts are also available. Alabama has a 223 volume G.R.C. set. The *Internal Revenue Assessment Lists 1865–1866* are on microfilm. A very large collection of recent county histories updates our earlier holdings.

Alaska

A very small amount of material on the 49th State includes some interesting genealogical sources. Some materials on Russian America are located in "The West" section. The Alaska section has 23 G.R.C. volumes.

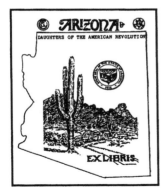

Arizona

Basic historical and genealogical sources are available. There are 74 G.R.C. volumes in the Arizona section.

Arkansas

Many county record abstracts, a 247-volume G.R.C. set with guide, and Allen's series of *Arkansas Land Patents* provide good sources. Original land grants tract books are available on microfilm.

California

A large number of county histories and record abstracts, the 1852 state census in typescript and microform, and a 432-volume G.R.C. set which includes the sub-series *Records of the Families of California Pioneers* highlight the California section. Nineteenth-century Los Angeles County marriages and birth, marriage and death abstracts from the *Sacramento Bee* (1857–1895) provide further coverage.

Colorado

County histories and record abstracts anchor the Colorado section, and a 195-volume G.R.C. set offers additional materials.

Connecticut

Many town histories and records compliment the Connecticut materials in microform. The latter include *The Charles R. Hale Collection of Cemetery Records, The Barbour Collection* (also in 55 published volumes), *The Hartford Times Genealogical Column Index*, and *Connecticut Revolutionary War Records from the Connecticut State Archives*. A 251 volume G.R.C. set includes much unique material.

Delaware

A good collection on a small state with includes 56 G.R.C. including 12 volumes of Bible records. Many early Delaware records are available on microfilm.

District of Columbia

With a G.R.C. set of over 700 volumes, which includes many abstracts of church and vital records along with extensive surveys of cemeteries in the District, the D.C. section is essential for researchers working on families in the Potomac Valley. The excellent publications of the Historical Society of Washington, D.C., the Columbian Harmony Society covering D.C. cemetery and other vital records, and most twentieth century D.C. city directories add valuable coverage to the basic historical sources for the Nation's Capital.

Florida

A growing county records collection coupled with 625 G.R.C. volumes provides good Florida coverage. The W.P.A.'s *Register of Deceased Veterans of Florida* and *Spanish Land Grants in Florida: Confirmed and Unconfirmed* offer helpful sources.

Georgia

A large collection of county histories and state and local record abstracts combined with an indexed, 819-volume G.R.C. set provide Georgia researchers with much material. Colonial and Revolutionary era records from the Georgia Archives in Atlanta are available on microfilm along with some county records.

Hawaii

Basic histories, some collected Hawaiian genealogies, 9 G.R.C. volumes and studies of early missionaries comprise the Hawaii section.

Idaho

A basic collection with some county record abstracts is available with 42 G.R.C. volumes.

Illinois

A large set of county histories and record abstracts provides the basis for a good Illinois collection. Illinois has a 706-volume G.R.C. set as well. In microform researchers will find *The*

Illinois County History Index, The Illinois Name Index to Early Records, Illinois Public Domain Land Sales, and *Illinois Marriage Record Index.*

Indiana
The Library has a very large Indiana collection. W.P.A. indices to vital records of Indiana counties are a major resource. Indiana has a 1,115 volume G.R.C. set.

Iowa
A good set of county histories and record abstracts coupled with a large number of publications from the Iowa Genealogical Society and a 259-volume G.R.C. set give substantial coverage for Iowa researchers.

Kansas
A basic collection of historical and genealogical materials, including the multivolume series *Forgotten Settlers of Kansas,* and 468 G.R.C. volumes, is available.

Kentucky
An ever–expanding collection of country record abstracts results in an excellent Kentucky section. Over 431 G.R.C. volumes complement this material. County tax lists prior to 1850 and early land records are on microfilm.

Louisiana
A detailed set of parish histories and record abstracts serves as the basis for significant materials on Louisiana. Hebert's *South West Louisiana Vital Records* and *South Louisiana Vital Records* are major sources, along with *The Diocese of Baton Rouge Catholic Church Records* and *Archdiocese of New Orleans Sacramental Records* sets. Studies on the German coast, and a G.R.C. set of over 323 volumes add further depth.

Maine
Many town record abstracts, a statewide index to marriages (1892–1966) on CD- ROM, and an indexed G.R.C. set of 422 volumes await Maine researchers. Massachusetts land grants in Maine after the Revolution are on microfilm.

Maryland
The Library has an excellent Maryland collection with extensive published county record abstracts, obscure local publications, and an indexed G.R.C. set of 276 volumes. In microform, researchers will find *Unpublished Maryland Revolutionary Records* by Margaret Hodges; historic Catholic Church records of the Diocese of Washington from the Georgetown University Archives; Anne Arundel County deeds, wills, and other sources; colonial county rent rolls; and Maryland Prerogative Court wills 1635-1714, v.1-13.

Massachusetts

One of the largest state collections at DAR, the Massachusetts section contains numerous town histories and record abstracts, some late nineteenth and early twentieth century town reports, published 1855 and 1865 state censuses for many towns, and a G.R.C. set of 502 volumes. The standard Revolutionary War source is *Massachusetts Soldiers and Sailors of the Revolutionary War*, and there is also a microfilm supplement. The *Corbin Collection*, the *Rollin H. Cooke Collection* (printed index), and the *1798 U.S. Direct Tax for Maine and Massachusetts* are on microfilm. On microfiche, the Holbrook Research Institute's collection of statewide vital records indices 1841–1895 and of early town records for many localities is a major resource, along with a collection of Boston city directories from 1789–1869. A microfilm version of the card index to the *Massachusetts Archives* series at the Massachusetts State Archives is a recent addition.

Michigan

County histories and record abstracts, including 53 volumes of Wayne County land transfers form the basis of the Michigan section. A card index to the 40 volume set *Michigan Pioneer and Historical Collections* is a useful finding aid not only for Michigan and Midwest research, but for New York as well. Michigan has a G.R.C. set of over 687 volumes. The 1894 state census is available on microfilm for those counties with surviving schedules.

Midwest Region

General histories and periodicals provide background information on the Midwest as a region and on the Old Northwest Territory in particular.

Minnesota

A good, basic selection of county histories and record abstracts and a 102-volume G.R.C. set constitute the Minnesota section.

Mississippi

A good selection of county histories and record abstracts is available along with a G.R.C. set of 177 volumes. *Mississippi Marriages* prior to 1926 (white) are on microfilm.

Missouri

The Missouri collection is one of the better ones for a Midwestern state. In addition to the many county histories and record abstracts, researchers will find extensive printed abstracts from newspapers of Springfield and Greene County from the 1880s to the 1990s (120 volumes) and 1,184 G.R.C. volumes. On 400 microfilm rolls is a statewide set of the major index books of county records, including deeds, wills and marriages in the nineteenth century.

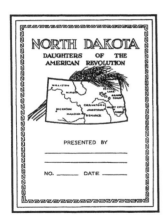

Montana

Basic histories and county materials are available with a G.R.C. set of 42 volumes.

Nebraska

Basic histories and county materials are available including 183 G.R.C. volumes.

Nevada

Basic histories and county materials are available with 59 G.R.C. volumes.

New England Region

Collectively, as well as individually, the six New England states are well represented in DAR holdings. In the New England section of the Library, researchers will find much Mayflower material, collected family histories, *The New England Historical and Genealogical Register* (also on CD-ROM) with its indices, and other standard studies and compilations for history and families.

New Hampshire

Many town histories, published state records and a G.R.C. set of 135 volumes provide the basis for the New Hampshire collection, and the indices to births, marriages, divorces, and deaths to circa 1900 on microfilm offer good New Hampshire coverage.

New Jersey

A large collection of New Jersey materials is enhanced by over 872 volumes of G.R.C. books containing much local information. County tax ratables (1778–1882) and New Jersey Revolutionary War records, including service records and damage claims, from the New Jersey State Archives offer many sources for research.

New Mexico

Basic sources on this Southwestern state include several studies of early Spanish and Mexican families along with materials on later settlers. There are 76 G.R.C. volumes in the New Mexico section.

New Netherland Region

A good, separate collection of materials relating to the former Dutch colony in America, along with sources in the New Jersey and New York sections provide researchers with considerable information.

New York

One of the Library's largest collections covers the Empire State. County abstracts, numerous church records, and a partially indexed G.R.C. set of nearly 1,130 volumes anchor the section. The liber–size *Index to the Public Records of the County of Albany* (37 volumes) provides information on settlers in major portions of northern and central New York when Albany County was much larger. The *Vosburgh Collection* of church records, *New York City Wills 1677–1879*, state Revolutionary War accounts and claims, and applications for state land grants 1665–1803 are available on microfilm.

North Carolina

The Library has an excellent collection of North Carolina county histories and record abstracts along with many other useful sources. In microform are *North Carolina W.P.A Pre– 1914 and Post–1914 Cemetery Card Indexes, North Carolina Revolutionary War Pay Vouchers, North Carolina Revolutionary War Army Accounts, North Carolina Treasurer's and Comptroller's Papers,* and various county court records. A microfiche *Marriage Bond Index of North Carolina 1741–1868* provides supplemental information to printed sources. A 511-volume G.R.C. set is also available.

North Dakota

A basic set of historical and genealogical materials, 24 G.R.C. volumes, and many county publications of the Red River Valley Genealogical Society represent North Dakota in the Library. Owing to a steady stream of donations in recent years, the North Dakota section has grown to a substantial degree with the addition of a number of church and town histories.

Ohio

A large collection of Ohio county histories and record abstracts is available and is supplemented by a G.R.C. set (with guide) of 873 volumes. In microform are such sources as *Annals of Cleveland: Cleveland Newspaper Digest 1818–1876; Annals of Cleveland: Court Record Series 1837–1850; Hamilton County Deeds and Wills; Ohio Civil War Regimental Histories; Ohio Revolutionary War Bounty Land Warrants in the Virginia Military District*, and *The Ohio Surname Index to County Histories* from the Ohio Historical Society.

Oklahoma

A good, basic collection of local Oklahoma materials along with books in the American Indian Collection on tribes in Oklahoma and a 355-volume G.R.C. set are available.

Oregon

Basic county histories and record abstracts comprise the majority of the Oregon collection and various genealogical periodicals and a 328-volume G.R.C. set supplement them.

Pennsylvania

An excellent collection of county histories and records, church histories and records, and genealogical and historical periodicals is the core of the Pennsylvania section. The

---

G.R.C. set contains over 786 volumes, and the published *Pennsylvania Archives* set is a popular source. Various county records are on microfilm along with *Abstracts Card File for Revolutionary War Active Duty Militia 1775–1783; Abstracts Card File of Revolutionary War Inactive Duty Militia; Military Abstract Cards, Philadelphia County, 1777–1783; Abstract Card File for Revolutionary War Continental Units 1775–1783; Pennsylvania Comptroller General Military Accounts, Militia 1775–1794;* and *Pennsylvania Comptroller General County Supply and Other Tax Lists.*

Rhode Island

An indexed, 96-volume G.R.C. set along with various county and town records is the basis for the Rhode Island section. On microfilm, the *Index to Military and Naval Records of Rhode Island 1774-1805* offers Revolutionary and post-Revolutionary military information.

The South Region

Many regional histories, periodicals, and record collections cover the states of the South as a region.

South Carolina

An excellent South Carolina collection is available to researchers. Beyond county histories and record abstracts, they will find a 225 volume G.R.C. set (with a microfiche index: *Name Index to Genealogical Records Collected by the South Carolina DAR*) and the following microform collections: *South Carolina Will Transcripts 1782–1868* (by county); *South Carolina Department of Archives and History Consolidated Index; South Carolina Auditor General's Records 1731–1775, Memorials COM Index; South Carolina Historical Magazine Index 1900–1983; Seventeenth and Eighteenth Century South Carolina Land Titles; South Carolina Department of Archives and History Individual and Combined Document Indexes to State Plats (Columbia and Charleston Series);* and *South Carolina State Plats, Charleston Series (1784–1860) and Columbia Series (1796–1868).*

South Dakota

A basic collection of sources and periodicals for South Dakota is supplemented on microfilm by a set of church vital and burial records and funeral home records numbering 160 reels from locations across the state. South Dakota has 17 G.R.C. volumes.

Tennessee

Excellent county record abstracts and histories form the basis of the Tennessee section. A 262-volume G.R.C. set provides further sources. Two important microfilm collections are *North Carolina Secretary of State Land Grants in Tennessee* and *Tennessee Index to Land Grants 1775–1905.*

Texas

A large, but by no means comprehensive, county collection comprises the majority of the Texas section. The Texas

DAR's G.R.C. has produced a set of 967 volumes. Many genealogical periodicals and early military record abstracts provide further depth of coverage.

Utah

A basic historical and genealogical collection of Utah materials is available along with 34 G.R.C. volumes.

Vermont

Many town histories and records, published state records, and an indexed G.R.C. set of 85 volumes give good Vermont information. The G.R.C. set contains many very complete cemetery listings from around the state. *The General Index to Vermont Vital Records to 1870* is available on microfilm.

Virginia

One of the Library's best state collections is that for the Old Dominion. County histories and many record abstracts, join with an indexed G.R.C. set of 431 volumes and all Virginia genealogical periodicals for detailed coverage. *The Virginia Civil War Regimental Histories* series expands the information available on that period. *Virginia Land Office Patents and Grants, 1623–1784, Virginia Revolutionary War manuscript volumes "War 0–62,"* and *Virginia Revolutionary War Bounty Warrants* and index are available on microfilm along with various county and church records. Many traditional and newer published indices to Virginia materials offer access to family information.

Washington

A basic collection of historical and genealogical books forms the basis of the Washington section. The G.R.C. set of 138 volumes includes the sub-series *Family Records of Washington Pioneers*.

The West Region

Overview histories and other studies provide background information on the Western states, on Russian America, and on the Spanish and Mexican periods in the history of the Southwest.

West Virginia

A good, growing collection of county histories, record abstracts, 147 G.R.C. volumes and genealogical periodicals forms the West Virginia section. The *Smith–Riffe Collection* of West Virginia and southwest Virginia families and a 184-roll set of microfilm reproducing abstracts of country records are available.

Wisconsin

Many county histories with recent indices and basic historical studies constitute this section. There are 145 G.R.C. volumes in the Wisconsin section.

Wyoming

Basic histories and some genealogical material with 48 G.R.C. volumes are available for Wyoming.

13.28
VITAL RECORDS

These essential sources are found throughout DAR collections and in many forms. Researchers will find marriage registers, birth and death registers, New England town vital records, church records, cemetery surveys and transcriptions, and other similar sources. In the catalog, check the name of the locality with the subheadings "Vital records," "Birth records," "Death records," etc.

New England vital records are the best in the country and are represented in large numbers at DAR. Besides published volumes of many of these sources, the following are available on microfilm:

- Index to Vermont vital records to 1870

- Indices to New Hampshire vital records to 1900

- The Massachusetts Town Records series on microfiche from Holbrook Research, Inc.

- The Barbour Collection and Index of Connecticut vital records

Other state–wide indices include:

- Mississippi marriages prior to 1926 (white)

- North Carolina marriage bond index 1741–1868; separate bride and groom indices

- Illinois Marriage record index

Many individual vital records have accompanied DAR membership applications as proof of lineage. These have included birth, marriage, and death certificates or register entries. Bible records abound as well. The DAR Library maintains the files of this material, **but does not make available for research or provide copies of post–1910 records obtained from state health and vital records departments** for privacy reasons. There are no exceptions to this policy.

13.29
WOMEN'S HISTORY

Records relating to women in American history are found throughout DAR collections. The Library maintains a growing Women's History Collection, which focuses on the role and experience of women. A natural focus of this and other materials is women during the period of the American Revolution, but coverage is much wider. The Women's History collection is located in the Library's Office. Also see sections 13.1 and 13.20.4.6.

The state sections include a subdivision "Women," which includes studies on women's experiences in the life and development of each state. Some books examine legal, cultural, and family ties in broad social contexts.

As a women's organization, the DAR owns much material on its own activities since 1890. The Office of the Historian General maintains the archival collections, which may require special permission to use, and the Historical Research Library, which includes various studies on American women's history. Catalogs and checklists from various exhibits on women's history and related topics in the DAR Museum are discussed in Chapter 10.

CITING, QUOTING AND REPRODUCING DAR SOURCES

D AR employees often see vague references in books or in letters to materials that are supposedly found in DAR collections. Such phrases as "in the DAR Library" or "in the DAR files" are all too frequent. They provide no useful information to help other researchers or the staff locate the material again. Proper citation or reference to documents and their locations is essential when noting a source from all libraries and archives. The examples of bibliographic records given in this chapter are for the most-frequently-used DAR sources and provide guidelines for proper citation.

Researchers should give proper credit for any reference in any publication or source they quote in their writing and note–taking. A proper credit line or footnote is important. This will avoid problems and misunderstandings in the future.

To reproduce or to quote extensively from any DAR publication, one must obtain permission from the appropriate part of DAR. Permission may or may not be granted, depending on the circumstances and purpose. For general DAR publications, write to the Corresponding Secretary General. For the *DAR Magazine*, contact the Publications and Printing Department. For publications from state organizations including *Genealogical Records Committee Reports*, write to the appropriate state regent. DAR appreciates a copy of any work including significant portions of DAR–produced material.

CITATION FOR DAR MEMBERSHIP APPLICATION
[See Section 6.6.1 for a discussion of membership applications.]

"Membership application of [member's name](National Number) on [ancestor's name (dates, state)]," National Society Daughters of the American Revolution, Office of the Registrar General, Washington, D.C., [date application was approved].

Fictitious example:
"Membership application of Elizabeth Jones Smith (1,911,111) on Josiah Walden (1750–1806, Vermont)," National Society Daughters of the American Revolution, Office of the Registrar General, Washington, D.C., April 19, 2003.

CITATION FOR DAR SUPPLEMENTAL APPLICATION PAPER
[See Section 6.6.3 for a discussion of supplemental applications.]

"Supplemental application paper of [member's name] (National Number, Add volume number) on [ancestor's name (dates, state)]," National Society Daughters of the American

Revolution, Office of the Registrar General, Washington, D.C., [date supplemental application was approved].

Fictitious example:
"Supplemental application paper of Evelyn Green Brown (1,999,001, Add volume 1,236) on Stephen Butler (1743–1810, Virginia)," National Society Daughters of the American Revolution, Office of the Registrar General, Washington, D.C., October 11, 2001.

CITATION FOR DOCUMENTATION FILE SUPPORTING A MEMBERSHIP OR SUPPLEMENTAL APPLICATION
[See Section 6.9 for a discussion of documentation files.]

"[type of record] in Documentation file supporting the Membership Application [or Supplemental Application Paper] of [name of member], approved [date application was approved], (National Number) on [name of ancestor, dates, state]," National Society Daughters of the American Revolution, DAR Library, Washington, D.C.

Fictitious example:
"Marriage record of Josiah Walden and Hannah Jones, 20 July 1772, Putney, Vermont, in Documentation File supporting the Membership Application of Elizabeth Jones Smith, approved April 19, 2003, (1,999,111) on Josiah Walden (1750–1806, Vermont)," National Society Daughters of the American Revolution, DAR Library, Washington, D.C.

CITATION FOR A *GENEALOGICAL RECORDS COMMITTEE REPORT*
The Genealogical Records Committee [G.R.C] *Reports* contain many genealogical materials that DAR members have collected since the late 1910s. There are now approximately 18,000 volumes of varying length, format and content.

These typescripts have arrived at DAR with numerous titles and much creativity in arrangement. Until 1988 there was little standardization and most state sets did not have proper volume numbering. In that year the Library imposed such a system on all new *G.R.C. Reports* for those state sets without one. Everything prior to 1988 automatically became "Series 1," and everything from 1988 to the present is in "Series 2."

To achieve uniformity, the Library's catalogers have assigned volume numbers for all books in Series 1 based on their compilation dates. Slowly order has arisen. The Library considers its national set of *G.R.C. Reports* as the master set. The volume numbering for Series 1 only applies to this set and not to any copies maintained by the states. This is primarily because there are no exact records showing where the state sets are located. A few states such as Maine, New York and Vermont, used a proper numbering system before 1988, and those systems remain in place from the very first book.

In addition to the volume numbering, the Library set the title for all of these volumes in both series as [a state's name + DAR] *Genealogical Records Committee Report.* The new titles are - followed by a descriptive subtitle, which would have been formerly the title.

The following fictitious models for a proper citation are given as guidelines. Note that sections of a specific report should be viewed as articles in a periodical and cited as such. For more detailed information, please check the Library's online catalog at **www.dar.org** or contact the DAR Library, Cataloging Section. Subsections of any such report should be treated like an article in a journal with appropriate inclusive page numbers included.

For pre–1988 reports:
    "Wauwatosa Congregational Church Records," *Wisconsin DAR, Genealogical Records Committee Report: Bible and Cemetery Records*, Series 1, Volume 64 (1955), 257-262, DAR Library, Washington, D.C. [Formerly referred to as *Wisconsin DAR, Bible and Cemetery Records*, 1955, with no other identifying information.]

For reports 1988 to the present:
    Sarah Davies Hogoboom, "The Anthony Hoskins/Haskins Family of Windsor, Connecticut," *Wisconsin DAR, Genealogical Records Committee Report: Miscellaneous Records*, Series 2, Volume 6 (1995), 1-30, DAR Library, Washington, D.C.

CITATION FOR *DAUGHTERS OF THE AMERICAN REVOLUTION MAGAZINE* (now: *AMERICAN SPIRIT*)

The DAR Magazine has had several title changes during its existence that affect bibliographic citations. [Note: Until v. 51 (July–December 1917) a volume comprised half a year or six issues.] See Chapter 9 for a discussion of *The DAR Magazine*.

- *American Monthly Magazine*, v.1 (July 1892)–v.42 (June 1913)
- *Daughters of the American Revolution Magazine*, v.43 (July 1913)–v.72 (December 1938)
- *The National Historical Magazine*, v.73 (1939)–v.79 (1945)
- *Daughters of the American Revolution Magazine*, v.80 (1946)-v.135, no.5 (June 2001)
- *American Spirit*, v.135, no.6 (July/August 2001) to present.

CITATION FOR NSDAR REPORT TO THE SMITHSONIAN

Annually, until 1974, the DAR was required to submit its annual report to the Secretary of the Smithsonian Institution. These then became United States Senate Documents and parts of the U.S. Government's *Serial Set*. Included within these reports over the years are various lists and compilations of Revolutionary War soldiers, cemetery records, and other genealogically important material. These volumes should be cited as is this last such report:

    Seventy–seventh Report of the National Society of the Daughters of the American Revolution, March 1, 1973 to March 1, 1974. 94th Congress, 1st Session, Senate Document No. 94–117. Washington, D.C.: U.S. Government Printing Office, 1975.

References to any subsection of these reports should be treated as an article in a journal with the inclusive page numbers shown.

    "The Ancient Burying Ground of Hartford: Names on the gravestones standing in 1835," Appendix C, *Third Report of the National Society of the Daughters of the American Revolution, October 11, 1898–October 11, 1900.* 56th Congress, 2d Session, Senate Document No. 219 (Washington, D.C.: Government Printing Office, 1901), 306–315.

Eric G. Grundset has been Library Director for the DAR Library since May 1983. He holds a B.A. in history from James Madison University, undertook graduate study in Russian history at the University of Wisconsin, Madison, and holds a Masters Degree in Library Science from The Catholic University of America. A native Virginian of Norwegian and colonial Virginia, Maryland, and Pennsylvania descent, he is active in historical and genealogical organizations in the Old Dominion. Mr. Grundset is a former employee of the Virginia Room, Fairfax County Public Library System (1976-1983) and a former president of the Virginia Genealogical Society. He is also a former Vice President and member of the Board of Directors of the National Genealogical Society and has served as national conference chairman and program chairman for that organization. A genealogist, historian, lecturer and writer, he specializes in Virginia genealogical research and the use of land and tax records in studying families. In 2004, he will complete a major publication for the DAR, an annotated bibliography of published materials on the history of America's women during the period of the Revolutionary War, 1760-1790, and will edit a series of papers for publication that were presented at the DAR's 2003 symposium, "Forgotten Patriots: African American and American Indian Patriots of the Revolutionary War."

Steven B. Rhodes was the Assistant Director of the DAR Library from March 1995 to April 2004. He holds a B.A. in History from Virginia Commonwealth University, an M.A. in History from Virginia Tech, and an M.L.S. from the University of Maryland. In the past he has held positions at university, government and law libraries. A native Virginian, he currently resides in Maryland and is employed by the National Archives and Records Administration.

L

M

N

O

P

President General's Project 2, 13, 24, 25, 39, 43

Presidents and First Families 63, 156

Q

Quilts 69–71

R

"Real Daughters" 59, 62, 98
"Real Granddaughters" 59, 98
Reddy, Ann Waller 25, 33
Registrar General, Office of the 41, 43, 46–56, 64, 67
Religious records 156
Rhode Island 25, 40, 44, 76, 83, 87, 95, 112, 113, 117, 135, 163
Roots 86
Russia and Russians 105, 107
Russian America 105, 157, 164

S

Santo Domingo 103
Scandinavia 105, 107
Scotland 105
Scots Irish 10, 33, 105, 107
Seimes Technology Center 17, 23, 27, 39, 40, 43–45, 47, 48, 52, 54, 64, 87, 92, 98, 100, 104, 108, 116–167 (passim)
Sierra Leone 102
Smithsonian Institution, DAR Reports to the Secretary of the 59–61
Society of the Cincinnati 110, 137
Sons of the American Revolution, National Society (SAR) 22, 43, 110, 132
Sons of the Revolution 32, 110, 137
The South 26, 29, 40, 115, 130, 141, 163
South Carolina 41, 44, 60, 77, 83, 88, 103, 107, 120, 127, 141, 163
South Dakota 77, 84, 163
Spain 10, 112, 126, 149–150
Spanish American War 149–150
State research sources 25–26, 29–30, 37–41, 59–62, 73–85, 96–98, 109–110, 157–166
Sweden 105, 107
Switzerland 105

T

Tennessee 29, 40, 44, 77, 84, 94, 102, 135, 136, 144, 163
Texas 38, 40, 77, 84, 163
Tories — see Loyalists

U

United Empire Loyalists — see Loyalists
United Kingdom 10, 85
United States Daughters of the War of 1812, 140
Utah 77, 84, 95, 141, 164

V

Vermont 41, 44, 60, 77, 84, 88, 95, 120, 130, 139, 164, 165, 167
Vietnam War 153
Virginia 25, 29, 33, 39, 40, 44, 77, 84, 87, 92, 94, 95, 98, 103, 107, 112, 113, 115, 119, 120, 123, 125, 130, 134, 146, 148, 156, 164
Vital records 22, 32, 34, 40, 44, 158, 159, 160, 165
The Vital Record Compendium 26, 40

W

Wales 105
War of 1812 112, 139–141
Washington (state) 77, 84, 164
Washington, George 63, 70, 113, 114, 117, 125, 155
Watkins, Linda Tinker 2, 39, 55
The West 70, 105, 147, 157, 164
West Indies 105
West Virginia 39, 41, 61, 77, 85, 102, 134, 164
Wisconsin 44, 77, 85, 95, 136, 164
Women's history and records 25, 31, 63, 69–71, 88, 123–124, 166
Works Progress Administration/Work Projects Administration (W.P.A.) 11, 32, 101–102
World War I 150–152
World War II 12, 152–153
Wyoming 77, 85, 92, 94, 147, 165